CAPITAL RESURGENT

Capital Resurgent

Roots of the Neoliberal Revolution

Gérard Duménil

Dominique Lévy

Translated by Derek Jeffers

HARVARD UNIVERSITY PRESS

Cambridge, Massachusetts

London, England · 2004

Printed in the United States of America

Originally published as *Crise et sortie de crise: Ordre et désordres néolibéraux,*

Library of Congress Cataloging-in-Publication Data

Duménil, Gérard.
[Crise et sortie de crise. English]
Capital resurgent : roots of the neoliberal revolution /
Gérard Duménil and Dominique Lévy ; translated by Derek Jeffers.
p. cm.
Includes bibliographical references and index.
ISBN 0-674-01158-9 (alk. paper)
1. Economic history—1990– 2. Economic history. 3. Capitalism.
4. Liberalism. 5. Globalization—Economic aspects. 6. Financial crises.
7. Unemployment. I. Lévy, Dominique. II. Title.

HC59.15.D8613 2004
330.12′2—dc22 2003067501

Contents

Introduction

"Neoliberalism" is the term now used to describe the transformations capitalism underwent at the turning point of the 1970s and 1980s. One salient fact was the decision by the U.S. Federal Reserve Board to allow interest rates to rise as much as the fight against inflation required. But this emblematic action, whose consequences were dramatic for large portions of the world population, can only be understood as one of many components of a change whose principal trait was restoring many of the most violent features of capitalism, making for a resurgent, unprettified capitalism.

From World War II to the late 1970s, the decades of the Keynesian compromise, full employment, social welfare protection, and universal access to education and health care had come to be accepted as important features of developed societies. The desire to tackle the challenges of the capitalist order and the fight against communism made development policies urgent necessities. These policies had led to institutional frameworks that were on the margin of the fundamental rules of straight-laced capitalism—more advantageous financing conditions for the nonfinancial economic sector, a high degree of state intervention in industrial policy, and an international monetary framework favorable to development, which placed certain limits on the freedom of decision for the owners of capital.

On both the domestic and the international level, neoliberalism has undertaken the destruction of this social order and has restored the strictest rules of capitalism.

It is true that the dynamics of capitalism generally escape the control of the protagonists involved, but collective political wills should not be underestimated, whatever form they may take. A central thesis of this book is that neoliberalism is the expression of the desire of a class of capitalist owners and the institutions in which their power is concentrated, which we collectively call "finance," to restore—in the context of a general decline in popular struggles—the class's revenues and power, which had diminished since the Great Depression and World War II. Far from being inevitable, this was a political action.

The rules whose imposition define neoliberalism are generally designated euphemistically as "market" rules, avoiding the direct reference to capital. In this use of the term "market," various types of mechanisms are at issue. The labor market refers to the tightening up of rules concerning hiring, layoffs, wages, and labor conditions. This market has been a favorite target of neoliberalism. The other market, directly at stake here, is that of capital. Neoliberalism has indeed completely changed the conditions under which the capital markets function. There are many aspects to this—the centrality of the stock market and of capital in general, free international mobility of capital, and so on. Finally, neoliberalism is indeed the bearer of a process of general commercialization of social relationships, and that is one of its more shocking aspects. But it is the logic of the capitalist relationship that extends and governs the whole process, in accordance with its rules.

These transformations are also commonly disguised as a material or technical necessity, as the necessary internationalization of the economy and, more specifically, as needed market globalization. The rule of the so-called international markets is nothing other than the rule of capital. Globalization, certainly, but capitalist neoliberal globalization, or better, globalization of this social order. And if one can speak of internationalization, its center is still situated in the United States.

May material, intellectual, cultural, and emotional exchanges be extended from one end of the planet to the other. May people and resources circulate for the greatest well-being of all. But neoliberal globalization is not the way to accomplish this.

The current processes, which are at the heart of this book, become more intelligible once they have been put into historical perspective. History does not repeat itself, but observing previous similar events—the ways in which the depression at the end of the nineteenth century and the 1929 crisis were overcome—is the imaginary laboratory of our hypothetical experiments.

This exploration will take us to the very core of the historical dynamic of the capitalist mode of production—the transformations of the relationships of production and the class structures—because the neoliberal order aims to reaffirm the fundamentally capitalist nature of our societies. Despite the reassertion of the power of capitalist owners, history, nevertheless, is still on the move. Is it possible to identify in which ways neoliberalism can be bypassed? Are they the ways we are hoping for?

PART

I

Crisis and Neoliberalism

CHAPTER

1

The Strange Dynamics of Change

How are the major evolutions of the world economy to be understood? What changes have taken place, and under which circumstances, creating, under the leadership of American finance, the conditions for the neoliberal order and the financial hegemony which it is the expression of?

In this discussion of how the world's affairs are conducted, good sense does not fit in. Only someone naive would imagine that men laid out a simple approach, starting with identifying the general problems, and then applying solutions. One, start with noting what is wrong; two, elaborate strategies; three, apply them. This three-point program is not what guides humanity.

If the world conducted its behavior in this way, the first stage of the approach, that of evaluation, would today be made up of strong self-criticism regarding the situation of the periphery, combined with an ode of great self-satisfaction regarding a portion of the classes within the main developed capitalist countries, particularly the United States. The arrival of the 2000 recession and the fall of the stock market barely made a dent in this neoliberal arrogance. Strange lack of harmony.

A balance sheet is drawn up every year by the international organizations, and it is hardly flattering. The United Nations 1997 *Human Development Report* painted the following picture: "More than a quarter of the developing world's people still live in poverty . . . About a third—1.3 billion people—live on incomes of less than $1 a day . . . And in industrial countries more than 100 million people live below the income poverty line."[1]

Perhaps even more shocking is the observation of the inequalities and their growth, as recounted in the 1999 report: "The income gap between the fifth of the world's people living in the richest countries and the fifth in the poorest was 74 to 1 in 1997, up from 60 to 1 in 1990, and 30 to 1 in 1960 . . . By the late 1990s the fifth of the world's people living in the highest-income countries had 86% of world GDP [output]—the bottom fifth just 1%."[2]

These reports emphasize that many events, in fact, go against what one might wish. Over half of the countries seeking to develop are ignored by foreign investors; the prices of the products that these countries can export have collapsed since the 1980s; high customs duties place a burden on potential exports; the agricultures of the most advanced countries are tremendously subsidized; the weight of the debt of the least-developed countries is crushing; and so on.[3] Have we plunged in an inert world, indifferent to all problems, incapable of reacting?

The purpose of this book is to determine the origins and the content of the new course of capitalism. The most general conclusion that can be drawn has much to do with the problem of poverty and inequalities. If the scope of human misery has not provoked any of the reactions that we might have naively expected, it is obviously because the economic and social transformations of recent decades proceeded not from the interests of the great masses, but from those of privileged minorities, who, in fact, did find themselves better off.

As soon as we shift from the point of view of the masses to that of these minorities, the commonsense analytical pattern, going from the appearance of difficulties to the application of solutions, again becomes pertinent. Once more the system retrieves its capacity to change; the course of events becomes intelligible. The transformations of the last twenty years were indeed prompted by the appearance of certain problems affecting privileged minorities. Through much trial and error, and given the numerous detours that characterize collective actions, the adjustments made actually did tend to resolve these difficulties.

In order to understand this, the analytical framework must merely be specified, and those involved, identified. It was not that humanity became conscious of the destitute situation of its least advanced fractions, or of the dire straits of its unemployed and outcasts, and decided to try setting things straight.[4] Rather, privileged minorities discovered the setbacks that they themselves had suffered and the dangers threatening them, and used their still dominant position to try everything possible to remedy this decline. In so doing, these groups contributed nothing to alleviating poverty, whether in the countries of the center (the United States, Europe, and Japan) or on the periphery, because they didn't care. This opinion may appear to be exaggerated. It will seem ridiculous to some to make villains out of rich people, the dominating classes. And yet.

This investigation thus takes us back to the center, to the heart of the capitalist world, and even, one may add, to the center of the center. This is where things have taken shape, following the struggles of dominated classes and countries within a relationship of forces that is constantly reaffirmed, where good intentions do not guide behavior.

This raises several questions. What problems caused the change? What is the nature of this center of the center? What is the content of the changes that have occurred and what were their effects?

The answer to the first question, which identifies the problems behind the changes, concerns the revenues of the ruling classes. This answer is precise and simple—in the 1970s the rate of capital profitability had significantly declined. In this proposition, each term should be underlined. The nature of the occurrence—a decline in the rate of capital profitability. Where and when?—in the most advanced capitalist countries, in the 1970s. Why was this phenomenon so important?—because it determined the action of the dominating classes in the following decades. Why is that shocking?—because the fight against unemployment, against social exclusion, and against destitution did not fit in with the approach of these classes, who in fact were making use of unemployment in this situation.

The answer to the second question concerning the nature of this center of the center, from which the initiative came, is that the center is made up of a particular fraction of the dominating classes, in which financial interests are preponderant. It had seen its revenues and power eroded during the 1970s. It was the great instigator of the transition to neoliberalism, and was its great beneficiary. The proportions of this restoration are difficult to imagine.

The third question is that of the content of the changes. Globalization and the liberalization of capital exchanges and movements are indeed its fundamental components. But they should not be considered independently from the reassertion of power by capital holders, which constituted the main aspect of the change. Finance reasserted its power and interests in relation to workers, company managers, those responsible for economic and social policies in governments, and public and semipublic institutions, both national and international. Prioritizing the fight against inflation, the new course of events refocused economic activity on capital profitability and payments to creditors and stockholders. This power was restored through the channels of globalization, which also marked it with specific features, in accordance with the interests of the owners of the means of production. But one should not confuse the way, globalization, with the goal, the revenues of finance and its hegemony. As for the effects of these transformations, they can be summed up in three words, poverty, efficiency, and opulence: perpetuated or aggravated poverty, reaching into the capitalist centers; the efficiency of the big groups led by capital in accordance with an unambiguous criterion, that of maximizing the profit rate and payments to the owners; and the opulence of the superior fractions of the dominating classes.

We would thus be wrong to remain paralyzed, given the complexity of the determinants of change. The economy is not governed by fates that are comparable to the effects of the natural elements—it is made by human beings. It would be mistaken to underestimate the sets of constraints within which collective actions maneuver and to a certain extent escape from, but these actions flow, in their own way, from motivations.

Starting from the experience of the advanced capitalist countries, Parts II and III illustrate the gap between the most obvious problems and the aims of those who preside over the transformations of the system. After the present introductory part, Part II is devoted first of all to the structural crisis at the end of the twentieth century and to unemployment, recounting the crisis itself, explaining unemployment within the crisis, and understanding why Europe was more affected than the United States. Could unemployment have been avoided? And is there light at the end of the tunnel, and is it possible to speak of an end to the crisis? Part III describes the reaction of finance to the crisis—how it used the crisis to its advantage and succeeded in restoring its position, increasing its revenues, and repositioning itself as hegemonic within the new capitalist order. Parts IV and V place this analysis in historical and theoretical perspective.

Information about sources and calculations can be found in Appendix B.

CHAPTER

2

Economic Crises and Social Orders

This experience of transformation is not the first for the developed capitalist economies. But recognizing that the events we are living through—the structural crisis begun in the 1970s, the affirmation of new trends, and the rise of a social order—are not completely original does not diminish their importance. History never repeats itself exactly, but all historical facts have precedents. The challenges of the present always appear enormous to those who pay little attention to the past.

It is no accident that the current transformations of capitalism followed a structural crisis. This should be seen as a general law of evolution. What the periods of major crises have in common is that they determine major changes. Here we find the old theory of violence as the midwife of history; crises share this function with wars.

In order to properly appreciate the significance of the last structural crisis, one should refer to what transpired at the end of the nineteenth century, rather than in 1929. Economic historians generally agree that a major crisis took place between 1875 and 1893 in Europe, and especially in France. Opinions differ on the geographic spread of the phenomenon and its features, but the fact of its occurrence is well established. At the same time the United States experienced a period of great instability between the end of the Civil War in 1865 and the turn of the century. These crises led to a deep transformation of capitalism in these countries. The economic, social, and political tensions expressed at that time created the conditions for shaking up the previous capitalist order. Capitalism after the structural crisis of the end of the nineteenth century was very different from capitalism before the crisis.

It suffices to recall that modern finance and the major corporations, which still rule over our societies, that is, over the entire social structure of contemporary capitalism, were born in the wake of these upheavals. One fundamental aspect of this transformation was the separation of capital ownership from management. The development of the major corporations created a class of stockholders, creditors, and financiers somewhat removed from direct corporate functioning. A complex system of financial institutions appeared, while monetary and financial mechanisms underwent a genuine explosion. Vast general staffs of managerial personnel were created, assisted by clerical personnel. The labor conditions for workers in the shop also changed radically. As has often been described, the direct producer became more and more an appendage of the machine.

The Marxists, and especially Lenin, realized the importance of the stakes, even if history finally did not agree with them in their anticipation of the radical destruction of capitalist society. At issue was not only the size of companies and monopolies, but also whether capitalism could revolutionize technology and management, which determine the efficiency of the system and therefore the possibilities of social compromises. And history went with capitalism, despite the imperialist war.

The successive shocks of the Great Depression and World War II once again shook up capitalist functioning. They precipitated capitalism's change in course and gave the change a new dimension, that of the institutions and policies to which the English economist and diplomat John Maynard Keynes gave his name. It is too much, however, to ascribe to Keynes all the features of the three decades of prosperity that followed World War II. Other labels, like "third road" or "mixed economy," were proposed, and though now out of fashion, did not lack in pertinence at the time.

What were the stakes and the methods of this period of compromise? While leaving private initiative free to act concerning investments and corporate management, the Keynesian state became involved in controlling the level of economic activity and growth through various regulations and policies (having to do with credit, the currency, and the oversight of financial institutions) and regulating state spending according to the economic situation, thus affecting global demand, and thus production. This macroeconomic responsibility of the state tended to recognize de facto the right to a job; long-term unemployment or its disguised forms were thus considered unacceptable. The idea of "sharing the fruits of growth," and therefore of an increase in wages, was established. The state became everywhere more involved in education, research, and industrial policy, sometimes directly taking over certain sectors of the economy. To this must be added the blossoming of social protection systems (health, family, retirement, and unemployment). Three elements were combined: (1) broad respect for private initiative, and the basic rules of the capitalist game; (2) state intervention to control the macroeconomic situation, growth (which meant certain limitations on private initiative concerning finance and a few industries), and technological progress; (3) guarantees concerning jobs and labor conditions, as well as an increase in purchasing power and social protection.

The importance of these changes, which followed two major crises, cannot be overemphasized. Behind the financial institutions and the great corporations of the beginning of the century, or behind the postwar Keynesian state, a profound transformation of the capitalist relationships of production, the ownership of the means of production and their control through management, and wage labor was taking shape (the labor power of wageworkers appearing less and less as an ordinary commodity). New class structures corresponded to this transformation of the relationships of production, particularly the development of intermediate classes of managerial and clerical personnel, breaking with the rigidity of the confrontation between capitalist owners and proletarians without anything in the middle.

At the heart of these movements was the great dialectic of the productive forces and the relationships of production that Marx's theory of history had described. The general principles are known—the development of the productive forces and the transformation of the relationships of production are interdependent; a class structure corresponds to each system of relationships of production; the class struggle is the motor force of this historical dynamic; and the state plays a key role. This analytical framework makes it possible to account for the different modes of production, as well as for the different phases that take shape within the same mode of production.

A central thesis of this book is that this historical dynamic is still on the march. The mechanisms that had governed the transformation of capitalism since its birth—still functioning at the end of the nineteenth century and during the first half of the twentieth century—have also governed the dynamics of the last decades of the twentieth century. The general approach, the analytical framework, should remain the same: the crisis begun in the 1970s once again created the conditions for deep transformations;

these transformations were gradually taking us to a new social order; relationships of production and class structures were at stake.

In many respects the crisis of the 1970s resembled that of the end of the nineteenth century. It was not limited to one passing incident, such as the 1974–1975 recession (a bit hastily ascribed to the first oil crisis); it was a deep and long-lasting phenomenon, a structural crisis, the first signs of which were already apparent in the United States during the 1960s. The list of its various components is long. Both growth and technological progress were affected; record inflation rates were registered in the advanced capitalist countries during the 1970s; wages entered into a period of near stagnation; the profit rate dropped, and above all, a great wave of unemployment supplanted full employment.

It is in the features of this crisis—a decline in capital profitability and its consequences for the revenues of the dominant classes—that the underlying reasons for the transformations must be sought.

During the first decade of the crisis, the revenues of these classes declined sharply. Profits were low and their distribution to stockholders in the form of dividends was reduced; inflation decreased the value of loans held. Corporate managers and the officials of public economic institutions in charge of policy had acquired, under the Keynesian compromise, a certain degree of autonomy in relation to the capitalist owners. In response to the crisis, at first officials put into place policies designed to favor growth and employment, but which did indeed penalize financial revenues. The ruling classes then turned this movement around, to their advantage.

One of the most resounding elements of this comeback was the coup of 1979, the sudden rise in interest rates, seeking to halt inflation whatever the cost. This blow triggered a spate of actions that spread to all of society and the economy, reorganizing them in accordance with this new social order and favoring the revenues and power of those fractions of the dominant classes that embodied capitalist ownership in the most direct way. The extension of this new order to the whole of the planet, at least to those countries where the perspectives for profit seemed sufficient, was meteoric.

This new course of capitalism confirmed what had already been obtained since the beginning of the structural crisis—an end to the previous decades' improvement of workers' conditions. Wage increases were interrupted or considerably slowed down; there were attempts to dismantle social protection systems; the lack of job security became more widespread; and so on. Major struggles that broke out against the initial pressures (particularly in the United Kingdom and the United States) were contained with the greatest determination. Popular strategies—both revolutionary (in the socialist countries, and on the far left in the capitalist countries or the countries of the periphery) as well as reformist (the policies of the left such as economic stimulation, nationalizations)—lost, or were losing, their credibility.[1]

How should the social order introduced by the crisis of the 1970s be characterized? And first of all, how should it be labeled? The term "neoliberal" has gradually come more and more into use—the crisis made us enter a neoliberal society.

Yet the term "neoliberalism" poses a multitude of problems. Let us first set aside the fact that this word is a *faux ami* for any American reader, because in the United States, a "liberal" is a man or a woman more or less on the left (liberal as opposed to conservative). Referring to the idea of liberty, the term sends us back to the heart of the ambiguities of the French revolution—liberty, equality, and fraternity of the *sans culottes* on the one hand, liberty of trade and industry (of hiring, and especially of firing) on the other. This liberty of trade and industry is, of course, what the neoliberals endorse.

In the eighteenth century, to demand this liberty, that of commerce and industry, was to attack the old feudal order; in our day and age it means attacking certain state interventions, some of the prerogatives of the state that go beyond, according to the neoliberals, the healthy limits that are in place to maintain order and the relationships of production and to promote the interests of the wealthy. Our states, coming out of the Keynesian period, are still partially the guarantors of past class compromises, and it is to that extent that they are rejected by the neoliberals. But these states are also the agents of the domestic deepening and the international dissemination of the neoliberal order. The states of the most powerful countries impose their law (their commodities, their capital, and their rules) and, at the same time, prevent other states from getting in the way. This liberty is that of the strongest.

The prefix "neo" is no less of a problem than the second element, liberal, which it qualifies. Speaking of a new liberalism implies that there was an old one. Which old one? But we shall leave the historians to their arguments on this question.[2]

Very generally, this return to power may be characterized as that of a capitalist class, which corresponds to the idea of a particularly violent affirmation of the ownership of the means of production. But this reference remains too general. In neoliberalism there is an obvious financial component, taking us to the heart of capitalist relationships, the various fractions of the dominating classes, and the institutional frameworks through which this power is exerted, and so on. We use the notion of "finance" to characterize this configuration, which is easier to wield than to define (Chapter 23). Note that by "finance" we do not simply mean the financial sector of the economy, but the complex of upper capitalist classes, whose property materializes in the holding of securities (stock shares, bonds, Treasury bills, etc.), and financial institutions (central banks, banks, funds, etc.).

The shift to neoliberalism had two types of consequences. First of all, finance managed the crisis according to its own interests, which prolonged the crisis; second, this stretching out of the crisis made it possible for finance to shift the course of history in its own interests. Both elements, the management of the crisis and setting up an alternative society, are indeed linked—the crisis created the conditions for destroying the old order.

What should be understood by "managing the crisis according to the interests of a particular social group"? The answer is operating according to a double standard, doing everything possible in order to preserve the revenue of the social group, even obtaining revenue through other means when it has declined in its traditional forms—whatever the consequences for other social groups and countries. Managing the crisis according to the interests of finance means being indifferent to unemployment, or even counting on its downward pressures on wage demands, on the level of social protection, on job guarantees—during the crisis and beyond. Attempting to generalize the neoliberal order in the world was and remains devastating.

"Shifting the course of history in its own interests" means, for finance, setting up the institutional frameworks for its power, which is that of the owners over the major portion of the group of managers; it also means reinforcing its alliance, its fusion, with the managing elites; it means breaking the rules that limit the discretionary power of the business world concerning hiring and firing and mergers; it means taking away from the state the means to guarantee the old social alliances; it means returning the central banks to the exclusive service of price stability and protecting the assets of creditors; it means making retirement and social protection into a profitable field of activity for retirement funds or private insurance companies (particularly concerning health care); it means breaking up the solidarity of wage earners in favor of a so-called partnership of wage workers and owners (the "everyone's a capitalist" approach); it means creating a comfortable cushion of unemployed and social outcasts, separated by flimsy barriers; and it means controlling the dynamics of the cost of labor. Some of these conquests of finance in relation to workers are now designated by the graceful term "flexibility"—leanness and the ability to flexibly adapt.

There are certainly political risks, but no one enters the best of all capitalist worlds without a few funds for maintaining order in each country and on an international level.

Finance also used the crisis of the 1970s on an ideological and political level to launch a kind of society reflecting its image and in accordance with its interests. Presenting itself as a savior, as the only force capable of getting capitalism out of the woods, it manipulated opinion with cynicism, in that in actually managing the crisis, it made sure first of all that its own interests were preserved, and with ease, in that its opponents were discouraged and silent.

The entirety of the actions taken by finance was presented to us as a therapy. The rise of a neoliberal society was supposed to be synonymous with the end to the crisis. The proof: the United States, more neoliberal than most European countries, experienced higher growth in the 1990s. The continuing secondary effects of this treatment are supposed to be temporary and part of a transitional period. These arguments did not survive the 2000 recession, be it in the United States or in the rest of the world.

The question of the possibility of another road remains wide open. The analysis undertaken in this book makes it possible to envisage this question from a dual point of view, technical and political. On a relatively technical level, the study of unemployment leads to the firm conclusion—which some will judge to be surprising, if not provocative—that the wave of unemployment experienced by our economies hung on very little. A slightly different course of the main economic variables could have profoundly changed the jobs situation, which directly calls into question the economic policies applied. Inflation was high and intolerable for finance; unemployment and social exclusion were intolerable for other social categories. Unambiguous choices were made.

Why did the former, post–World War II compromise turn out to be incapable of dealing with the crisis? Did it die because of the intrinsic weaknesses or because of the strength of finance? Did these two elements combine their effects—the weakness of the Keynesian system when faced with the crisis and the renewed aggression of finance? Why have economic and social structures, such as those of Europe and Japan, so far from the American model, ceded to a large extent to neoliberal expansion? How was this new rise in the power of finance organized? All these questions are of paramount importance, because it is at this level of analysis, that of the political contest, that the principal determinants of the developments observed must be sought. The first point of view, which is more technical, clearly speaks for the contingent nature of these movements, but the political point of view, that of the confrontation of social forces, is obviously more difficult to define. However, it may be asserted that the weakness of popular struggles played a central role.

History, briefly invoked in this chapter, has much to teach us. These lessons will be at the heart of Parts IV and V. Part IV initially uses them in discussing the possibility of an end to the crisis and the current dangers of crisis. Did we get out of the 1970s crisis in the same way that society emerged from the crisis at the conclusion of the nineteenth century? To what extent can this comparison be made? Does this end to the crisis threaten us with another crisis, such as the Great Depression, which followed the upturn at the beginning of the twentieth century? And then, what do the policies of the thirty years following World War II teach us concerning political alternatives? Can these patterns be extended? Part V further broadens this historical perspective. What was the contribution of Keynesian theory and practice? In other words, is it possible to conceive of a capitalism in which finance is not hegemonic? Finally, how does Marxist analysis allow us to view the historical dynamics of capitalism, and its current transformations? What are the transformations of the relationships of production? What are the new class structures?

PART

II

Crisis and Unemployment

The contrast between this second part (as well as the third) and the preceding is considerable both in content and in method. Chapter 2 left us facing the image of finance triumphant. From now on we must grasp another, harsher, side of reality, that of crisis and unemployment. Leaving the great historical panoramas, we will now take up the analysis of the mechanisms, of the relationships between the variables characterizing technology, distribution, growth, and employment. Such a study may be drier, but the stakes are major. What was the origin of the structural crisis, the first signs of which can be situated in the late 1960s? Is it possible to establish a single diagnosis capable of explaining the evolution of the European and U.S. economies?

Chapters 3 and 4 put forward a general pattern, shared by Europe and the United States and centered on the decline of the profitability of capital in the 1970s. But this approach is extended in the comparative analysis of Chapter 5, in which the less advanced state of the European economies in relation to the American economy coming out of World War II and their gradual catching up play a central role. Intelligibility is only one of the motives of this analysis—its purpose is also to demystify. The depth of unemployment in the European Union and its permanent character reflect structural differences, but not those put forward by neoliberal propaganda.

This analysis of the crisis and unemployment concludes in Chapters 6 and 7 with two questions. Was the big wave of unemployment of the 1970s and 1980s inevitable? Are we emerging from the structural crisis? Initial elements of the answer are proposed, which the study of the monetary and financial processes will later make it possible to complete. The analytical apparatus of Part II, which shows the general trends of technology and distribution, is fundamental in the etymological and strongest sense of the term, but it is also limited. Must one refer to Marx in order to see the grounding of the analysis in technical and distributional trends, a requisite point of departure?

CHAPTER

3

The Structural Crisis of the 1970s and 1980s

A crisis struck the developed capitalist countries from the late 1960s to the early 1980s. The growth of unemployment was one of its most outstanding aspects, especially in Europe. But aside from unemployment, this crisis was evident in a series of problems—slowing of growth and of technical progress, increased frequency of overheating and recessions, runaway inflation, and monetary and financial crisis. And this list is not exhaustive. The multiplicity of these dimensions makes clear the structural character of the crisis, which was major.

This structural crisis has obviously not gone unnoticed. Even if everyone points to a particular event, limited in time, all are compelled to agree that something has gone awry. In the United States the degradation of the situation is generally traced to the end of the 1960s, during the first recession in which the decline in economic activity was accompanied by continuing inflation (hence the term stagflation). In Europe the interruption is most often dated to the 1974–1975 recession, which coincided with the rise of oil prices. The expressions "before the oil crisis" and "after the oil crisis" are at the center of many analyses of the beginning of the crisis in Europe, whatever their origin. But the oil crisis is never considered fully adequate for explaining a lasting, multifaceted crisis. As to its possible conclusion, everything depends on the indicator that is focused on—for example, employment or the stock market.

In the analysis of the structural crisis one must carefully distinguish a trigger factor, which explains the suddenness of a few movements, from a deeper deterioration of the situation, which results from a confluence of underlying trends—the historical trends of the major variables characterizing technology and distribution (labor and capital productivity, real

Box 3.1
Rate of profit: Productivity of labor and capital, and wage rate

The rate of profit is the indicator of the profitability of capital. It relates the mass of profits realized during a given period, one year, to the total sum of funds invested in a firm, a sector or the entire economy. Determining it is a delicate procedure, whether it be a question of profits or of the stock of capital that has been advanced. Profits are calculated by subtracting from sales all the expenses involved (raw materials, depreciation, the cost of services, and wages), but they may be figured in various ways, according to whether interest is paid or taxes are deducted. Therefore, the definitions used should be specified: for example, profits before or after interest payments, before- or after-tax profits. Measuring the total mass of the funds advanced is even more difficult, because it has been constituted over the years, during the life of a company. At a given point, these investments are materialized in different types of assets, such as fixed capital—buildings and machines (in the broader sense, including cars, computers, and the like)—inventories of raw materials or of as yet unsold products, financial assets, liquidities, without forgetting the mass of debt that companies have incurred, which must be deducted from the total value.

It is worth remembering that the profitability of capitalist business is not measured by the share of profits (as opposed to that of wages) in the total revenue generated by a line of business. What interests the capitalists is not to know whether they must pay out wages of one or ten million dollars in order to obtain a one million dollar profit, but rather what is the total amount of capital they must invest in order to turn a profit of that magnitude. This is

(continued)

wages, and rate of profit). The shift in the course of these variables is at the heart of this chapter and the next: what is the nature of this unfavorable change—common to the United States and Europe—which, in a very general sense, makes it possible to contrast the 1970s and 1980s with the two preceding decades?

It is difficult to orient oneself within the complexity of these processes. The interplay of cause and effect quickly dissolves into that of interdependencies. However, one idea emerges, that of the importance of the profitability of capital, measured by the rate of profit. The rate of profit is the ratio between profits made in one year to the capital used; it indicates to what extent the investment of capital is successful (Box 3.1). The rate of

(continued)

what the rate of profit measures. It is easy to understand the importance of this question of profitability in the evaluation of how lucrative a business is. As for interest rates, they measure the return on a loan and not on that of production or commercial activity.

Fundamentally, what determines the rate of profit is technology and wages. Besides the rate of profit, we therefore attach special importance to what we call the *major variables:* both the productivity of labor and that of capital,[a] and the wage rate, in a broad definition which includes all costs related to employment (social taxes). These three variables make it possible to calculate the rate of profit on fixed capital in an initial definition, which leaves aside the payment of interest rates and taxes.

$$\text{Rate of profit} = \frac{\text{Profit}}{\text{Fixed capital}} = \frac{\text{Profit}}{\text{Output}} \times \frac{\text{Output}}{\text{Fixed capital}}$$

$$\text{Rate of profit} = \text{Profit share} \times \text{Productivity of capital}$$

$$\text{Profit share} = 1 - \frac{\text{Rate of real wage}}{\text{Labor productivity}}$$

a. Respectively, the ratio of output to an indicator of employment (for example, the number of hours worked) or to a quantification of capital (in general, the stock of fixed capital). The notion of the productivity of capital does not imply that capital creates value in the sense of the Marxist theory of value. It is simply a question of a ratio.

profit is not the original cause of everything, but it does occupy the key position in the analysis. Many aspects of the crisis were determined by the low level of profit rates. The central thesis of this chapter is that the structural crisis at the end of the twentieth century, and indirectly unemployment, flowed from a decline in the rate of profit since the 1960s, a decline suspended only during the 1980s before the assertion of the new rising trend of the profit rate thereafter.

The reality of the decline in profit rates has been well established empirically. Figure 3.1 shows the rate of profit in Europe (restricted to the three main countries: Germany, France and the United Kingdom)[1] and in the United States over roughly a forty-year period (from 1960 to the end of the century).[2] This measurement does not take into account the weight of

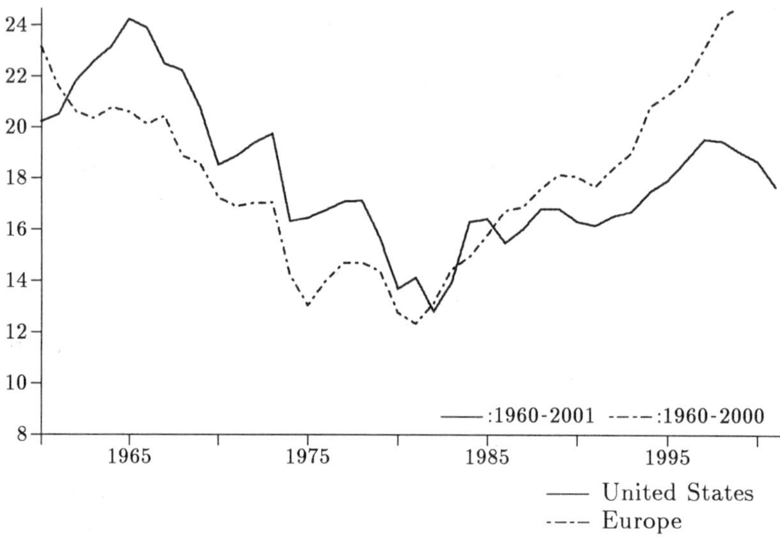

Figure 3.1 Rate of profit (percent): United States and Europe (Germany, France, and the United Kingdom). The unit of analysis is all firms. The rate of profit relates a broad-based measurement of profits (net output minus the cost of labor) to the net stock of fixed capital after depreciation (Box 3.1). Profits therefore still include tax, interest, and dividend payments.

taxes and interest rates (which will be analyzed in Part III). With the exception of the decline in the United States since 1997, the degree to which the movements are parallel is striking. The decline is very pronounced from the 1960s until the beginning of the 1980s. An upward trend can also be seen from this period onward. The levels of 1960 were regained in Europe at the end of the 1990s.

The pattern of the decline in the profit rate was not exactly the same in Europe as in the United States. It decreased very regularly in Europe, despite a certain interruption at the beginning of the 1970s. The level of the profit rate was stimulated by strong economic activity, culminating in 1973, just before the oil crisis. This was the period of Keynesian support policies. The drop was then abrupt, which explains why the first oil crisis of 1973 is so widely referred to as the starting point of the economy's deterioration even though the trend had already begun. This break was not as strong in the United States. The most striking difference concerns the high point reached in 1965 in that country. The 1960s in the United States were marked by a vigorous upswing after the 1960 recession, and then by the

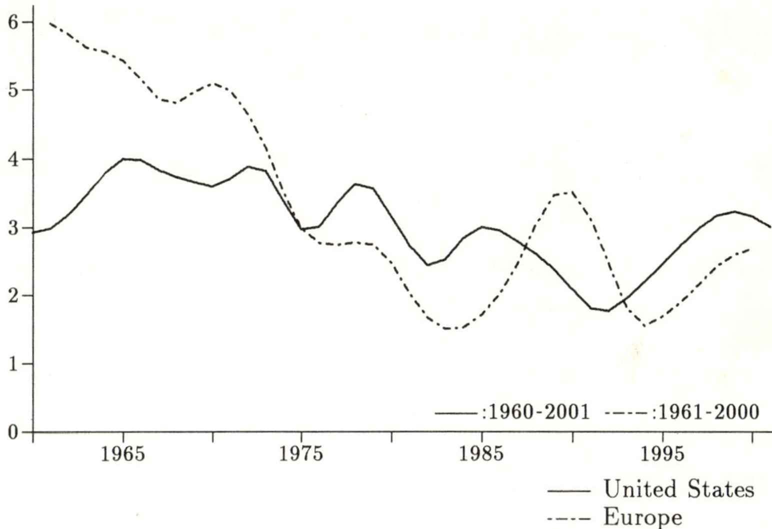

Figure 3.2 Rate of accumulation (percent): United States and Europe (Germany, France, and the United Kingdom), all firms. The rate of accumulation is the rate of growth of the net stock of fixed capital. The data have been slightly smoothed in order to leave aside short-term fluctuations.

outlays linked to the Vietnam War. In the United States as in Europe these events made it possible to temporarily postpone the effects of the decline of profit rates. In addition to these policies there was a reduction of interest rate charges given the rate of inflation, as we shall see. This only deferred the opening of the crisis. These policies could not, on a long-term basis, remedy the decline in the rate of profit, whose existence and origins were, moreover, not clearly identified by contemporary observers. To designate the respite that was accorded the U.S. economy in this way, we speak of a *Keynesian* (and inflationary) *reprieve,* underscoring its necessary limitation in time and its relation to policies of a particular inspiration.

However, referring to the decline of the rate of profit does not conclude the analysis of the crisis, because this decrease itself has origins that have to be accounted for. Temporarily setting aside certain retroactive mechanisms, we can say that the profit rate makes it possible to separate out causes and effects:

Causes of the decline in the rate of profit → Decline in the rate of profit → The crisis as an effect

This chapter discusses only the effects of the decline in the rate of profit and not its causes (the second element of the diagram and not the first). The discussion is even limited further to two effects among several: the slowing down of capital accumulation and unemployment.

The general relationship between profit rates and the crisis may be summed up in a simple idea: the rate of profit is the motor force of capitalist production, and when it is low or declines, firms are in trouble, disrupting the general functioning of the economy (Box 3.2). This thesis was at the heart of Marx's analysis in *Capital.*

To a certain extent the economy can adapt itself to reduced profitability, but this adaptation is complicated and takes time. Companies have to learn to act differently, in more difficult conditions; they have to better manage their liquidity and obtain new financing; moreover, it is necessary to modify the functioning of the financial system (the ways in which capital is raised and remunerated) and carry out macroeconomic policies capable of responding to these difficulties or to the slowness of accumulation. These adjustments are possible, but not automatic.

Still to be established is the relationship between the crisis and unemployment. On this point we can supply a clear answer. The main cause of the wave of unemployment that developed between 1975 and 1985 was the low level of investment, the insufficient accumulation of capital:

Decline in the profit rate → Slowdown of accumulation → Unemployment

As for the impact of technical change on employment, along with the crisis came a slowdown of technological progress, which was—in its direct effects, that is, rather than in its impact on the profit rate, which will be taken up later—favorable to employment: slower technical progress means less labor saving, therefore comparatively more employment.

The decline in profit rates described in Figure 3.1 was coupled with a lowering of the accumulation rate. This pronounced slowdown is illustrated in Figure 3.2.[3] This decline contributed to a reduction of the growth in the employment rate. Table 3.1 presents the average values of the rates of profit, accumulation, and unemployment in the United States and the three European countries for two ten-year subperiods, before and after 1974.

The slowdown in accumulation and the decline of the profit rate clearly coincided in time. The lowest rate of profit was reached at the beginning of

Box 3.2
The consequences of a decline in profitability

A low level of profitability confronts companies with cash-flow problems, a shortage of liquidity, and difficulties in making reimbursements and in obtaining financing, leading to stricter management, particularly concerning investment and production decisions.

Levels of profitability are also reflected in rates of investment, or capital accumulation. Profits make investment more attractive; companies finance it directly or take advantage of more favorable conditions for issuing stock or borrowing; an insufficient rate of profit lowers the rate of investment. A slowdown in investment likewise leads to a slowdown in the growth of output and employment, two essential aspects of the crisis.

A recession may be analyzed as a cumulative contraction of output. Declines in output and in demand become tied together, one leading to the other. Less output means fewer purchases of capital goods and fewer salaries being paid out—that is, reductions that diminish demand—therefore leading companies to lower their output. The intensity of a recession is a function of the intensity of reactions, particularly companies' sensitivity to their difficulty in selling their products, and that is where the effect of profitability is particularly felt in the short term. Continuing to produce too much when the company is experiencing poor sales and unsold inventories are accumulating leads to a continuing depletion of funds, which is not sufficiently built back up through income from sales. Thus the decline and low level of companies' profitability leads them to vigorously adjust output to demand by passing the difficulty of selling on to production. Following rather intuitive mechanisms, such behavior, when it becomes generalized throughout the economy, creates increased instability—the shocks in the economy take on a cumulative character. Such spirals account for the intensification of cyclical fluctuations during a structural crisis, particularly in the increase in number and deepening of recessions.

the 1980s. Accumulation resumed later, more rapidly but fleetingly in Europe and after a delay in the United States.

The slowness of accumulation is in fact an explanation for spreading unemployment, as is fairly intuitive. Along with economic growth comes jobs growth. The slowing of the growth of capital was coupled with a slowing of the growth of the number of people engaged in production. Since roughly the mid-1970s, economic growth has decelerated; it no longer

Table 3.1 Consequences of the fall in the profit rate (in percent)

	United States		Europe	
	1965–1974	1975–1984	1965–1974	1975–1984
Profit rate	20.6	15.4	18.1	13.8
Accumulation rate	3.8	3.0	4.8	2.3
Unemployment rate	4.6	7.7	1.8	6.1

generates a sufficient quantity of jobs compared with the population available to work; this insufficiency has provoked the rise in unemployment. Whatever the other variables may be that complicate these relationships, accumulation and growth are at the heart of the employment problem.

The considerable duration of the crisis gave new life to stagnation theories, which have already gone out of style because of the resumption of growth during the 1990s: the slowdown of growth was interpreted in the 1980s as characteristic of a new era in which demand would no longer grow as before. Humanity, or at least a privileged minority, had been carried away by growth and abundance, until its needs were saturated. And with the end of demand came the end of the increases in employment. Here we run into another theme, also popular at one time, that of the end of labor linked to the excesses of technological progress. The next two chapters, which deal with the relationships between unemployment and technical progress, refute both these theories.

This initial investigation therefore concludes with the assertion of a diagnosis: the profit rate is central to an explanation of the crisis, of the slowdown of accumulation, and of the rise in unemployment. Other variables (concerning technology, growth, or inflation) confirm these common features: the structural crisis struck Europe and the United States in a similar manner, and the same causes had the same effects.

As we have noted, the profit rate reached a low at the beginning of the 1980s and has since been increasing. This chapter therefore concludes with a paradoxical observation: accumulation diminished with the drop in profit rates, but the more recent trend toward a rise in profit rates has not been coupled with a corresponding recovery of capital accumulation, despite the upward swing of the rate of accumulation at the end of the 1990s. Here it is implicitly a question of financial relationships; we shall return to them in Chapter 9.

CHAPTER

4

Technical Progress: Accelerating or Slowing?

To what extent can technological progress explain unemployment? The question deserves careful examination. The growth of unemployment is often attributed to the acceleration of technical progress, but it must be said without equivocation that this explanation is wrong. Yet this does not mean that technological progress and its varying tempo are not at the heart of both the crisis and unemployment—they are, but in another way. It is not because technological progress has accelerated that the crisis has occurred and that a wave of unemployment has developed. Rather it is because something has gone wrong in the course of technological progress.

The logic that makes the acceleration of technological progress responsible for unemployment is simple—mechanization makes labor unnecessary and workers are replaced. This analysis, combined with other, particularly environmental, concerns, fits well into a perspective that calls progress into question.

But this interpretation is not borne out by the facts. In no way may one speak of the acceleration of progress. To the contrary, the rate of technological progress has declined during the decades of growing unemployment. There is no doubt that production is more and more mechanized and that it requires comparatively less and less labor. Yet the speed of this progress hasn't stopped slowing down since the mid-1960s. It was stated in the preceding chapter that the wave of unemployment had other causes: the slowness of economic growth, that is, the slowness of the increase in output and the slowness of the accumulation of capital.

A simple indicator of technological progress is the progress of labor productivity (Table 4.1). This variable measures the evolution of the average output of a worker in one hour. During the 1960s, when near full em-

Table 4.1 Productivity and unemployment (in percent)

	United States		Europe	
	1965–1974	1975–1984	1965–1974	1975–1984
Growth rate of labor productivity	2.1	0.9	4.8	2.9
Unemployment rate	4.6	7.7	1.8	6.1

ployment prevailed, labor productivity advanced comparatively rapidly. Conversely, the years of structural unemployment were years of slower progress—every year production saved on labor, but to a constantly diminishing extent. These observations therefore associate full employment with vigorous technological progress, and not more rapid technological progress with a growth in unemployment.

These findings may be surprising, but they are also intuitive. The speed of technological progress is a sign of an economy that is healthy and dynamic; the same is true for full employment. When technological progress is doing well, the economy is doing well.[1]

This slowing down of technological progress is well known to specialists and provoked a wide-ranging controversy. The debate was more heated in the United States than in Europe, because it raised the problem of American preeminence, particularly as regards Japan, which for a long time sustained much more rapid progress than the rest of the world.

Figure 4.1 traces the course of labor productivity for Europe and the United States since World War II. The flattening out of the curve over the years reproduces the decline in the growth rate of this variable. The decrease in the pace of overall progress is obvious. In the United States, for the period 1946–1970, the average annual growth rate of hourly labor productivity was 3.3 percent. It did not go beyond 1.5 percent in any of the subsequent decades.

Is it possible to observe a recent upturn in the growth of labor productivity in the United States? Over the last five years of the twentieth century, the average growth of labor productivity did reach 1.6 percent. The recovery was real, but remained weak.[2]

These observations contradict the image, firmly rooted in many minds, of technological change backed by a continuous flow of new goods and services. The expanding performance of computer and communications technology, for example, is the subject of ongoing amazement.

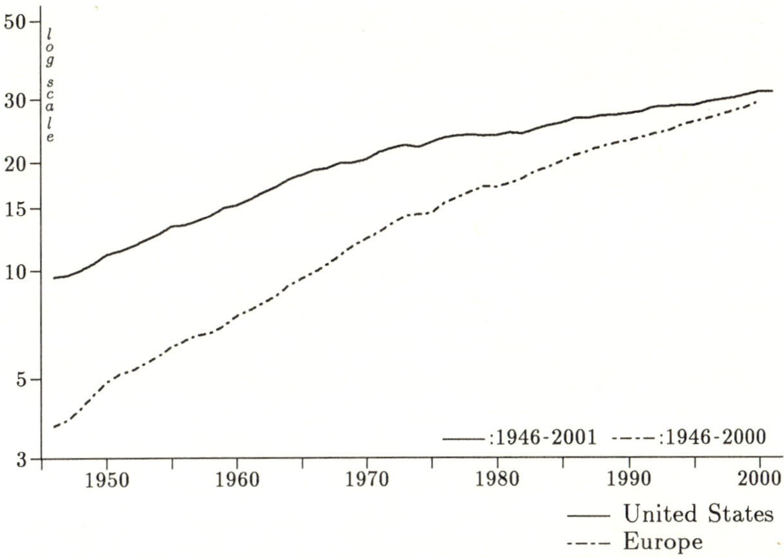

Figure 4.1 Labor productivity (1990 dollars per hour): United States and Europe (Germany, France, and the United Kingdom), all firms. Labor productivity is net output, corrected for inflation, over the number of labor hours. This figure is the first in the book to use a logarithmic scale—the slope of the curves is proportional to the growth rate of the variables. Recurrent fluctuations (small in this figure) are the effects of overheating and slowdowns in activity.

Two remarks should be made here. First, this view cannot be given full credence. The most recent innovations should be compared with those of previous periods—the industrial revolution, the end of the nineteenth century, the beginning of the twentieth century, or the first postwar decades. Wasn't the progress accomplished during these years also sizable? What about electricity or the radio? Many of the innovations prior to World War II became widespread in postwar Europe—even those from much earlier, like the automobile. The same is true for the mechanization of domestic life, made possible by the development of household appliances or the invention of plastic. Certainly, cellular phones, home computers, and the Internet are fascinating, but previous decades also had their share of products.

Second, this flow of innovations expresses another phenomenon, different from that manifested in the change in labor productivity, even if the two processes are in some ways related. The ability to economize on resources needed for the production of a good or service (which is measured by the progress of labor productivity) is distinct from the arrival of consumer goods. In our analysis of unemployment, the term "technological progress" must always be understood in the sense of "production technology progress" (combining mechanization and organization), from the strict viewpoint of the capacity to economize on resources used in the production of a good or in providing a service. It is this form of technological progress that is important for profitability and for employment when the economy is considered globally.

If the acceleration of technological progress is not the problem, what then is the relationship between this progress and unemployment? In our opinion the link is indirect but very simple. It is, on the contrary, the slowing down of technological progress that is the problem. To grasp this, we must return to the first diagram of Chapter 3, which describes the chain going from the factors of the decline of the profit rate to the effects of this decline, among them unemployment. We arrive at the following result: technological progress is at issue in the analysis of unemployment because of its role in the evolution of the rate of profit. Hence we must specify what comes before the previous diagram by making technological progress one of the determinants of the rate of profit:

Slow technological progress → Decline in profit rate → Slowdown of accumulation → Unemployment

Technological progress is linked to unemployment by this indirect path. As one of the determinants of the profit rate, it stands at the origin of its decline; the decline of the profit rate slows down accumulation; this slowing down is reflected in the insufficiency of job growth; unemployment is the expression of this insufficiency.

We now examine the first link of this chain—the relationship between technological progress and the ups and downs of the rate of profit. What happens to technological progress that may explain the decline in the profitability of capital?

The first clue that we had to the existence of problems in technological progress was the slowdown in the growth of labor productivity depicted by Figure 4.1. During the 1950s and 1960s considerable savings were made on the quantity of labor required for the production of a good or a service; the rate of these savings later slowed down.

In order to grasp the reasons for this slowdown, one must recall that the principal way to save labor is mechanization. Relatively less labor is utilized because more use is made of fixed capital (or of more costly items). The term "mechanization" is a bit restrictive because, strictly speaking, it means the increased use of *machines* in production, whereas fixed capital includes other items, such as buildings, but is commonly used in a broad sense. It is therefore not sufficient to compare the labor consumed in the production with the product obtained in order to speak of progress. One must also question the quantity of fixed capital required by production, that is, the increased amount of capital demanded by the labor savings.

In the same way that labor productivity measures the product obtained per hour of labor, the productivity of capital measures the products obtained per unit of capital, that is, per dollar of fixed capital (Box 3.1). How many dollars' worth of products are produced each year for one dollar of buildings, machines, or vehicles? That is the question. The change in the productivity of capital is a crucial element in the transformation that occurred in the 1970s.

The examination of capital productivity in Figure 4.2 for the United States reveals quite a spectacular result. Whereas capital productivity had fluctuated since World War II, without the emergence of a clear trend, it started dropping sharply beginning in the second half of the 1960s, just prior to the crisis. A similar, more regular, development also appeared in Europe, at least after 1960 when the statistics begin (Figure 4.3).

These trends in the productivity of capital make considerably less credible the notion of "technological progress," an expression that we nevertheless use. Savings continued to be made in production, in labor, but they were paid for by an increased need for capital—less on the one side, but more on the other, progress on the one side and, in a certain sense, regression on the other.

The existence of this increased use of fixed capital (mechanization) is well known, but one must examine its characteristic features. This increased weight of capital reached such proportions that its total price, in relation to that of the goods and services produced, didn't stop growing until the early 1980s, as the decline in capital productivity indicates. Although mechanization made labor productivity growth possible, its cost limited its potential in terms of profitability. Mechanization may have turned out to be effective in making it possible to save labor, but it was expensive.

This very particular course of technological progress, burdened with

Figure 4.2 Productivity of capital and profit share (1966 = 1): United States, all firms. The productivity of capital is net output over the stock of fixed capital (Box 3.1). Profit share is profits broadly defined (before taxes, interest and dividend payments) over net output. For both of these figures the data has been divided by its value in 1966, in order to come out to 1 for that year. The vertical and horizontal scales are identical in both Figures 4.2 and 4.3.

Figure 4.3 Productivity of capital and profit share (1966 = 1): Europe (Germany, France, and the United Kingdom), all firms.

growing masses of capital, was understood by Marx in the mid-nineteenth century. He placed it at the center of his analysis of the trend toward the decline of the profit rate, in Book III of *Capital* (Box 4.1). For this reason we call "technological progress à la Marx" progress where capital increases not only in relationship to the labor used, but also in relationship to out-

Box 4.1
The tendency of the rate of profit to decline

In Book III of *Capital,* Marx gave a detailed description of a set of "historical trends" characteristic of capitalist production. This notion of *trend* refers to long-term evolutions of technology and distribution—broad movements that may be observed independently of cyclical fluctuations (the succession of overheating and recessions). The most famous of these trends delineated by Marx is the falling rate of profit, but the description given by Marx also includes the progress of labor productivity, the increase of the composition of capital (the capital-labor ratio), the continuing accumulation of increased masses of capital although the rate of growth of the stock of capital is diminishing, and the increase of employment. At issue, therefore, is a trajectory of growth and progress of labor productivity, but in which the profit rate declines. The fundamental intuition of Marx is that progress in labor productivity generally demands expensive mechanization. Instead of an increase in the composition of capital, we usually refer to a decline in the productivity of capital to characterize the profile of such mechanization. We call these "trajectories à la Marx."

In earlier work we have interpreted Marx's intuition in terms of "the difficulty of innovation." This difficulty refers to a contradiction between individual and collective interests in research and in the development of new procedures. Elaborating procedures is expensive, and it is difficult to protect their results, which tend to become widely available. Moreover, strict legislation to protect patents would have the disadvantage of holding up the spread of progress.

What is interesting about this analysis is that the capitalist system is effectively inclined to place itself on such trajectories, although it may avoid them during certain periods, given the effect of countertendencies or of more or less deep transformations of its functioning.

Periods of decline in profit rates lead to great structural crises, which capitalism has, until now, been unable to avoid, but has been capable of overcoming. The conditions of change, the arising of countertendencies after such crises, are created by the tendency itself, even though there is nothing automatic.

put—less and less labor, but relatively more and more machines. The period of the decline in the productivity of capital in Figures 4.2 and 4.3 may thus be labeled as a period *à la Marx.* This character is important because it is responsible for another feature: such technological progress is coupled in general with a decline in the profit rate (Figure 3.1).

This unfavorable course of technological progress is not permanent. A historical investigation going back further into the past reveals that the United States came out of World War I in a quite advantageous position with regard to the speed and forms of technological change (Chapter 16). Real progress was demonstrated at all levels: from one year to the next less labor and less capital were required per unit produced. The profit rate increased, even though real wages were increasing at a particularly fast pace. The drop in the profit rate, hence the slowing of accumulation, hence the insufficient jobs growth, hence unemployment, should be ascribed to the disappearance of those advantageous features of technological change.

The profit rate depends not only on technology but also on wages. Many therefore place the responsibility for the decline of the profit rate on the excessive increase in wages. Indeed, something did change from the point of view of wages during this period: their increase slowed down, as Table 4.2 indicates. But this change had the opposite effect of one that could make it responsible for the decline in the profit rate.

Not coincidentally, the period of crisis led early on to the strict control of increases in wages and in social taxes. The wave of unemployment that accompanied the crisis helped a great deal to slow these increases down. The rate of wage hikes never stopped declining all during the crisis, until it was reduced to practically nothing or eliminated (Chapter 6). It was only revived during the late 1990s in the United States, as we will discuss later on.

Faced with the slowdown in technological progress, employers sought to put all its weight on the shoulders of their employees. In this they suc-

Table 4.2 Wages and profit rate (in percent)

	United States		Europe	
	1965–1974	1975–1984	1965–1974	1975–1984
Rate of wage cost increase	2.4	1.1	5.5	2.7
Profit rate	20.6	15.4	18.1	13.8

ceeded somewhat belatedly. But these chains of events should not be inverted. Too rapid wage increases did not disturb a peaceful world. It is the interruption of the course of technological progress that laid out a new economic trajectory; wages were adjusted.

Despite lower wage increases, labor costs gradually began to weigh more on the profitability of capital. In the United States this burden continued to be moderate until the mid-1970s, as long as the slowdown in the rise of labor productivity remained limited. Thus profit share in total income decreased slowly until this point, as can be seen in Figure 4.2.[3] The decline in profit share, resulting from a sharp slowdown in the growth of labor productivity, contributed significantly to the decline in profit rates in the 1970s. A similar evolution took place in Europe (Figure 4.3).

Those who place the responsibility for the drop in profit rates on wages mean in fact that wages should have immediately and entirely adapted to this unfavorable course of technological change in order to fully maintain the profitability of capital. But in this regard, what was the attitude of the other social groups? We shall return to this.

To sum up, events took place as follow. Unfavorable conditions for technological change appeared in the 1960s or even earlier. Despite the gradual throttling of the rate of wage increases, the profitability of capital dropped and economic growth (the rate of capital accumulation) was significantly affected, both in Europe and in the United States. The European economies in particular were incapable of generating a mass of jobs equal to the available population—hence the wave of structural unemployment. The chain went from technological progress to unemployment, passing through profitability of capital and accumulation. It was a question not of too much progress, but of its deficiencies.

At the risk of getting ahead of our study, one cannot avoid noting in Figures 4.2 and 4.3 the specific features of the last decades, since the beginning of the 1980s. A trend toward the increase in the productivity of capital and profit share, related to the increase in profit rates (Figure 3.1), may be clearly seen—an essential element in the change of the course of capitalism which denotes the beginning of a new phase.[4] No significant improvement concerning labor productivity, however, is noticeable (Figure 4.1). The recent decline in the profit share in the United States since 1998 (Figure 4.2), also apparent in the profile of the profit rate, is the consequence of the recent increase in the growth rate of the labor cost (Figure 6.1).

CHAPTER

5

America and Europe: The Creator of Jobs and the Creator of Unemployment

The structural crisis that began in the 1970s was common to both the United States and the European Union, but the problem of jobs and unemployment did not develop to the same extent in both economic areas. The wave of structural unemployment that grew in Europe between 1975 and 1985 was much more sweeping and has not gone away, whereas in the United States the rate of unemployment has diminished significantly, to the point of giving the impression of a return to normal or overemployment before the 2000 recession. Because of the growth of temporary jobs and the transformation of labor conditions, this idea of newfound full employment in the United States cannot be given complete credence. Nevertheless, the decrease in the official statistics for unemployment in that country contrasts strongly with the stagnation or slow decline of unemployment seen in Europe in the late 1990s. The time has now come to give an initial answer to this puzzle.

Why this divergent development? Must one see here the effects of a wonderful degree of flexibility in the United States? This step is quickly taken by the advocates of neoliberalism—according to them, the United States was capable of evolving in a way that the old continent refused because of cumbersome social constraints. America has once again become a model—precisely a neoliberal model that we should import. Dynamism on the one side of the Atlantic, ossification on the other, or, by combining the United States and the United Kingdom, dynamism in that part of the world most firmly engaged on the neoliberal road on the one hand, and ossification in the countries of the European continent on the other. The purpose of this chapter is to refute these statements.

These differences in unemployment may be simply explained: similar rates of growth and accumulation generate an increase in employment in the United States and its stagnation in Europe, because technological progress has been much more rapid in Europe than in the United States. The virtues of flexibility are not at issue here, but rather the relatively slow pace of American technological progress—the slowness of the growth of labor productivity. To be more precise, the problem is the more rapid substitution of capital for labor in Europe (the more rapid increase in the capital-labor ratio, that is, the quantity of fixed capital, of machines, per worker). European economies were less advanced, but performed much better in terms of technological progress since World War II, perhaps too much better. They are now making less progress, but still more than the United States.

When Europe emerged from World War II it was far behind the United States. This is a well-known fact, which one statistic suffices to measure. Figure 5.1 presents an estimation of the capital-labor ratio in the three European countries on which we are focusing and in the United States. This figure gives a striking image of the catching-up phenomenon of these countries in relation to the United States. The capital-labor ratio, which measures in a simple manner the degree of mechanization, was nearly three times lower in the principal European countries than overseas. Three times less fixed capital, let's say three times fewer machines, or machines three times less expensive, characterized Europe in relation to the United States at the end of the war. Over the next thirty years these economies made up for their backwardness, thanks to much more rapid technological and organizational progress.[1] Of course, this was not a uniform phenomenon for all sectors; here we are talking about averages.

It is easy to imagine the consequences in terms of employment of this race to modernization—growth in employment on the one hand, stagnation on the other. The difference is glaring. To become convinced of this, it suffices to examine Figure 5.2. Two curves of private employment are to be found there, for the United States and the three countries of the European Union, for the period ranging from 1946 to the end of the century. The population employed in the private sector in the United States has continually increased since World War II at an average rate of 1.6 percent per year; in Europe it has grown little and fluctuated around a basically stable level of the workforce since the 1970s.[2]

The level of employment shown in this figure does not include public employees. Whereas in the United States the ratio of public civil servants to

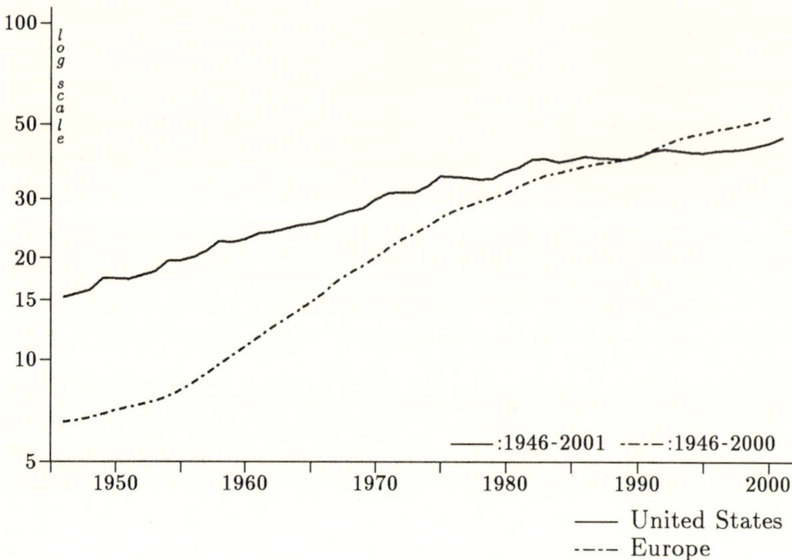

Figure 5.1 Capital-labor ratio (thousands of 1990 dollars per hour): Europe (Germany, France, and the United Kingdom) and the United States, all firms. Capital is the net stock of fixed capital, adjusted for inflation; it has been divided by the number of hours worked.

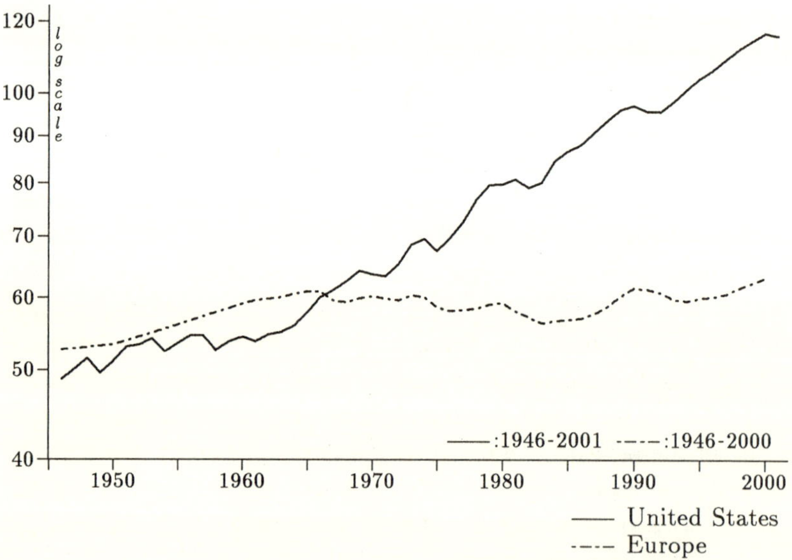

Figure 5.2 Total private employment (millions): United States and Europe (Germany, France, and the United Kingdom).

private employees remained fairly stable over this period, this ratio increased in Europe.[3] The difference between the job trends in the three European countries and the United States is thus less for total civilian employment than that concerning private employment in Figure 5.2, but this difference does not change the general observation regarding the much greater job growth in the United States—which is explained by the slower increase in the capital-labor ratio in that country.[4]

The consequences of the different rates of technological change for employment were spectacular over this entire period. In Europe they were compensated by rapid growth (capital accumulation) before the 1970s, but had dramatic effects during the crisis. Since 1974, that is, since the crisis has held sway, the capital-labor ratio has increased in the United States by 1.0 percent per year, against 2.7 percent in the three European countries, or at more than double the same rate. Had these countries not continued their catching up since 1974, in other words, had their mechanization evolved similarly to that of the United States at the slow rate of 1.0 percent per year, then private employment would have encompassed—all other factors being equal, particularly the rate of accumulation and the reduction of the workweek—around 36 million people more than it did in 2000, when there were officially only 9 million unemployed. To avoid unemployment completely it would have sufficed for the growth of mechanization to take place at a rate of only 2.2 percent per year, or twice as rapidly as in the United States.[5]

Must one deduce from this robust technological progress that Europe possesses better know-how than the United States? Obviously this question must be answered negatively. This opinion is already contained in the notion of "catching up." The United States was more advanced than Europe. Europe imported American technology and management. It goes without saying that this does not mean Americans invented everything—to a certain extent, every country made its contribution. In a world of multinationals, the limits of research and innovation are no longer the traditional borders. Nevertheless, it is well known that American methods were very widely disseminated in all the advanced countries. Certain European or Japanese organizational types were sometimes perceived as alternatives to the American model, capable of taking over, but recent developments have somewhat relegated those analyses to the background, rightly or not.

Simplifying considerably and leaving aside the widespread heterogeneity among sectors and countries, the United States may be seen as the cutting-edge country for technology and management up until the 1980s. Innovation in such a country fully merits its name because it implies exploring up to the limits of the unknown. It has a high cost because it operates in this manner at the frontiers of knowledge. Technological change there follows its own laws that may be analyzed intrinsically. Conversely, the other countries progress below this frontier. Technological change there is governed by other mechanisms and other laws. This does not mean, however, that it is easily obtained or more or less guaranteed. There we have all the complexity of the problems inherent in catching up—the one that is less advanced potentially benefits from progress made elsewhere but is also dominated by the world market, and that domination may force it to stand still or to lose ground. Its companies may be crushed by foreign competition if they are too suddenly exposed to it. Should they wait for the flow of foreign investment? And what if it never comes? And what if the quest for immediate profit by these international investors and their fear of risk provokes an unbearable instability?

The real miracle accomplished by the latecomer countries (Europe and Japan) after World War II was to have been able to go ahead and catch up, despite the difficulties, while still protecting the job situation. This success was based on a careful mixture of opening up to foreign competition and protecting national economies, made possible by the national and international monetary institutions set up at the end of the war. The state got involved in this development via its macroeconomic and industrial policies, by directly taking charge of fundamental sectors, and by financing research and training. No excessive monetary discipline was imposed and inflation was not demonized. The dynamics of national and international investment were adjusted by means of continuous monetary adjustments (Chapter 21).

The lessons suggested by Europe's catching up are simple. Concerning technology, it is not good to catch up as rapidly as possible and to modernize production capacities in a period of structural crisis; concerning policies, it is premature to give up one's tools when the task has not been completed.

The explanation of the differences between the two economic areas given in this chapter contrasts sharply with the theses of Chapter 4. We argued there that the wave of unemployment in the 1975–1985 decade could not be ascribed to the rapidity of technological progress, as it had slowed down considerably since the beginning of the crisis. The previous level of full employment had been coupled with much stronger rates of progress. What is now being considered, however, is not the formation of structural unemployment in the crisis since the 1970s, but the differences between the United States and Europe. The explanation of the global phenomenon differs from that of the differences between the various zones. There is nothing disconcerting here. The acceleration of technological progress cannot account for unemployment in the crisis, because this progress slowed down everywhere. But it is possible to understand why the problem of unemployment was much sharper in Europe than in the United States, because that country saves, year after year, much less labor than Europe does.

CHAPTER

6

Controlling Labor Costs and Reining in the Welfare State

Full employment is detrimental to the fructification of capital because it entails wage increases and, more generally, makes employees less amenable to the demands of their employers. If labor costs increase too much, profit rates are affected. The same is true if workers refuse to adapt to the workweek or to labor conditions. Unemployment and lack of job security are the best guarantors of this discipline, whether the employee goes through the experience himself or whether the threat hangs over his or her head. Permanently assuring the maintenance of a reserve of individuals without work or seeking to work more—what Marx called the "reserve army"—is a fundamental feature of capitalism.

Globally, the 1950s and 1960s had been characterized by near full employment, making it necessary for countries to resort largely to immigration. Coupled with rapid technological progress, struggles by workers had made possible a relatively sustained improvement of their purchasing power, winning certain guarantees concerning social protection and gradual recognition of a right to a job.

The enormous wave of unemployment which expanded during the second half of the 1970s, therefore, formed a powerful means of pressure to bring labor costs back under control. The most direct way for company owners and officers to improve their profit rate was to obtain concessions from their employees. A pure and simple reduction of purchasing power would have been welcomed by the owners and officers, and, moreover, was obtained in certain countries for certain categories of labor, but workers resisted this challenge to their standard of living. Lowering social taxes would have had the same effect on the profit rate, but there also it was not simple to take on these social conquests, solidly rooted institutionally and culturally.[1]

Rather than seeking to drive down purchasing power and social benefits, employers have sought to block any further increases. The deterioration of the conditions of technological progress and the concomitant drop in the profit rate, and the structural crisis that this drop provoked, were followed by an attack on both the direct and indirect cost of labor. The simplest way to demonstrate this is to describe the evolution of the total average cost of an hour of labor (wage cost) for an employer in Europe and in the United States, all social taxes included.

The slowing down of the growth of labor costs in the crisis was striking in both areas, echoing the increase in unemployment rates (Table 6.1 and Figure 6.1). As the figure shows, European wage costs remain below those of the United States, despite the difference in the rates of increase (in 1960, the average cost of an hour of labor in the three European countries was 50 percent of one in the United States; in 2000 it represented 91 percent of it).[2]

Wage costs do not directly measure workers' purchasing power for various reasons. They include social taxes and not benefits; because costs are seen from the employer's point of view, adjustments for the effects of inflation are made according to the price index of total output instead of that of goods bought by workers, and it is hourly costs that are considered, whereas the length of the workweek has been reduced. In total, the decrease of the growth of purchasing power was even more severe than what Figure 6.1 suggests.

Moreover, it is obvious that the population of wage workers is extremely heterogeneous, and the differences are even stronger in the United States than in a country such as France. In the United States there exist a category

Table 6.1 Unemployment and wages (in percent)

	United States		Europe	
	1965–1974	1975–1984	1965–1974	1975–1984
Unemployment rate	4.6	7.7	1.8	6.1
Rate of wage cost increase	2.4	1.1	5.5	2.7

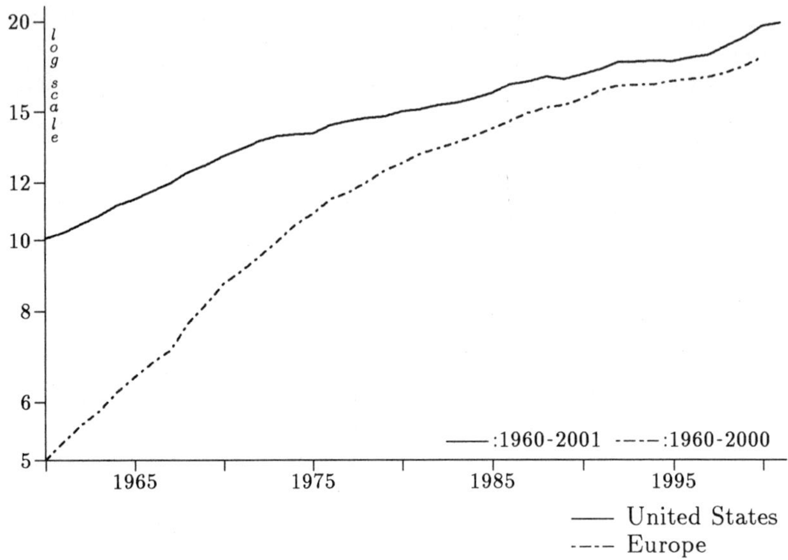

Figure 6.1 Cost of one hour of labor (1990 dollars): United States and Europe (Germany, France, and the United Kingdom), all firms. These values have been corrected for inflation and are expressed in a common unit of purchasing power, which makes it possible to compare not only the rate of growth but also the absolute values.

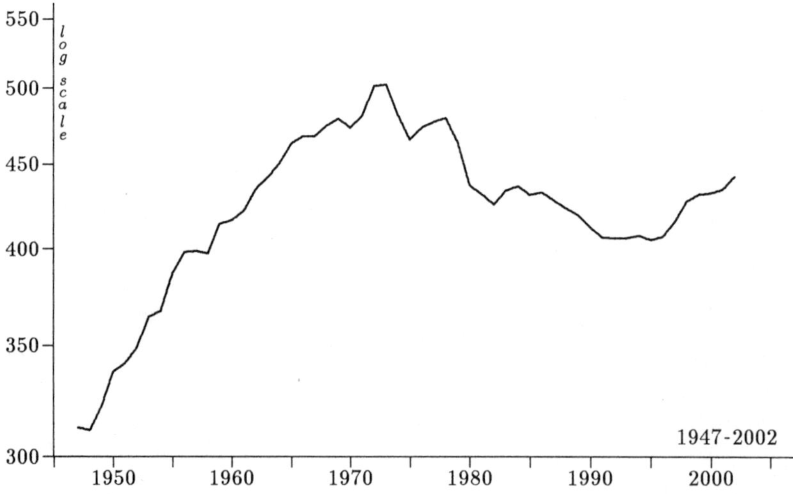

Figure 6.2 Weekly pay of a production worker (1996 dollars): United States.

of production workers (80 percent of the workforce) and statistics describing the weekly pay of these workers (that is, given the length of their work). The profile of this weekly pay has been drawn in Figure 6.2. The transformation that occurred at the beginning of the 1970s and that was amplified in the 1980s is breathtaking. The weekly pay of a production worker in the 1990s dropped back to its level at the end of the 1950s. Despite a slight increase in the very last few years, in 2002 it was 12 percent below its maximum level in 1972. A nice example of what keeping wage costs under control means.

It is the social taxes, and therefore the benefits they finance that, in France, have been the subject of the bitterest complaints from employers. Here we limit ourselves to the case of that country, since the differences between the benefit systems would overly complicate the analysis.

As long as economic growth and wage increases held up, that is, until the mid-1970s, benefits (retirement pensions, health care, family and unemployment allocations) could grow regularly without raising any big problems. In 1960 they represented an amount equal to around 11 percent of total French output. This proportion slowly grew (15 percent in 1974), reflecting the increase in health care expenses and the aging of the population. These developments were evidence of a society that was progressing, that was providing better medical care, and whose life expectancies were increasing. The total amount of employee and employer social taxes required to finance expenditures had stabilized at the beginning of the 1970s at a little more than 42 percent of the salary actually received by employees, or, if one prefers, these taxes represented a little over 29 percent of total wage costs.[3]

The structural crisis upset the balance between expenses and revenue. It added to certain expenditures, such as those relative to unemployment, and decreased revenues (which are linked to total wages). The slowing down of the increase in wages and in the number of jobs resulted in new problems, given the expenses, such as medical costs or pensions, that developed through their own dynamic.

No one will be surprised when we state that expenditures related to unemployment allocations increased a great deal in the crisis. But they were also quickly brought under control. In inflation-adjusted francs, the average cost of an unemployed worker fluctuated considerably from the 1960s on, but without a clear trend toward an increase or a decrease emerging. When this cost began to increase,[4] the laws were modified in order to avoid a swelling of expenditures. Since wages were rising, though at a slow pace, the result was a relative degradation of the situation of the unemployed.

As for the rest, the general dynamic of expenditures and revenues is fairly simple to perceive. The main base for the social taxes is total wages.[5] Their rate of growth (in real terms) was wiped out by the crisis. From 1959 to 1974, the annual average growth rate of total wages had been 6.6 percent; since 1974 it has attained only an average of 1.9. Against this sudden slowing down of the revenue base, expenditures, as one may easily imagine, tended rather to continue their expansion. Besides unemployment allocations, the number of retirees continued to swell (as a result of the increase in life expectancy)—at an even greater rate because of early retirements aimed at reducing the number of unemployed. The health system was driven by its own, similar, internal dynamic, borne by the evolution of consumer modes and the progress of medical technology.[6] The difficulties came from the conflict between the slow progression of total wages resulting from the crisis and the dynamic of social expenditures.

In order to put a stop to the progression of benefits, it was necessary to exert constant and strong pressure. Figure 6.3 describes the growth rates of total benefits and total wages. The constant decline, generally in a fairly parallel fashion, of both these rates is easily perceived; the slowing of the growth of social benefits was indeed a reality. But, as the figure reveals, this slowing down was a bit less rapid, particularly between 1975 and 1986, than that of total wages. The consequences of this gap are easy to imagine. Benefits, and therefore the taxes necessary to cover them, increased more quickly than output and wages over the ten years.

The difference that Figure 6.3 describes seems moderate, but its cumulative effect over ten years was considerable. The slow increase of taxes and benefits led to a very significant gap. The ratio of benefits to national output leapt some 5.7 percent, of which 1.7 percent was for unemployment allocations and 4.0 percent for other benefits. This movement took place between 1974 and 1982. Subsequent years saw a reversion to prior rates. The slowing of the growth of total wages was so pronounced that between 1975 and 1986, despite the curbing of expenses, social taxes went from 42 percent to 68 percent of directly received wages. This percentage remained approximately stable until 1996, after which it declined significantly (Figure 6.4).

It is therefore important not to invert the terms of the diagnosis that may be made of the high growth rate of social taxes and spending in the

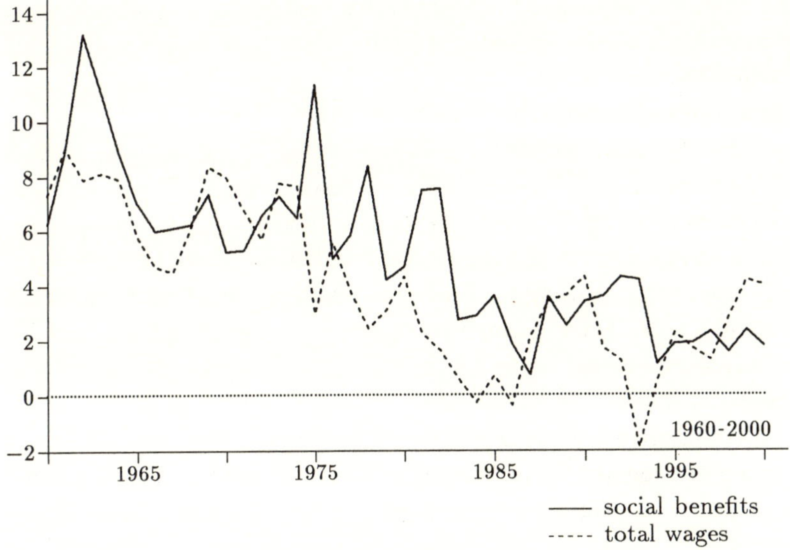

Figure 6.3 Growth rate of social benefits and total wages (percent): France.

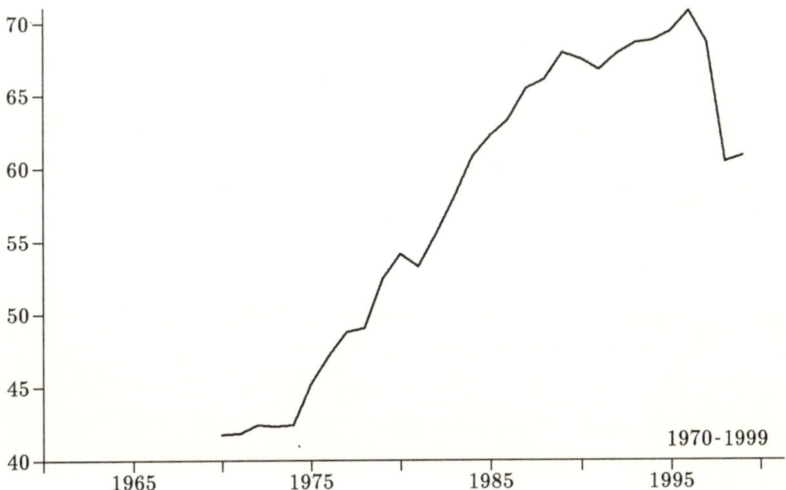

Figure 6.4 Ratio of (employer and employee) social taxes to net wage (percent): France.

crisis, both in relationship to output and in relationship to wages. It is not the unbridled increase in social spending that created an unsustainable growth rate of total wage costs, particularly in France, because wage costs, both direct and indirect, grew relatively slowly; it was not that benefits took off, as some people strive to make us believe, since, on the contrary, they grew more slowly; this pronounced slowing down was just a bit less rapid than that of direct wages—hence the problem.

What was the impact of getting wage-cost dynamics back under control? With wage costs growing very slowly, companies and finance kept for themselves virtually the entire benefits of the savings made from technological progress, which at first during the crisis was very slow, and later came back. The decline in the profit rate was interrupted and a certain growth of profitability was experienced. The increase in profit share played there a preponderant role in Europe and an important one in the United States despite the stagnation of labor productivity (Figures 4.2 and 4.3).

CHAPTER

7

Unemployment: Historical Fate?

It is always easier to state after the fact that things could have gone better when they have not turned out as we wished, but rewriting history is a difficult business. At the same time, not all behavior and practices can be retrospectively justified. Is it ridiculous to assert that unemployment in the 1970s and after could have been avoided or that it could have been eliminated earlier?

This chapter will advance the thesis that the wave of unemployment in these decades was in no way inevitable. The problem was not primarily a technical one, but a political one. Unemployment hit our economies in such proportions and for such a long time because the political goal advanced was not in fact the fight against unemployment, contrary to all the declarations. No country was able to halt this dynamic, because neoliberal policies were applied and generalized through capital's neoliberal globalization. The message was clear: function within the movement according to its rules or be excluded from it—from now on there is no third road.

It is the statistics, above all, that militate in favor of rejecting the thesis of the inevitability of unemployment. What was the extent of the problem? Unemployment in Europe during the period 1975–1995 corresponded to a deficit in jobs growth of only about 0.5 percent per year. In other words, if the annual average jobs growth rate had been a half point higher than what it was for years, there would not have been massive unemployment in Europe.[1] Before going into the details of the arithmetic, we will review the main aspects of the creation of the wave of unemployment.

Europe and the United States both suffered from a comparable slowdown of accumulation in the structural crisis. But the problem of employment was not of the same nature in both cases. As was demonstrated in

Box 7.1
Measuring unemployment

Defining and measuring unemployment remain a headache, and a simple unemployment indicator does not suffice to characterize a country's jobs situation.[a] There exists a battery of seven official indicators that make certain comparisons possible. They go from estimating the long-term unemployed (more than thirteen weeks) to broad measurements that record discouraged workers and half of those employed part-time. Figure 7.1 utilizes the most commonly used indicator: the ratio of the number of people without jobs, ready to work and looking for a job (during the four weeks preceding the survey), to the active civilian population (employed or unemployed). The various indicators evolve in a fairly parallel manner, and the official figures generally reflect evolutions over time.

However, these indicators give only a limited vision of the jobs situation.[b] For example, in 1996 unemployment in France affected 3 million people, according to the International Labor Organization (ILO) definition, in addition to 350,000 workers in training programs. If one adds people forced to work part-time but who wish to work more, we reach 5 million. An additional half million cannot look for work or state that they are discouraged, which gives us a total of 5.5 million. If we take into account early retirements, which may be forced or voluntary, we come to 6.7 million people affected.

The employment situation in France may also be grasped with the help of other indicators that are linked to the previous categories. The percentage of French people who are at an age to work and who are effectively employed has declined since 1975 from around 65 percent to 60 percent; during the same period the rate of men aged fifty-five to sixty-five and not working has increased from 30 percent to almost 60 percent, and the percentage of jobs held by temporary workers has gone from 3 percent to 14 percent, and so on.

(continued)

Chapter 5, the United States has since World War II created more jobs, and in a fairly consistent manner, because of its less rapid rate of technological progress. Dealing with a decline of accumulation in Europe was a much taller order, due to the more rapid substitution of capital for labor in Europe.

The curve of Figure 7.1 recalls the main features of the growth of unemployment in Europe, still limited to three countries, using the indicator most commonly referred to (Box 7.1). By taking all the data as is, we can

(continued)

It is easy to see how this complex situation can be manipulated into an excuse. The decline in recent years of the official rate of unemployment in the United Kingdom tends to puzzle specialists.[c] Through constant changes in the way statistics are compiled, only those unemployed receiving benefits are still counted (benefits now run out after six months instead of twelve); between 1992 and 1996, over 40 percent of the jobs created in that country were part-time (as against 15 percent in France).

---

a. Cerc-Association, Chiffrer le Chômage, Les dossiers de Cerc-Association, no. 1, 1997.

b. Commissariat Général du Plan, *Chômage: le cas français,* Paris : La documentation française, 1997.

c. "When Margaret Thatcher won her first election in 1979, the United Kingdom counted 1.3 million officially unemployed. If the method of calculation had not changed there would now be a little over 3 million unemployed. A Midlands Bank report published recently even estimated their number at 4 million, or 14 percent of the active population—more than in France or Germany" (S. Milne, "How London manipulates the statistics," *Le Monde diplomatique,* May 1997).

say, in a purely descriptive manner, that until the mid-1970s the unemployment rate oscillated between 1 and 2 percent. Starting in 1975 it took off rapidly, culminating in 1985 at 9.9 percent. Between 1985 and 1990 the rate began to decline quite significantly, but that did not continue and the 1985 record was almost reached again in 1994. The creation of this wave may therefore be dated back to the 1975–1985 period, a dark decade. Since then unemployment rates seem to have oscillated around 8 or 9 percent. It required ten years to build up the wave of unemployment, and it continued for fifteen years or more. The decline in 2001 remained fairly modest.

The dotted lines in Figures 7.1 and 7.2 indicate the general trend of these evolutions, the "structural" component of unemployment. The fluctuations around this trend set out what is commonly called its "cyclical" movement, which follows the fluctuations of economic activity (output increases during overheating and declines during recessions lead to corresponding declines and increases in the unemployment rate).

Despite the increase in structural unemployment at the beginning of the crisis that was common to both Europe and the United States, the profiles observed are significantly different. The extent of the wave of structural

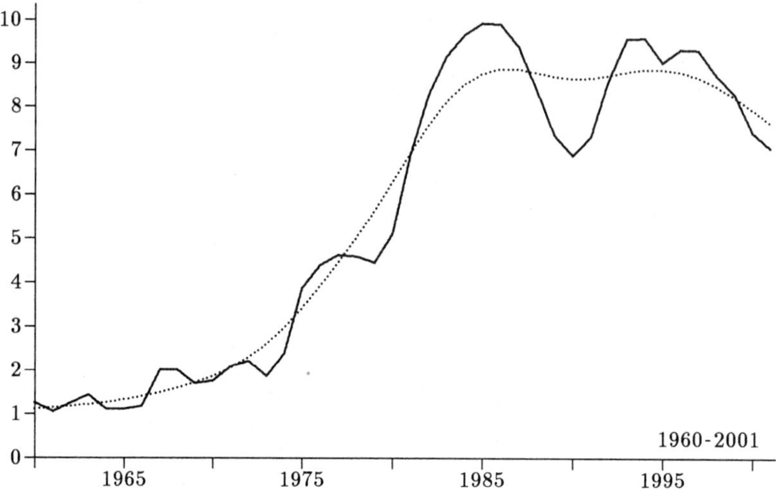

Figure 7.1 Unemployment rate and its trend (percent): Europe (Germany, France, and the United Kingdom).

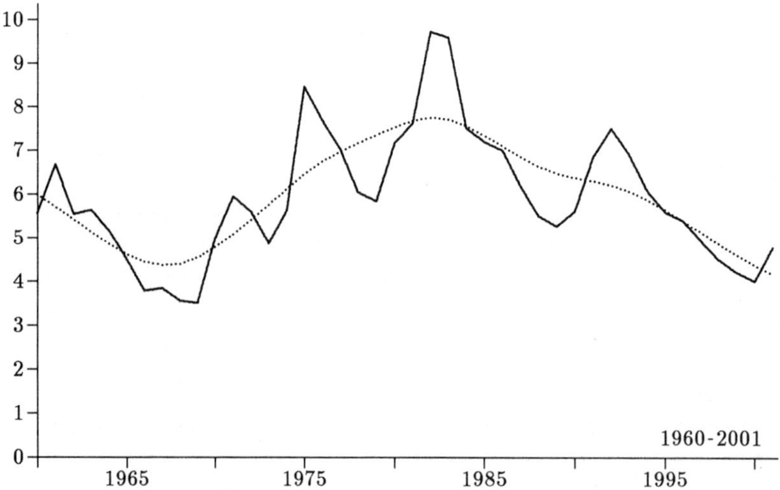

Figure 7.2 Unemployment rate and its trend (percent): United States.

unemployment was less in the United States (Figure 7.2). Rates above 9.5 percent were reached there, but only briefly (at the worst of the 1982 recession), and after having started out at initially high rates of 5 percent.

These disparities are due to fundamental differences, whose nature is not the same for the trend (structural unemployment) and the fluctuations (cyclical unemployment). The fact that the structural wave was much bigger in Europe than in the United States may be explained, as we have said, by the completely different jobs growth rates for the two areas: stagnation or loss of jobs in Europe, sustained growth in the United States. These features are linked to the rapidity of technological progress, which is much greater in Europe. Flexibility plays no role here. Conversely, the cyclical component of unemployment is more significant in the United States, because employment responds more energetically there to fluctuations in economic activity. In other words, American employers hire during periods of strong activity and lay off during the recessions at a much greater rate than in Europe. This is indeed flexibility.

We shall now look at the structural component of unemployment in Europe. Assessing how credible a different strategy to avoid unemployment would be depends entirely on the half-point of jobs growth mentioned at the beginning of this chapter—the extra 0.5 percent annual growth in employment that would have been necessary in order to avoid unemployment. Is that a lot? Was it out of reach? In order to answer these questions, it is necessary to compare this figure to that of economic growth and to the rate of technological progress.

First of all, unemployment may be ascribed to insufficient growth. For the three European countries, the annual rate of growth was 4.3 percent between 1960 and 1970, that is, before the crisis. Since 1975 this rate has been reduced to 2.3 percent (Figure 7.3). Everything is there—in order to preserve jobs, it would have been necessary that this rate drop to only 2.3 percent plus 0.5 percent, that is, 2.8 percent. We are not stating that the growth rate of the European economies should have increased or should not have dropped during the crisis in order for the level of employment to be preserved. The problem is the scope of the decline—instead of going from 4.3 percent per year down to 2.3 percent, that is, 2 points, it should have only dropped 1.5 points. It wasn't a miracle that was needed, but a slight improvement, or a lesser evil.

The sensitivity of jobs to the rate of growth is demonstrated very well by the two periods of fairly significant upturn. The recovery of economic

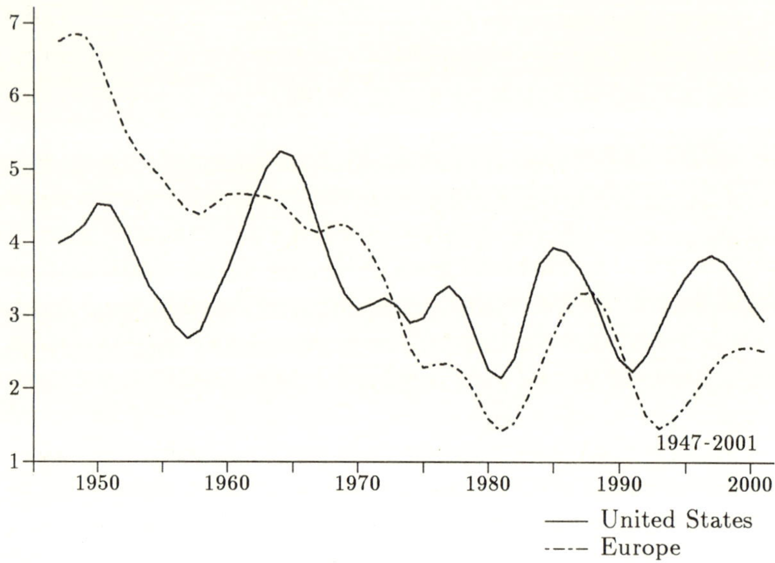

Figure 7.3 Rate of growth of output (percent): United States and Europe (Germany, France, and the United Kingdom). This figure gives a picture of growth close to that of Figure 3.2, which described the rate of growth, not of output, but of the stock of fixed capital. The statistics have been smoothed out a bit in order to eliminate short-term fluctuations.

growth, which began at the end of the 1980s (even if it still remained mediocre in relationship to the 1960s), provides one example of this. Comparatively high growth rates were registered at the end of the 1980s—it didn't take long for this improvement to affect jobs. In order to realize this, it suffices to look back at Figure 7.1. The decline in unemployment in Europe during these years, like the upturn that caused it, was, however, fleeting. The second period of resumption of growth, in the second half of the 1990s, had similar effects.

This reasoning takes the rate of technological change as a given and therefore does not question the speed with which Europe was catching up. In order to assess its effects we need to return here to the discussion in Chapter 5. The capital-labor ratio, which measures mechanization, grew very rapidly in Europe between 1960 and 1974, at an average rate of 6 percent per year (Figure 5.1). The speed of mechanization slowed down considerably during the crisis—the previous rate of 6 percent gave way to a rate of 2.7 percent after 1974. In order to protect jobs, all else being equal, the rate of mechanization would have had to ease up a little more—to 2.2 percent, instead of 2.7 percent, that is, at a still higher rate than the United States (where, on an average since 1974, it attained 1.0 percent). This would have postponed Europe's catching up, but only for a few years.

Between output and employment there is not only technology, but also the length of the workweek. During the period under consideration it did not cease to diminish. There, too, more could have been done.

Growth, technological change, length of the workweek—possible steps to influence these variables were not at all mutually exclusive, but, on the contrary, could have been combined. For example, one could make up the following brew: 0.2 percent more growth, 0.2 percent slower mechanization, and 0.1 percent reduced workweek.

Why was it not so simple? We should first question how independent these processes were. If, for example, by increasing the rate of growth, it was necessary to accelerate the rate of technological change (or vice versa), it would have been more difficult to positively affect employment. What would be gained on the one hand would have been partly lost on the other. In a symmetrical fashion, slower technological progress could have made the crisis more severe and hindered growth and therefore employment.

But this was not the problem. Until the 1970s, Europe improved both technology and growth at very high rates. It did so via a set of institutions and policies that assured it a certain degree of protection and relative autonomy. The process of continuing to catch up in the 1980s was done under extremely different conditions. It was necessary to adapt to strong external constraints (resulting from less advantageous exchange rates) and to strict policies within the neoliberal world, which was giving precedence to the fight against inflation. This system was once known under the attractive name of "competitive disinflation."

Disinflation certainly, but why competitive? Some saw in these policies an attempt to accelerate the process of catching up. The general idea was that restrictive policies could put pressure on the European economies, tending to eliminate inefficient companies and leaving no other exit than modernization. Given the way they were carried out, these policies had two negative consequences for jobs—slowing down of growth and sustaining technological progress (even if it was slower than previously). Therefore, the policy choices made during the crisis both went in the direction of *increasing* unemployment. Europe was not a victim of a choice between growth and technological progress, making it necessary to lose out in at least one area from the point of view of jobs. Both developments led in the same direction—jobs lost on both levels.

Many other reasons add to the difficulty of reducing unemployment. It is difficult to reinsert into the workforce the long-term unemployed who still hope to work. One must also wonder, after so many years, whether the unemployed hold the qualifications required in case accumulation starts up again, given the technological changes. This explanation is often put forward in relationship to difficulties companies encounter when hiring certain categories of personnel. It seems to be confirmed by the selective character of hiring during the phases of upturn: the most qualified workers are the first to benefit from the improvement in the jobs situation. Does this failure of qualifications on the part of other workers—or the failure of the wages offered to match what companies are now requiring—condemn certain sections of the workforce to perpetual unemployment or exclusion? Continued unemployment in a country like France cannot be interpreted in this manner, at least given the level that country has reached. Lasting unemployment tends to generate permanent unemployment.

However severely one judges recent decades, the future of employment in that country is henceforth dependent on the perspectives of growth. Has Europe emerged from the structural crisis? Given the absence of political motivation to reduce unemployment, everything hangs on this question.

CHAPTER

8

The End of the Crisis?

Has capitalism finished with the structural crisis begun in the 1970s? Over the last few years, and despite possible recessions, have the countries of the center, Japan excepted, entered into a phase of growth for which the United States, at least up to the 2000 recession, was supposed to be providing a brilliant demonstration, for which it was supposed to be the driving force, as we sometimes read? Unprecedented performances? A new economy? What is the status of technological progress, wages, and unemployment? The previous chapters have already revealed certain aspects of this renewed vigor during the 1990s. We shall now attempt to bring these scattered elements together and complete them.

What should be said about the growth of output and of the stock of capital? In these respects we have already had the opportunity to compare the three European countries and the United States. For Europe, the expression "thirty glorious years" accounts well for the first decades that followed World War II until the mid-1970s, particularly in terms of growth (Figure 7.3). Even the upturn in economic activity at the end of the 1980s cuts a sorry figure in relation to the 1950s and 1960s. The same figure makes clear that growth was more moderate in the United States than in Europe during the first postwar decades. The new element is that since the 1980s the United States has experienced somewhat higher growth rates than the European rates, especially during the 1990s. Thus in contrast to Europe, the United States has almost been able to again reach its precrisis rates.

Figures 8.1 and 8.2 provide the means to make a more detailed comparison of France and the United States on the basis of quarterly data. They describe output growth rates from the mid-1970s until 2002 by comparing

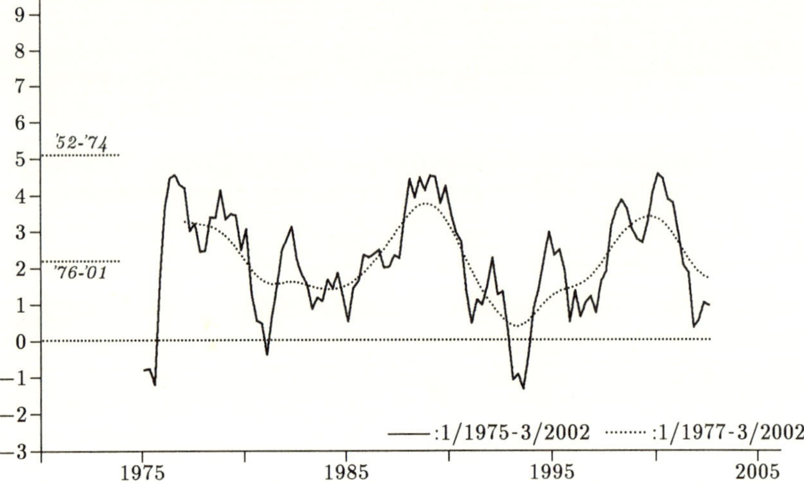

Figure 8.1 Rate of annual growth in output for each quarter and its trend (percent): France. The variable is the rate of growth per quarter as compared with the same quarter one year earlier. The dotted line represents the trend, after having eliminated the shorter-term fluctuations. The small horizontal lines indicate average values for the two subperiods of 1952–1974 and 1976–2001 for both this figure and Figure 8.2.

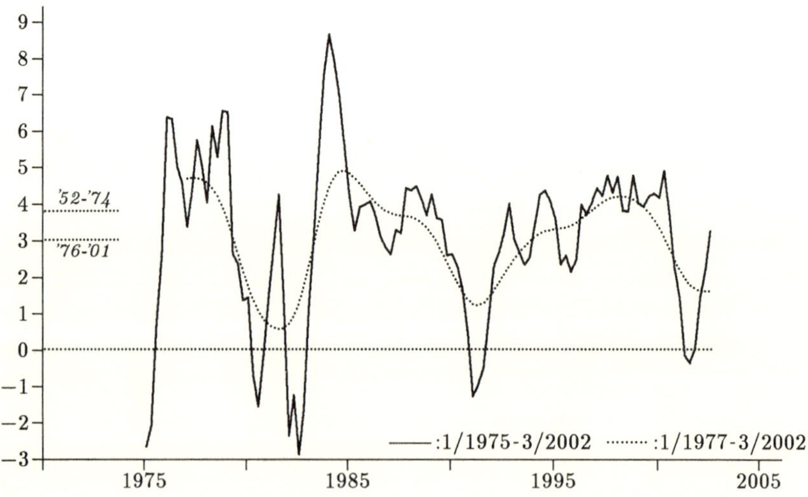

Figure 8.2 Rate of annual growth in output for each quarter and its trend (percent): United States.

the output of each quarter to that of the same quarter of the previous year (thus at an annual rate).

Both economies are constantly fluctuating. But what interests us here is above all the general level around which they fluctuate. The average level of 2.2 percent per year, which has prevailed in France since 1976, is low, both in relation to years prior to 1975 (the rate was 5.1 percent from 1952 to 1974) and in relation to the United States, which grew 3.0 percent on the average over the same period.

Miracle or American mirage? In accordance with what was stated above, one can see in Figure 8.2 that, at the end of the 1990s and prior to the 2000 recession, the United States caught up with its average growth rate of the 1952–1974 period, which was prior to the structural crisis.

This lack of growth of the French economy in relation to the American economy since the mid-1970s is an important phenomenon. It stands in striking contrast to the relative progress made in the first decades after World War II. By one measure (that of purchasing power parities), which gives a certain meaning to relative sizes, French output represented 18 percent of that of the United States in 1952. In 1982 this percentage attained its maximum, at nearly 25 percent, after having made fairly regular progress for a third of a century. Since 1997 it has sunk beneath 20 percent, that is, it has gone back to its 1958 value. This accentuation of the ascendancy of the American economy has taken place between 1983 and 1984 and since 1992. Why were the neoliberal years so comparatively unfavorable to France? We shall return to this question.

One may also wonder about how stable growth was (that is, how regular the curves from Figures 8.1 and 8.2 were—see Box 8.1). Fluctuations in economic activity remained modest in the United States between the 1991 and the 2000 recessions, that is, over nearly a decade. The country found itself in 2000 at the height of a growth cycle that was somewhat longer-lasting than the previous ones and a great source of pride, before growth rates again contracted.

Will the 2000 recession be transformed into a deeper crisis? The onset of such collapses in economic activity is a recurring, run-of-the-mill fact. However, this one is taking place in a threatening context, which combines a drop in stock prices, a strong degree of instability in the peripheral countries (notably Argentina), growing domestic and external disequilibria (surging household and external debt), and the political shock of the events initiated by the September 11, 2001, attacks. We shall return to this

Box 8.1
Fluctuations in growth since 1975: Comments on Figures 8.1 and 8.2

Growth has not been regular either in France or in the United States. One may observe a first set of fairly simple and slow fluctuations, which are suggested by the dotted lines in Figures 8.1 and 8.2—a kind of cycle of growth. The term "cycle" should not be misleading—these movements follow one another, but do not repeat themselves within certain defined periods.

Recurrent and sharper upturns of growth, and, especially, sudden downturns in growth are also apparent. When, after such collapses, the growth rate becomes negative, that is, when output effectively decreases (instead of increasing less), it is possible to speak of recessions, like those of 1979, 1982, and 1992 or 1993.

Both categories of fluctuations are common to both countries and are fairly well synchronized, with a few time lags and exceptions. The concomitance of the slowest movements defines a simple breakdown into periods. The first period is characterized by sustained growth, following the 1975 recession to around 1980. Profit rates had already dropped, Keynesian policies were being applied in order to bolster economic activity, and inflation was strong. The 1979 recession was continued in the United States by that of 1982, the deepest postwar recession, which was avoided in France by the coming to power of the left. Policies were then radically changed. A second period of stronger growth appears here, with an upturn in the United States in 1983. This level of economic activity was characteristic of the second half of the 1980s. However, a cyclical swing drove both economies downward until the recession of the early 1990s (1993 in France, 1991 in the United States). Then a new phase of growth, the last of the century, emerged, before a decrease in growth rates asserted itself, leading to the recession of the end of the century.

point in Chapter 20, after having recalled the conditions that led to the Great Depression.

One must therefore give qualified answers to the questions raised at the beginning of this chapter concerning the return of growth. More vigorous than Europe, the United States again reached growth rates in the 1990s on the level of the average rates of the period prior to the crisis. The three European economies, which performed particularly well before 1976, especially France, are far from that. The onset of a new recession shows that there has been no radical transformation of the conditions that govern macroeconomic stability.

Besides the growth of output, we can also examine the growth of the stock of capital (the rate of accumulation from Figure 3.2). The growth rates of the net stocks of capital remain fairly low in both geographical areas; in comparison with the 1960s and 1970s, Europe and America have accumulated little.[1]

As for jobs and unemployment, we have shown that the situation differs between Europe and the United States. At first view, the permanent character of the wave of unemployment in Europe goes against the thesis of an end to the crisis. The period of a still very limited reduction of unemployment at the end of the 1990s is actually an effect of the resumption of growth and accumulation, which corresponds in France to the latest phase of macroeconomic fluctuations (Figure 8.1 and Box 8.1).

The central role that we give to the rate of profit in our analysis leads us to favor a different perspective, one that focuses on the trend toward an increase in the profit rate since the mid-1980s (as well as on the determinants behind this increase, technological change and wage adjustments). The turnaround in the trend of the profitability of capital is indeed pronounced (Figure 3.1). In the United States in 1997 the rate of profit again reached its level of the early 1970s; in Europe, even the rate of the mid-1960s was reached. In spite of the recent decline in the United States, is it possible to make out of this vigor the criteria for determining the beginning of a new phase?

The difficulty in interpreting this upturn in the rate of profit resides in the fact that there are two ways, which are not mutually exclusive, of reestablishing the profitability of capital—one that may be labeled regressive, and the other that may be labeled progressive. This distinction is crucial in the assessment of the current period and the present-day trends of capitalism. From the point of view of the immediate capitalist interests, both means are equivalent, but they do not have the same historical import. The regressive means consists of freezing wages with slow technological progress; the progressive means consists of promoting a flow of technological progress (the speed of technological progress making wage increases—which continue to depend on the degree of struggle by workers—possibly easier). We must therefore again pick up the thread of the various observations that have been made up until now, keeping the following question in mind: how was the profit rate restored?

The increase in the rate of profit during the last two decades had two origins: the growth of the productivity of capital and the slowing down of wage increases. The rise in the profit rate since the mid-1980s combines both aspects—progressive concerning the increased efficiency of capital, despite the stagnation of labor productivity, and regressive concerning wage controls. Obviously it is the first movement that bodes well for the future.

One difficulty in assessing recent trends has to do with the relationships between the different variables. The persistence of low rates of accumulation is striking, but if the productivity of capital increased sufficiently, more could be produced on the basis of a relatively slowly growing stock of capital. A second difficulty has to do with the ambivalence of certain trends. If the capital-labor ratio is evolving slowly in the United States, is that because of the effects of the slow progress of mechanization or because of a transformation of the forms of technological change, requiring less capital from now on (the sign of the emergence of technologies that economize capital or of a drop in the price of capital)?

To sum up, the balance sheet that this chapter draws regarding a possible end to the crisis is uneven. The positive element is that trends in technology and in the profitability of capital, some of whose aspects are promising, are asserting themselves. We are now beyond what we have characterized as trajectories à la Marx, whose essential feature is the growing amount of fixed capital required by production (in relation to labor and especially to the quantities produced); the traits of the years since the mid-1980s have been different. In correlation, a certain upturn in growth has asserted itself. The United States has attained growth rates similar to those prior to the crisis, but this is far from the case in Europe. Whatever side of the Atlantic one may be on, it is necessary to keep in mind that growth is always a cyclical phenomenon with its ups and downs, and that the period at the end of the 1990s, up until the 2000 recession, corresponded to a phase of strong economic activity.

Nevertheless, this chapter continues to recognize the paradox raised at the very beginning of this part (Chapter 3)—the strong restoration of the rate of profit should have resulted in a much more significant resumption of capital accumulation and growth, carrying employment with it. This contradiction makes the significance of recent trends somewhat ambiguous. If it were possible to associate the rise in the profitability of capital in Europe with a restoration of the rate of accumulation and of growth, the hypothesis of an end to the crisis (linked to escaping from trajectories à la Marx) would be strengthened. The *for* side: the increase in the profitability of capital (more precisely, its progressive component, the increase in capital productivity); the *against* side: the slow pace of growth (and continuing unemployment) in Europe, despite the strong rise in profit rates.

Why was the restoration of the rate of profit not coupled with a parallel resumption of growth in Europe? The key to this enigma may be found in the monetary and financial mechanisms, which we shall now take up. This investigation shows that the continuing poor performances of the American and European economies with respect to capital accumulation are actually the effect of the specific dynamics of neoliberalism. One can, therefore, assert that the structural crisis is over and blame neoliberalism for poor accumulation rates.

PART

III

The Law of Finance

Part III is devoted to the law of finance. It continues the approach of the previous chapters, which, although they leave aside the financial mechanisms, have already made it possible to describe certain aspects of neoliberal policies.

The analysis of the origins of the crisis does not directly implicate finance, as defined in Chapter 2, at least not beyond what the capitalist mode of production implies. The crisis was the product of immanent trends of the production mode: the drop in the profit rate resulted from its inability to maintain a sustained rate of technological progress, which slowed down capital accumulation, prompting a tremendous wave of unemployment. Its scope was more limited in the United States than in Europe, not by virtue of any flexibility, but because of the relative rapidity of technological change in Europe. Taking advantage of the failure of Keynesian policies and of runaway inflation, finance was able to withstand workers' struggles and impose its law.

Getting wages under control even preceded the neoliberal turn. One can only be struck by the speed of the reaction at the beginning of the crisis. The slowdown in the growth of social spending was a little more difficult to obtain, leading to its relative growth. The creation of a reserve of unemployed was a cornerstone of this neoliberal plan. As we shall see, the concerns of the ruling classes were elsewhere—and, in many ways, crude.

Are these tensions part of the past? Are we beyond the structural crisis? The last chapter of Part II only made it possible to formulate the problem. On the one hand, the term "end of the crisis" is ambiguous—are one's eyes fixed on American or European growth; is one talking about how the productivity of labor or of capital has progressed, how wages or how profit rates have progressed? Why is European growth still so weak, although profit rates have attained their precrisis levels? Once again, the hegemony of finance—whose center, as we know, is situated in the United States—has deeply marked the economic processes with its stamp. Better to be the one who dominates than the one dominated. Europe, particularly France, is only an example—and not the most dramatic one.

The restoration of the domination of finance in neoliberalism is an event of a political nature, a direct expression of the class struggle. Its stages and historical conditions will be discussed in Part IV, which will use the lessons of history to explain them. Only once things are placed in historical perspective will it be possible to raise two major questions. First, we shall wonder about the possibility of a crisis of broad scope, recalling the depression of the 1930s and affecting the capitalist countries of the center (Chapter 20). The Great Depression took place at a time when finance occupied a dominant position; will the return of finance to power have similar consequences? Second, in relation to the first decades of the twentieth century and to what are commonly called the "thirty glorious years" (from World War II to the mid-1970s), we shall raise the question of the role of finance in the assertion of a new technological course that has been apparent since the mid-1980s (Chapter 21).

Why venture out into the twists and turns of financial relationships, which is the goal of Part III? Because a few simple statistics—profit rates, total revenue, financing—placed next to descriptions of financial crises and American hegemony, tell us a lot about neoliberalism. From now on, we shall look at the violence of these figures.

In what follows we shall have to abandon the joint treatment of the three principal European countries (Germany, France, and the United Kingdom) and limit ourselves to the lone case of France. This option reduces the scope of the analysis, but it is forced upon us by the complexity of financial mechanisms, the heterogeneity of monetary and financial institutions, and our insufficient access to the pertinent data. Furthermore, the analysis will be limited to corporations—we shall distinguish between financial and nonfinancial corporations.

CHAPTER

9

The Interest Rate Shock and the Weight of Dividends

From a financial point of view, the most spectacular element in the restoration of the hegemony of finance was the change in monetary policies at the end of 1979: the 1979 coup. One should not see here the hand of a mysterious market, but, in fact, a centralized decision, a deliberate policy. At a time when inflation was taking off, priority was given to its eradication, whatever the price for some and after having taken into account the advantage for others. Diverse procedures were conceivable, such as price controls or direct quantitative rationing of credit; such measures had been used previously, in other circumstances. The method chosen was a hike in interest rates—they would go up as much as necessary, and any recession or unemployment would not change matters. Furthermore, the qualities of such a policy were praised. High interest rates would encourage savings, driving everyone to save—this prediction was not borne out. Such rates would be at the origin of a rigorous weeding-out in which the weakest would be eliminated in favor of more vigorous elements—no doubt true, but unemployment is still present in Europe. This propaganda hid a simple, determining fact: inflation was eroding financial revenues and holdings; it was necessary to put a halt to these losses.

Figure 9.1 traces the evolution of interest rates on long-term credits in France and in the United States, corrected for inflation: real interest rates. One may clearly distinguish there the relatively low level of the 1960s, the drop in rates in the 1970s, their increase at the beginning of the 1980s, and then their stabilization around still high levels of about 4 or 5 percent. The sudden increase at the beginning of the 1980s reflected simultaneously the movements of nominal rates, linked to the change in policy, and the de-

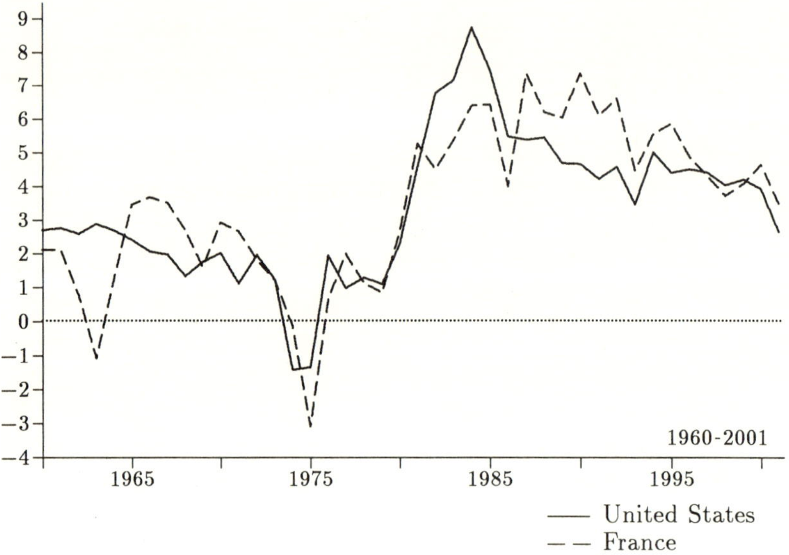

Figure 9.1 Real long-term interest rates (percent): United States and France.

cline in inflation that was the consequence. Globally, the profiles are similar in the two countries.

Long-term credit rates are represented in Figure 9.1, but short-term credit rates experienced a similar evolution. A significant difference was that short-term rates decreased in the United States rapidly, strongly, and fleetingly during the first half of the 1990s, whereas they culminated in France at exceptionally elevated levels.

As we have said, the policy of high real interest rates did not create the crisis—but it did deepen it and extend its effects. Too often the problem of investment is reduced exclusively to a problem of interest rates. The rate of accumulation underwent its fall, which was related to the decline in profit rates, well before the increase in interest rates. The truth is that this increase added to the deterioration of the situation because it perpetuated the low level of profit rates calculated after payment of interest rates—the rates that directly influence the workings of companies. At the worst of the crisis, an extraordinary levy was thus made on company profits. At the same time that the pressure of wages on profitability loosened up, the continued high-rate policy extended the harmful effects of the crisis into the 1990s.

The question is therefore posed: what was the scope of the effects of the rise in interest rates on companies between the beginning of the 1980s and the end of the 1990s?

Nonfinancial companies are at one and the same time both debtors and creditors. They can, for example, borrow from their bank, while still granting credit to their clients, or possess treasury bonds, that is, make loans to the state. They therefore pay out interest on the one hand, and receive interest on the other. They also hold debts or liquidity that bear no interest.[1] Both from the point of view of indebtedness and from that of interest, it is useful to consider net values—the net debt (debt less monetary and financial assets) and the net interest (interest paid out less interest received). Taken globally, nonfinancial companies are more debtors than creditors and pay out more interest than they receive; their net debt and their net interest are therefore positive.

Inflation complicates the assessment of the burden of indebtedness, because it devalues debts and assets held in monetary units. Its effect is felt on all debts and monetary and financial assets posted at their nominal value, especially those that are not reevaluated on a market (as a stock portfolio is), and likely to adjust to changes in the general level of prices.

The effect of the increase in real interest rates on corporate profitability is described in Figure 9.2 for France and Figure 9.3 for the United States.[2] These figures compare two evaluations of the profitability of nonfinancial corporations (once all taxes have been paid). In the first one, the interest paid by firms is still counted as part of the profit; this evaluation therefore sets aside the burden of debt. The second one takes that into account, that is, subtracts interest paid out (once interest received has been deducted) from profits and adds benefits that correspond to a devaluation of net debt (once losses from financial assets have been deducted), due to inflation.

The profiles are fairly different for both countries, but the weight of interest payments appears to be indisputable. As long as real interest rates were fluctuating around a very low level, near zero, the impact of debt on corporate profitability was practically negligible. Corporations paid interest, but this expense was compensated for by the devaluation of debt from inflation. This situation continued until the beginning of the 1980s, as the proximity of the curves on both figures indicates. After that point, the profit pump started up again, more generally draining the profits of corporations toward their creditors, and the increase in real interest rates weighed heavily on corporate profitability.

This strongly accentuated weight of indebtedness is common to France

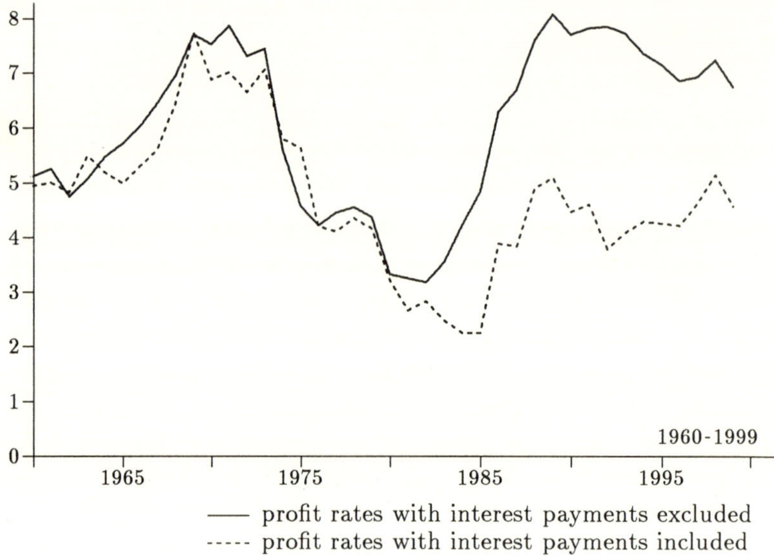

Figure 9.2 Profit rates, with interest payments excluded and included (percent): France, nonfinancial corporations. In the first measurement (with interest payments excluded), net interest (what was paid out minus what was received) has not yet been deducted from profits. The second measurement is identical, with this difference: net interest has been deducted from profits and the devaluation of net debt (debt less monetary and financial assets) from inflation has been added in. Profits have been divided by net worth. (See Appendix B for definitions.)

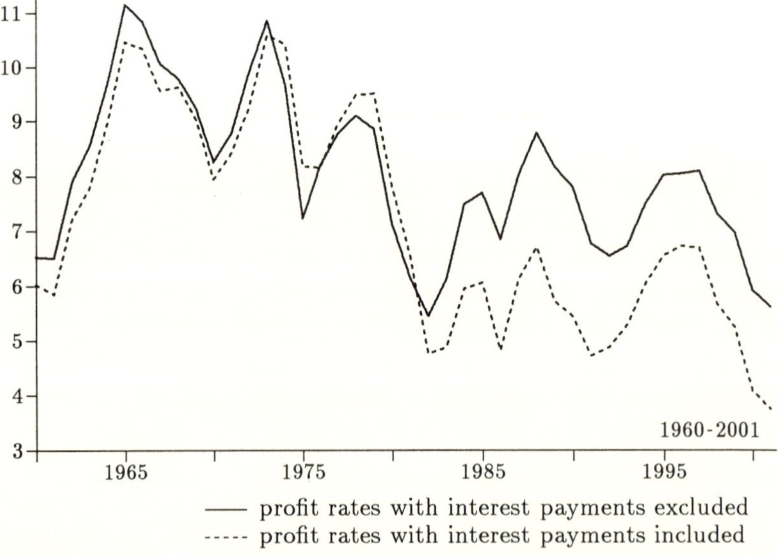

Figure 9.3 Profit rates, with interest payments excluded and included (percent): United States, nonfinancial corporations.

and the United States, but it was of greater scope in France. The explanation is simple: French firms were more indebted than American firms at the time of the 1979 coup.

This relative over-indebtedness in France in relation to the United States is illustrated in Figure 9.4. The variable used is the value of net debt (debt less monetary and financial assets) of nonfinancial corporations, divided by their real assets (fixed capital and inventory), in order to adjust their dimensions to the size of the companies. The difference between the levels and the similarity of the evolutions is striking. We see that after a strong increase in indebtedness in the 1960s, firms in both countries reduced their levels of debt during the 1970s. They were able to do this because of negative real interest rates. The ratio was reduced by a quarter of its maximum value in both countries over a ten-year period. The rise of indebtedness in France between 1988 and 1992, during the brief upturn of accumulation, was strong but fleeting. The reduction of debt levels during the 1990s is marked in both countries (to the point that the net debt became negative in the United States). Finally, since the beginning of the 1980s, nonfinancial firms appear to be very clearly more heavily in debt in France than in the United States, which explains the much more negative effect of the increase in real interest rates.

One must incidentally note that the favorable picture of the corporate balance sheet in the United States in the 1990s, as seen in Figure 9.4, is subject to the inclusion, within corporations' financial assets, of the excess of the purchase price of other firms over the fair value of the net assets acquired. These amounts are known as "goodwill." During the period when corporate net debt declined, as is evident in the figure, stock market fever led to strongly overestimated values of corporate acquisitions. The data do not allow, however, for the identification of these amounts.

The evolution of dividend distribution reveals a transfer of profits outside of nonfinancial corporations, similar to what happened for interest. Figure 9.5 presents the share of profits of nonfinancial corporations distributed as dividends to stockholders. The profile obtained for the United States confirms the unfavorable character of the 1960s and 1970s for the holders of financial assets, in this case stocks. The proportion of profits distributed dropped from over 50 percent to around 30 percent. But the beginning of the 1980s indicated a new turnaround, and the rate of distribution reached 94 percent in 2001. In France, dividend distribution was at a low level before the structural crisis (around 25 percent of profits).

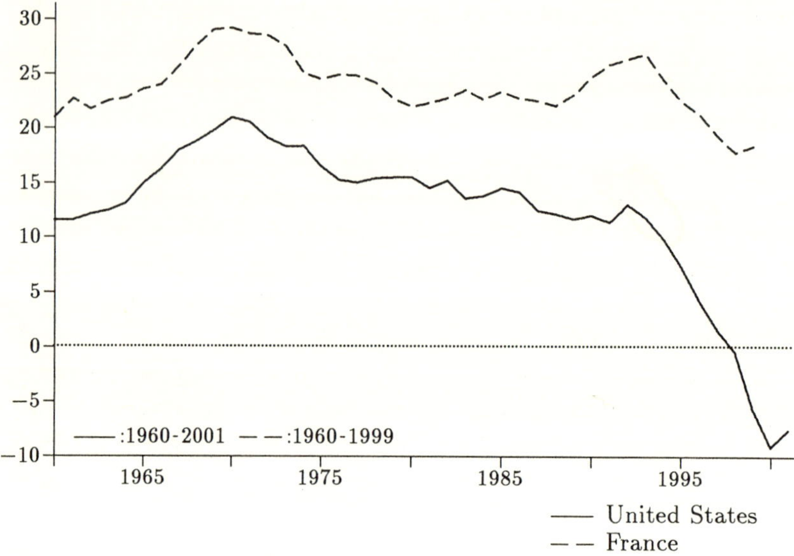

Figure 9.4 Ratio of net debt to tangible assets (percent): United States and France, nonfinancial corporations. Net debt is made up by the difference between total debt and monetary and financial assets; tangible assets are the sum of fixed capital and inventories.

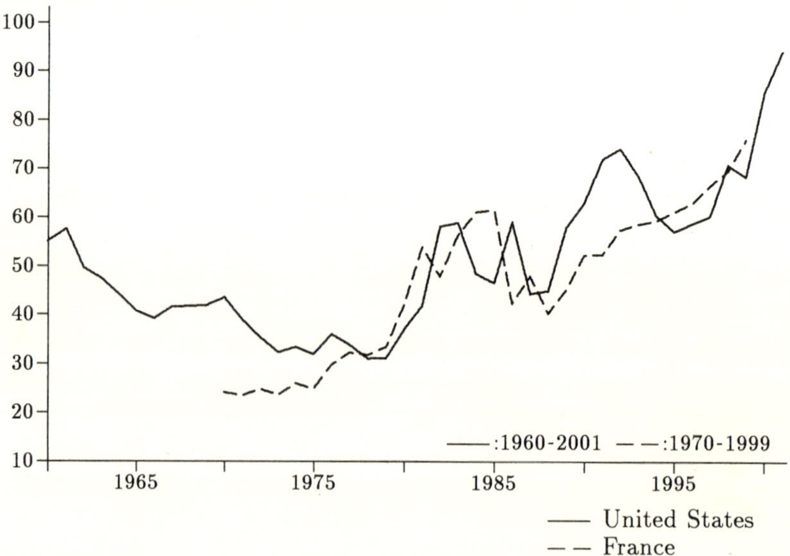

Figure 9.5 Share of profits distributed as dividends (percent): United States and France, nonfinancial corporations.

As for the neoliberal course, the figure speaks for itself: France is deeply into it.

As in the case of interest, these changes in level indicate a transformation of the relation of forces and powers. During the crisis, before the neoliberal blow, companies, which were gradually lowering their dividend distributions, held back an ever-larger fraction of their profits, which, at the same time, had been reduced. Since the beginning of the 1980s, despite the absence of a genuine restoration of the profit rate once interest was paid, the opposite situation prevails.

Altogether, the neoliberal decades appear to be a period of high return on capital, not from the point of view of the corporate profit rate, but from that of lenders and stockholders. For companies, it is a period of expensive financing, in the sense that they must compensate the holders of capital with very high interest payments and dividends, respectively, in relation to the loans and profits made. This increasing burden of the levies made by finance, interest payments and dividends, is sharply contrasted to the reduction of corporate taxation. In both countries the state went to the aid of corporate profitability, which had been reduced by the appetite of finance. The burden of taxes on profits decreased significantly.

Once dividend payments have been registered (in addition to taxes and real interest), we have a measurement of the profitability of capital that better brings out the strength of the link between profit rates and rates of accumulation (still for nonfinancial corporations). Figure 9.6 illustrates this relationship for France. The profit rate used is calculated on net worth, with real interest, taxes, and dividends being subtracted from profits. We shall call it the "rate of retained profit." The similarity is striking—the growth rate of fixed capital evolved in the same way as this rate of retained profit.[3] These observations suggest that the profits levied by finance do not return to nonfinancial corporations to finance real investment, a thesis we shall defend in Chapter 14.

These results confirm the essential role of the profit rate in the dynamics of capitalist economies. We have now become conscious of the weight of capital earnings, interest payments, and dividends in the dynamics of accumulation, which leads us to favor the rate of retained profit in the diagram introduced in Chapter 3:

Change in the rate of retained profit → Change in accumulation → Changes in employment and unemployment

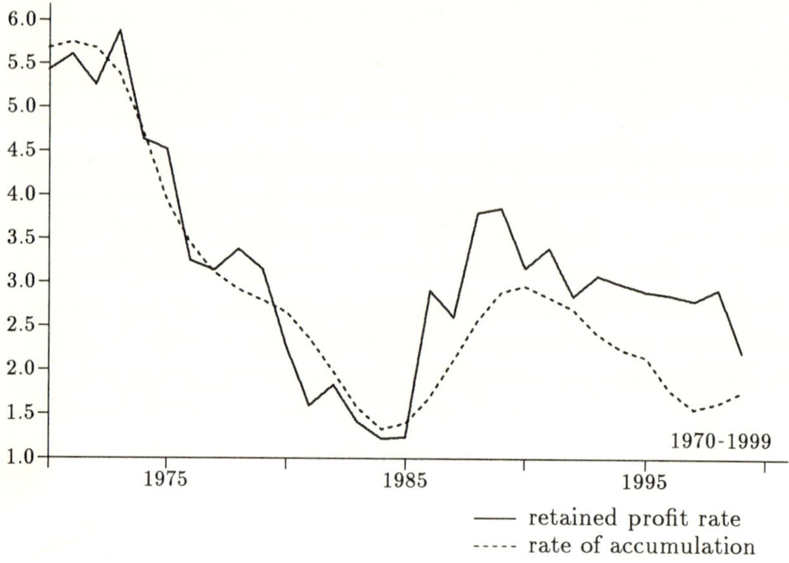

Figure 9.6 Rate of retained profit and rate of accumulation (percent): France, nonfinancial corporations. The rate of profit is that of Figure 9.2 (with interest payments included), with the lone exception that dividends paid out have been subtracted from profits. The rate of accumulation is the rate of growth of fixed capital.

Figure 9.6 reveals a limited difference between the rate of retained profit and the rate of growth of the stock of fixed capital since the mid-1980s. These differences suggest that a proportion of the retained profits reaches a destination other than accumulation—purchases of French stock shares, exporting of capital (direct or indirect investments abroad), or debt reimbursement. We shall concentrate here on the last element. (We take up the purchases of French stock shares in Chapter 14 and the exporting of capital in Chapter 12.)

Instead of investing, French companies paid their debts. This was an indirect effect of the rise in real interest rates.[4] In France this strategy led to very high rates of self-financing of investments (higher than 100 percent) at the end of the 1990s. Similar difficulties were noted in the United States, but to a much lesser degree, because U.S. companies were less dependent on credit. This is one of the reasons explaining why the United States took the lead over France in terms of growth in the 1980s and especially the 1990s.

The thesis developed in this chapter may thus be summarized as follows. The decrease in profit rates in the 1970s led first of all to a surge of inflation. Since real interest rates were low or negative, the consequence was a transfer of wealth from lenders to nonfinancial companies, which compensated almost exactly the amount paid out in interest. Dividend distribution was at its lowest. The situation was turned around in the course of the 1980s. Finance decided to stop inflation in order to protect its revenues and its investments, whatever the cost might be for others, and to restore the claims of stockholders to profits. The rate of accumulation declined accordingly, and the crisis and unemployment found themselves extended.

The paradox identified at the beginning of Part II is resolved here. After having associated, in Chapter 3, the decline in the rate of profit and the decline in the rate of accumulation in the crisis, until 1982 (the year when profit rates reached their low), one expected a symmetrical development: the profit rate trend, now on the rise, would prompt a resumption of accumulation—which was not the case. We now know the answer: the rate of accumulation is controlled by the rate of retained profit and the rise in the rate of profit before the payout of interest and dividends was confiscated by finance.[5]

This confiscation of the effects of the new course of technological change, which underpins the new rise in profitability, appears all the more shocking because governments, through tax policy, and labor, through the fact that its purchasing power practically ceased to increase, contributed very positively to the increase in the profitability of capital. How can it be claimed then that wage restraint and docility in carrying out jobs are the necessary conditions for a decrease in unemployment? These concessions have generally been made—but the benefits went not to labor but to the holders of capital.

CHAPTER

10

Keynesian State Indebtedness and Household Indebtedness

The policy of high interest rates affected not only companies but governments and households taking out loans as well. The problem of public spending and how to fund it is one of the most widely discussed. Large deficits widened during the structural crisis, and government debt ballooned. In France the increase in the rate of mandatory deductions, in social and other taxes, which reached 46 percent of total output in 2001, became the subject of permanent lamentations.[1] Keynesian governments and their propensity to spend were accused of everything under the sun: they were nothing less than the reason for the increase in interest rates (which explained the slowdown in investment, which in turn explained unemployment). A crowding-out effect was also invoked—public spending was preventing private investment. These arguments should be turned on their head: in reality, it was the high rates that created the deficits.

The evolution of public spending and revenues should be placed in the general framework of the structural crisis. These mechanisms are identical to those observed for France (Chapter 6) concerning social spending, which is part of public spending, our subject in this first part of the chapter.

The inordinate growth of public spending was the expression of the time lag between the increase in public spending and the growth of output. But this was not a slow, permanent change. The rise of the ratio between spending and output is clearly situated in time: it is concentrated over a ten-year period. What was happening at that time?

In this analysis, we must isolate interest costs from the cost of other state spending. We shall first take up spending, except for interest payments. This leads us to distinguish three subperiods: before 1975 (that is, in France, before the structural crisis), between 1975 and 1982, and since 1982.

Until 1974, public spending grew at the same rate as output without raising any problem of financing, because revenues were increasing in similar fashion. Growth of the French economy slowed down considerably starting with the 1974 recession and dropped from 5.1 percent (1952–1974) per year to 2.8 percent (1974–1982) (Figure 8.1). Between 1975 and 1982 public spending continued to grow, with surprising regularity, at its former rate of 5.3 percent per year. In this context of slow growth in output, the ratio of spending to output leapt. The rate of social taxes continued to increase in the proportions required to maintain a balance, and public debt did not increase any faster than output. Finally, after 1982 the growth rate of public spending was rapidly reduced to 2.1 percent per year, a rate that has continued since that date, slightly lower than the rate of growth of output.

To summarize: before the structural crisis, output and spending grew rapidly and balanced out, without any relative rise in social taxes. In the first phase of the crisis, before 1982, the growth of output declined considerably, whereas spending continued to rise, but the imbalance was contained thanks to the rise in social taxes. After 1982 the growth rate in spending dropped to a level lower than the growth rate of output, even though this latter rate was low itself.

One would therefore expect a balance between spending and revenue to have been continually assured. This was indeed the case—without interest payments there would not have been any government deficits in France, only fluctuations around a balance of zero.

Concerning public deficits, it is therefore necessary to be aware of the following fact: the deficits are due entirely to the rise in interest rates at the beginning of the 1980s. The same was true in the other primary European countries (with the exception of Italy). Figure 10.1 illustrates this assertion for France. The first curve traces the evolution of public surpluses or deficits as a percentage of total output. This is a first, traditional measurement, which includes all spending. Then a second measurement excludes interest payments. We will not take time here to discuss the fluctuations of these balances over the years; they flow from the sensitivity of public revenue to economic activity (high when economic activity is strong, low in a recession), whereas spending is more rigid. The major fact is that without the interest payments, the deficits disappear. Even the 1975–1982 period,

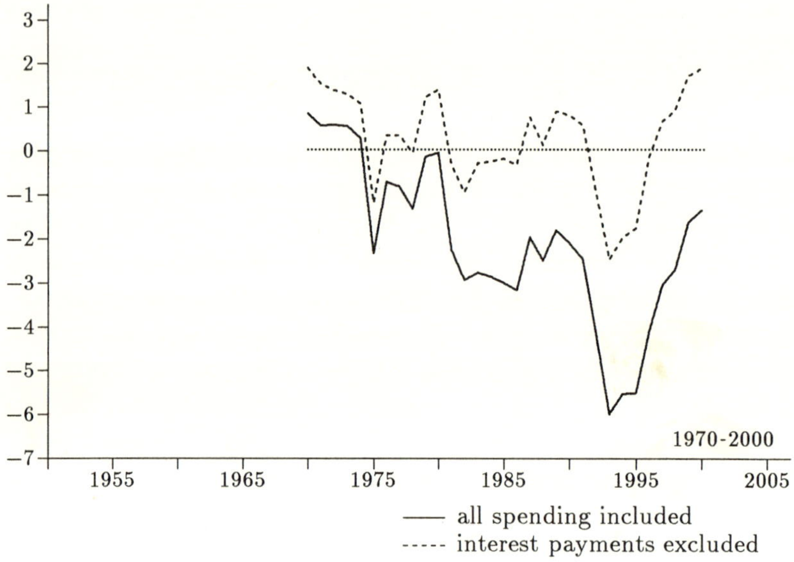

Figure 10.1 Public administration surpluses or deficits, with all spending included or with interest payments excluded (percent of output): France.

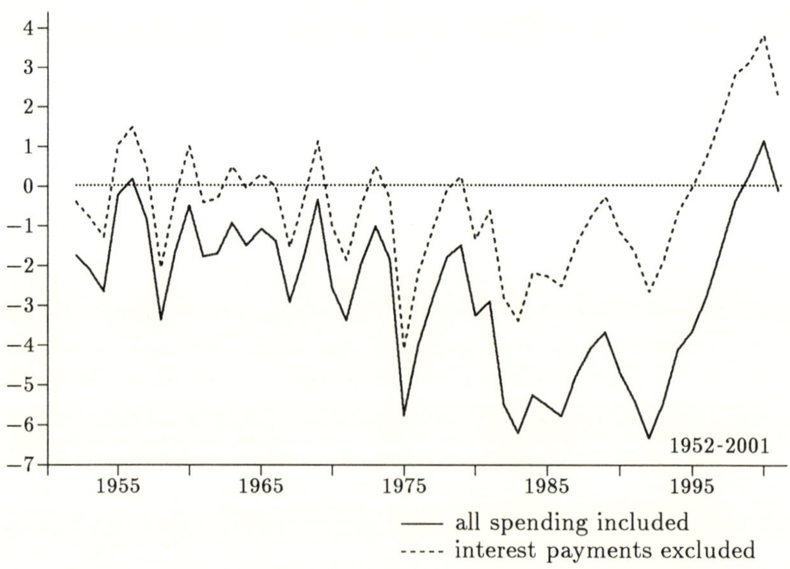

Figure 10.2 Public administration surpluses or deficits, with all spending included or with interest payments excluded (percent of output): United States.

when the growth rate of spending had not yet significantly declined, is not an exception to the rule.

Figure 10.2 introduces the same analysis for the United States. Unlike in France, in the United States a deficit existed before 1975, given interest payments, but it remained very modest. The effect of the rise in rates in the 1980s and 1990s was then obvious, as in France, until the late 1990s, when the situation improved.

In passing, let us clear up an ambiguity. The deficits of the 1980s were not caused in order to stimulate growth, in accordance with the rules of Keynesian macroeconomics, which call for public spending to take over from deficient private demand. In the United States, deficits were endured in a context that saw weak growth combined with the difficulty of slowing down the increase in public spending, and inflated by the increase in interest rates. Reagan was not the greatest Keynesian of all!

How could the increase in interest rates have represented a burden before the emergence of large deficits? When interest rates rose, the various governments were already in debt to different degrees. These debts had tended to decrease after World War II with the help of inflation. Short-term securities financed a large share of these debts. When rates went up it was necessary to renew these securities at higher rates. This operation was at the origin of the deficits of the 1980s and 1990s.

It is impossible to make market mechanisms, linked to public deficits, responsible for the increase in interest rates. These deficits appeared *after* the increase in interest rates, and disappear once the burden of interest payments is put aside.

Another argument is also put forward to the effect that an increase in rates was vital in order to force governments to control their spending. This supposes that governments could not have slowed down spending through other policies; they had to pay interest and go into debt in order to become reasonable like everyone else. The burden of the debt and the decline in revenue didn't create sufficient pressure. In other words, it was necessary for finance to increase government spending—and its own revenue at the same time—to the point where the deficits would become absolutely intolerable. This fallacious argument also leaves aside the fact that a less restrictive policy—interest rates that were not as high—would have made possible more rapid growth and thus provided a more sustained flow of tax revenues and social taxes. A more lenient policy would also have made it possible to avoid both the resulting poverty and the payment of unemployment benefits. That it was necessary to manage the crisis is an undeniable fact. That the neoliberal strategy was particularly harmful is another one.

We now take up the problem of household debt. Despite certain common points, its terms are distinct from corporate or public debt. French households provide an excellent illustration of the dramatic consequences of the structural crisis and of neoliberal policies.

The debt of households, like that of companies, cannot be examined as an undivided whole. Obviously, it is necessary to distinguish two groups—lenders and borrowers. Certain households belong structurally to one group or the other; others go from one to the other (in order to borrow to, say, buy a house, it is necessary to save beforehand, and hence to make, for a time, a financial investment such as the purchase of a bond). The available records, however, do not make it possible to isolate the pertinent itemized data, and we shall have to be satisfied with aggregates.

Figure 10.3 traces the annual amount of household loans (once loan payments are deducted). These loans represented a fairly stable total each year until 1985, but they increased suddenly in 1986 and 1987, eventually doubling.

In order to grasp the meaning of these events, we must situate the problem of indebtedness in the general framework of the structural crisis and the way in which households faced it. Total wages make up the primary component of household income, which until 1974, before the crisis, rose at a rate of over 6 percent per year in real terms. From 1974 to 1982 it continued to increase, but at a slower rate. Given this slowing down in the increase of their income, households lowered the rate of increase of consumer spending, and even more their purchases of housing. In this way they avoided going into debt. The years 1982–1987 were the worst—total wages remained almost stable because of the low increases in salaries and the decrease in employment (stability in total wages means increases for some, and decreases for others). Households—some of them—reduced their spending, but not in the same proportions as their decline in income, which led them into debt. The loans resorted to were the sort that sought to make ends meet in the final days of the month—debt that was generally involuntary. This increase was especially a result of short-term credit (Figure 10.3), for which interest rates rose very sharply. From this flowed a wave of excessive debt, which justified considerable governmental intervention (in the form of commissions on excessive debt). The features of

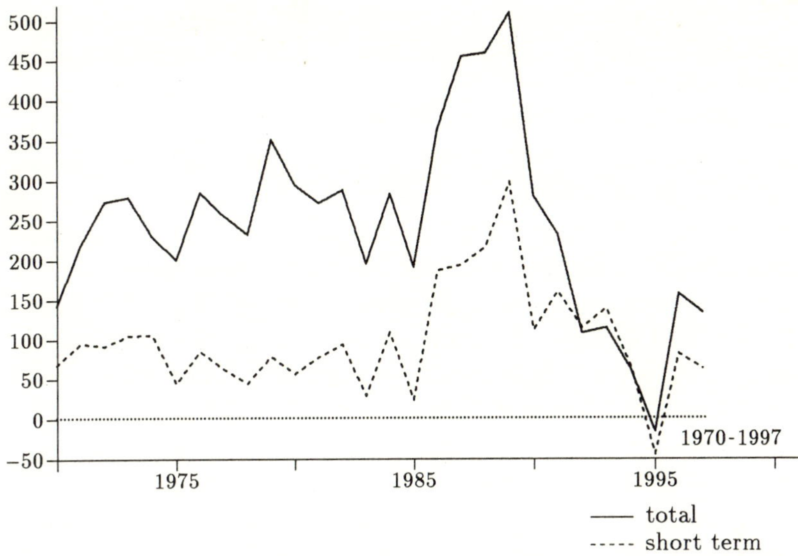

Figure 10.3 Annual new household loans, total and short term (billions of 1995 euros): France. Loans are always calculated after subtracting loan repayments.

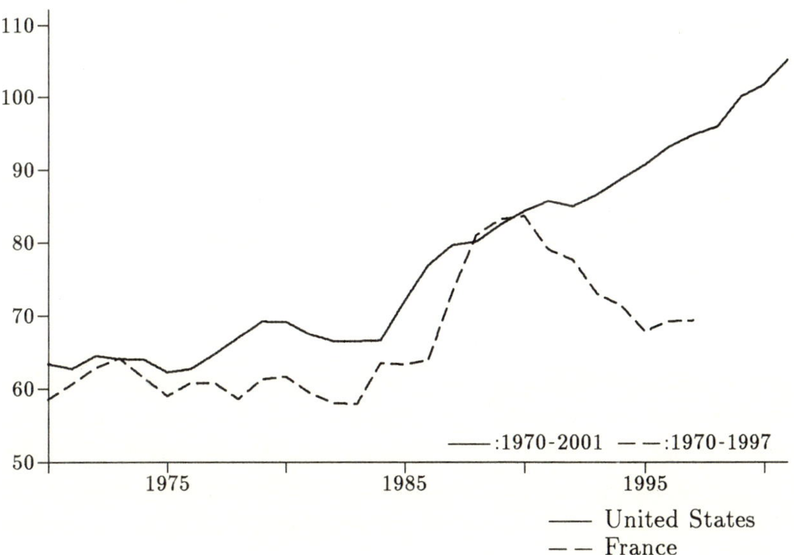

Figure 10.4 Ratio of debt of households to their disposable income (percent): United States and France.

this growth in indebtedness have been analyzed in various studies that reveal its relationship to the structural crisis.[2] Consumer credit is the problem in nearly 90 percent of the cases, either alone or in addition to real estate loans; in nearly half the cases, the difficulties are tied to unemployment.

The fact that this indebtedness occurred several years after the rise in interest rates at the beginning of the 1980s does not diminish the responsibility of the policy change. Households, facing difficulties directly due to the crisis (unemployment, lack of job security), were victims of this policy twice over. First, incomes were the subject of severe cutbacks, leading to a complete stagnation of total wages: the rise in rates extended and deepened unemployment and this unemployment—more generally, neoliberal policies—contributed to the wage freeze. Second, the burden of interest payments is one of the components of household spending, and the increase of real interest rates weighed heavily on many households. In 1987 interest payments were equal to nearly half the amount of all loans. Going further into debt, in order to make one's interest payments—the logic of such a cumulative deterioration is well known.

This flow of increased loans was naturally reflected in the increase of the mass of household debt (with a slight time lag). In Figure 10.4 one can see, standing out clearly, the profile of the inflation of household debt, which until the beginning of the 1980s had represented around 60 percent of households' available income, and which rapidly increased to nearly 90 percent. But although excessive debt remained a problem, this excess was not permanent. The period of austerity finally came to an end at the beginning of the 1990s and growth picked up (Box 8.1); unemployment stabilized and total wages began to increase again while household spending continued to increase moderately. This episode of indebtedness thus had a fleeting character. At the end of the 1990s, however, rates of indebtedness in France were still a little higher than the rates of the 1970s.

The growth of household debt was more pronounced in the United States than in France (Figure 10.4). As of the early 1960s, the total debt of U.S. households represented about 60 percent of their income, not very far from the rate for France. This rate then took off, as in France. However, it continued to increase, exceeding 100 percent from 1999 on. The growth of household debt in the United States and its lasting character are due to certain features of the macroeconomic situation in the United States that we shall analyze in Chapter 12 (focusing on the low level of savings in that country and the financing of the American economy by foreign sources). As we shall see, neoliberalism initiated a very specific sequence of cumulative disequilibria in the United States. A growing indebtedness was observed in both France and the United States. France was not able to maintain this trend because of the constraint of its external balance of payments, while the United States was.

CHAPTER

11

An Epidemic of Financial Crises

The indictment we have formulated against neoliberal finance is already substantial. The 1979 coup extended the effects of the structural crisis, particularly unemployment, and deepened both public deficits and the debt of a proportion of households already made vulnerable by the slowing of growth, the increase in unemployment, and the lack of job security. This chapter will add to the indictment. It examines the epidemic of monetary and financial crises of the 1980s and 1990s for which neoliberalism sowed the seeds.

Such crises fall into several categories. Those of the 1980s, whether at the periphery or at the center, were direct effects of the rise in interest rates, combining with monetary and financial deregulation. The crises of the 1990s were linked above all to the globalization of markets, a particular aspect of neoliberalism in its international dimension. The first crises expressed the beginnings of the neoliberal economy; the monetary and financial crises that followed were characteristic of the globalization of neoliberalism. However, this frontier was not impermeable.[1]

We shall first review the two major financial crises linked directly to the rise of interest rates in 1979: the crisis of the debt of the peripheral countries and that of the financial systems of the center countries.

Here we must return to an episode that took place twenty years ago, at the beginning of the 1980s, but whose consequences were still just as dramatic at the end of the period covered by this book. This was the crisis begun by the declaration by Mexico in August 1982 that it was incapable of meeting its commitments. Mexico was only the first, however, in a long series. By October 1983 twenty-seven countries had already rescheduled their debt payments and others were to follow. The four most indebted countries, Mexico, Brazil, Venezuela, and Argentina, were responsible for 74 percent of the debt held by less-developed countries.

How was it that these countries all found themselves suddenly driven to cease payments? The shock of high interest rates and disinflation, that is, the rise in real interest rates, dealt body blows to countries pursuing policies of borrowing at variable rates. The violence of this shock was reflected in the sudden rise in the apparent real interest rate for these countries' debts—the ratio of the total amount of interest to the total amount of debt, minus the American rate of inflation (Figure 11.1). We see, as for the capitalist center countries, the low (here negative) rates of the 1970s, their dramatic rise following the change in policy, and then the particularly elevated rates of the 1980s. It is easy to understand that, in such conditions, indebtedness became unbearable.[2]

Debt began growing before the 1980s, and the change in monetary policy of 1979 does not bear the entire responsibility for the crisis, but a good part may be ascribed to it. At the beginning of the 1970s, the debt of the developing countries, according to the World Bank definition, represented only about 7 to 8 percent of the total output of these countries. This rate was multiplied by two by 1979, with a large increase in the short-term portion of these debts, indicating a growing threat. Between 1979 and 1987 this ratio went from 16 percent of output to 39 percent. Debt payments on interest and principal, which had represented 7 to 8 percent of exports, suddenly rose to around 23 percent in 1986.

Combined with the decline in the price of raw materials exported by these countries and the low level of demand emanating from the center countries, which were in crisis, this tremendous charge for interest payments had a catastrophic effect. Figure 11.2 describes the output of developing countries, expressed in 1992 dollars. This variable does not directly account for the variations in the standard of living of populations, but it does measure the purchasing power that the production of these countries represents in relation to that of the United States. It is difficult to be clearer. This was a collapse, contrasting with the progress made in the 1970s. Of course the dollar fluctuated a great deal at the beginning of the 1980s, distorting these movements, but fifteen years later, in 1996, the level of output in these countries had still not attained, by this gauge, the maximum level of 1979.

The second major crisis of these neoliberal years, directly linked to the rise in interest rates, struck financial systems in the center, including the

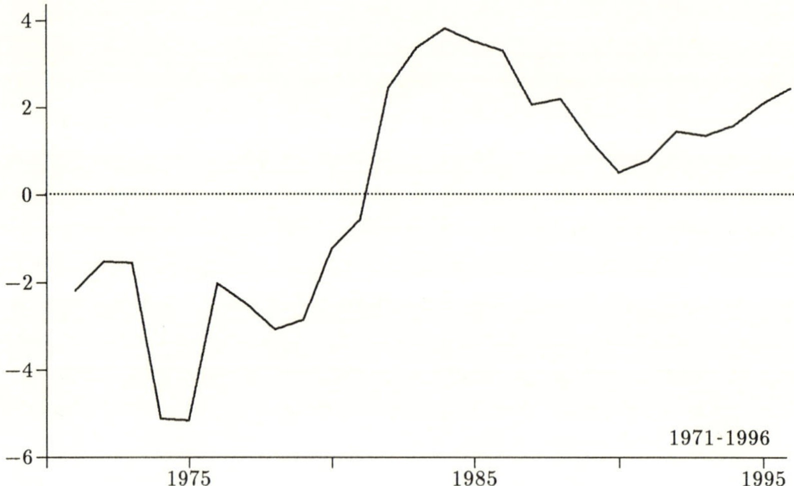

Figure 11.1 Apparent real interest rates (percent): developing countries. This is the ratio of the total amount of interest payments over total debt, minus the U.S. rate of inflation.

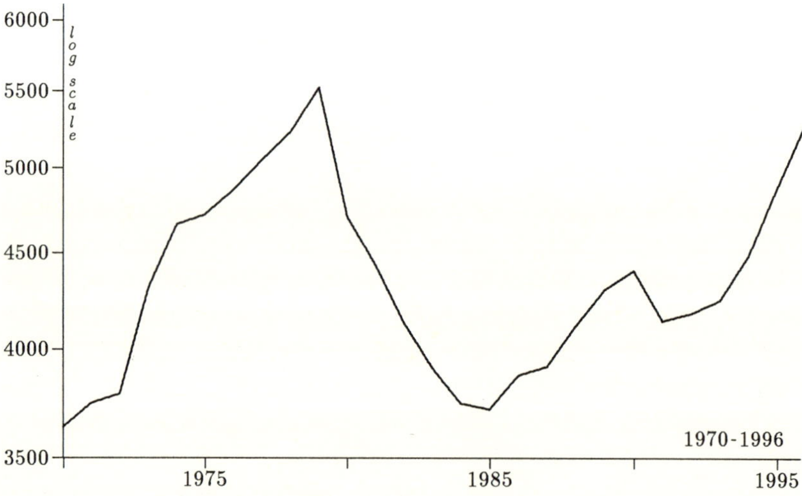

Figure 11.2 Output (billions of 1992 dollars): developing countries.

United States. Many of the problems were the direct consequences of the rise in rates, but they continued into the 1990s, following national and international deregulation.

Since the beginning of the 1980s, few banking systems have been spared. Besides Germany, which is cited as the exception that confirms the rule, all, or almost all, of the major capitalist countries were affected: the United States, Japan, France, the United Kingdom, and the Scandinavian countries. The financial institutions in the United States were struck by a wave of bankruptcies unprecedented since the Great Depression. The case of Japan is well known, and everyone in France is familiar with the problems of the Crédit Lyonnais, the Comptoir des Entrepreneurs, and the Crédit Foncier. The Scandinavian countries also provide an excellent example: it may be recalled that the bailout of Finnish banks cost the state the equivalent of one-sixth of a year's total output. Southern Europe was no better off, given the volume of bad credit that had accumulated.[3] The press reported widely on the bankruptcy of the English bank Barings and the bailout of the American fund Long-Term Capital Management.

We shall take up here in more detail certain aspects of the American financial crisis of the 1980s and the beginning of the 1990s—the crisis of banks and the savings and loan associations (Box 11.1). Between 1984 and 1994, almost 1,400 banks and 1,200 savings and loans (out of a total of around 14,500 banks and 3,400 savings and loans in 1984) went into bankruptcy or required intervention by the Federal Deposit Insurance Corporation (Figure 11.3).[4]

A few general features emerge from the analysis of this turmoil. An essential factor was the rise in interest rates at the beginning of the 1980s. In this connection, one may speak of the "backlash" of 1979. The primary cause of the crisis of the American banking system was the insolvency of the borrowers, particularly the international borrowers, because of the rise in rates. Among the affected borrowers, in addition to the peripheral countries, there was American agriculture, the energy sector, and especially office buildings, which had gone through a speculative binge. Thus the rate of profit of the financial sector took time to increase in the 1980s, despite the rise of real interest rates.

The American banking crisis and the debt crisis of the peripheral countries are closely linked. Note that the loans of U.S. banks to these countries were equivalent to about half of their own net worth in 1977 and to more than their net worth in 1987. In 1983, one year after the beginning of the

Box 11.1
The crisis of the savings and loan associations in the United States

The American savings and loan associations are investment institutions that traditionally focus on financing housing. The deposits they held represented between 55 and 60 percent of those held by banks before the crisis (1965–1988)—and only 19 percent in 2000. The principle behind the savings and loans' activity was to pay short-term rates on their deposits that were lower than the (long-term) rates at which they granted mortgages. The maximum rate paid on deposits was regulated in 1966 at the request of the savings and loans, who were concerned for their profitability.[a] For this reason, households placed their savings elsewhere when interest rates increased at the beginning of the 1980s, in order to obtain better returns, following a process called "disintermediation." An initial crisis occurred at the beginning of the 1980s, when the net worth of all savings and loans had been virtually reduced to zero. The activity of the savings and loans was then subject to extensive deregulation, and mergers were encouraged by the government. The result of this was unrestrained and disorderly activity between 1982 and 1985. The savings and loans engaged in all kinds of supposedly lucrative activities—increasing loans to casinos, ski resorts, and especially office buildings, the market for which had gone sky-high at the time. Beginning in 1986, the losses turned out to be colossal, especially in relation to the drop in the price of real estate. George H. W. Bush launched a major bailout program in 1989, whose cost has not yet been determined.[b]

---

a. T. F. Cargill, *Money, the Financial System, and Monetary Policy* (Englewood Cliffs, N.J.: Prentice-Hall, 1991), p. 304.

b. This cost has been estimated at $160 billion over many years (the total budget of the United States in 1998 was $2,500 billion). On these questions see the picture painted without any prettification in: Federal Deposit Insurance Corporation, *History of the Eighties: Lessons for the Future* (Washington, D.C.: Federal Deposit Insurance Corporation, 1997), note 1.

crisis, about a quarter of the debt of the four most heavily indebted countries (Mexico, Brazil, Venezuela, and Argentina) was owed to the eight largest American banks, representing 147 percent of their net worth. Despite a number of warnings, the stock prices of these banks continued their ascent. Only in 1987 did Citicorp, for example, make provisions for losses in

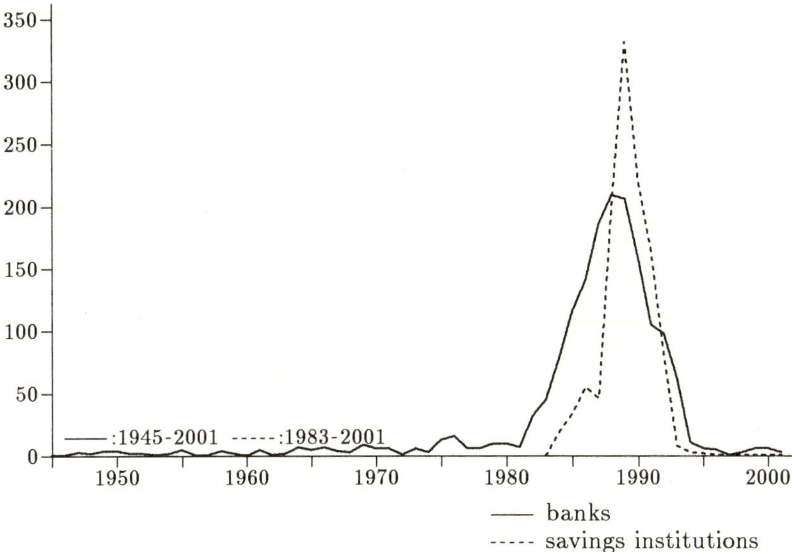

Figure 11.3 Number of banks and savings and loan associations in bankruptcy or being aided: United States. Banks and savings and loan associations, the deposits of whose clients are insured by the Federal Deposit Insurance Corporation, which were shut down, or which were bailed out by that institution.

its statements. In 1989, about half of these debts to the banking system were covered by such provisions.

The consequences of the waves of deregulation and re-regulation were also crucial, and the way in which the savings and loan crises were handled was particularly revealing in this respect. During the first phase of the crisis, the Reagan administration, carried away with market values, did not want to get involved in bailing out and restructuring the sector. All the neoliberal formulas were utilized—the encouragement of mergers, and the freedom to pay whatever interest rate on deposits was desired and to engage in all types of questionable activities, especially the most speculative. The federal government later modified its attitude and did everything that had to be done to prevent the financial crisis from degenerating into a crisis similar to that of the 1930s; in particular the government guaranteed the financing for the insurance of deposits.

Much has been written recently concerning neoliberal crises of the second type, which are less tied to the rise in interest rates, but which are directly related to the globalization of markets and the international mobility of capital.

Besides its debt crisis, Mexico provided an early example of this second type of crisis in 1994–1995. After six years of economic policy judged exemplary by the International Monetary Fund (IMF), at the end of December 1994 Mexico had to suddenly allow its currency to float against the dollar (Box 11.2). Over one year the peso lost half its value, the market dropped in the same proportions, interest rates took off, and the economy was driven into recession, with tremendous social consequences. The average purchasing power of Mexican workers dropped by half and the poverty rate rose from 30 percent to 50 percent; but Mexico paid its debts.

The Mexican crisis put an end to a stage of euphoria, to a period of stability of the peso against the dollar and of the massive arrival of foreign capital. It was a precursor to the crisis of East Asia, three years later, in 1997. First came the collapse of the Thai baht, then that of the currencies of the Philippines, of Indonesia, and of South Korea. The stock markets ac-

Box 11.2
The roots of the Mexican crisis of 1994–1995

At the end of the 1980s Mexico experienced a very high rate of inflation (prices approximately doubling annually). Large reforms were carried out. They bore traditional macroeconomic features, particularly the elimination of state budget deficits and maintaining a stable exchange rate for the peso, but their significance was much broader. This change, of course, may be characterized as a movement of liberalization: privatization, deregulation, reorientation of the economy toward foreign markets (which would lead to the signing of NAFTA in 1993), and the boom of the financial sector. According to its internal criteria, this program was crowned with success in all fields, although Mexico never again reached the level of its growth rates prior to 1982.

The rate of inflation, which was declining, remained at the end of this period higher than that of Mexico's commercial partners, despite wage moderation. The relative prices of national and foreign goods continued to evolve favorably for the latter. The entire period was characterized by a growing deficit in the balance of trade—ever more imports relative to exports, despite the sale of oil. Under these conditions it became impossible to maintain the parity of the Mexican currency. Mexico was compelled to resort to more and more perilous schemes in order to retain foreign capital. When the necessity of an adjustment became obvious, capital funds fled, prompting a widespread crisis.

companied the currencies in their fall, just as the number of bankruptcies increased, especially those of certain Korean conglomerates, the chaebols. In all these countries, the consequences of the crises were dramatic—unemployment, poverty caused by the rise in the prices of basic commodities, a rise in petty and serious crime, and so forth.

Figures 11.4 and 11.5 illustrate the violence of these shocks in the case of Korea. The rate of unemployment, around 2 percent prior to the crisis, suddenly rose to 7 or 8 percent. Stock prices, already declining since the beginning of 1995, dropped suddenly, and were divided by two in one year. Economic activity, especially in industry, strongly benefited from the devaluation of the won against the dollar by one-third, but unemployment did not return to its previous levels.

To these examples should be added the near-bankruptcy of Russia after the drop of the ruble in August 1998, the effects of the Asian crisis on Brazil at the end of 1998, then on Turkey, and the crisis in Argentina beginning in 2001, another major illustration of this neoliberal instability with dramatic consequences.

It is difficult to explain these monetary and financial crises. A certain number of factors have been cited: the fragility of the banking system, along with deregulation (both in the center and on the periphery); poor management of certain public and private financial institutions, and the lack of supervision of banking activity both nationally and internationally; the flexibility of exchange rates, or, conversely, the pegging of certain currencies to the dollar (according to the countries and the periods); the free international mobility of capital (which concerns the periphery more directly). To this must be added the high interest rates, which led to nonpayment.

Still absent from this picture, however, is an important element: the wild growth that the financial sector went through during the 1980s and 1990s. We shall treat that question in Chapter 13. This growth was financed by the net flow of interest payments, which this sector levied on the remainder of the economy, and the capital inflow spurred by this profitability. Whatever the circumstances, such a boom would put the financial system at risk. This one happened to coincide, and not by accident, with a tremendous degree of deregulation. At the same time that the total amount of available funds was increasing, finance abandoned some of the safeguards it had been using; in a situation that required increased caution, everything was done to limit the rules that imposed restraint and discipline.

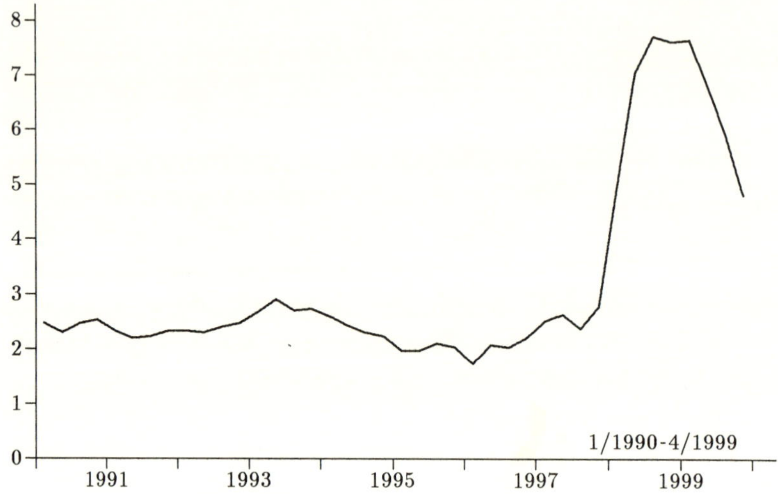

Figure 11.4 Rate of unemployment (percent): Korea.

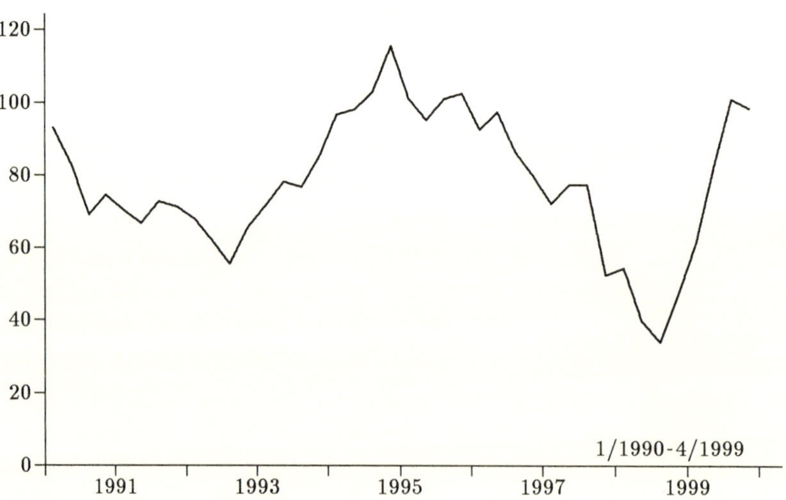

Figure 11.5 Stock prices (1995 = 100): Korea.

There is no doubt that the activity of financial institutions must be regulated and subject to certain controls (from the perspective of monetary and financial stability). This control was exercised in the decades prior to neoliberalism by the central banks, under government supervision. The fact that this surveillance has been loosened and is weak on an international level raises in an acute manner the problem of the emergence of substitute rules and of setting up supranational bodies capable of imposing them on a global scale. Rules of management, termed prudential, are being gradually set up; calls to order are being formulated; bailout operations are being organized. It is difficult to argue that these measures have been useless, but they have not prevented the crises from recurring.

The mechanisms governing currency exchange added to these troubles. In the 1990s the world monetary system combined rates that were practically fixed, tending to link certain currencies to the dollar, and floating rates, which led to steep variations in exchange rates, as between the dollar and the yen—a strange cocktail of extreme rigidity and flexibility. Pegging certain currencies to the dollar seemed to insure international capital against exchange risks and therefore allow it to circulate under the most satisfactory conditions for finance. But the fact that other currencies were floated and the differences in inflation rates were likely to undermine the system. So it was that certain East Asian countries, like Korea, which were deeply tied to the Japanese economy, had nevertheless pegged their exchange rates to the dollar (used in international transactions). That was quite advantageous as long as the dollar was depreciating. But the steep variations in exchange rates between the dollar and the yen,[5] in particular the 27 percent revaluation of the dollar between June 1997 and August 1998 (that is, over fourteen months), also revalued the currencies of these economies, creating the conditions for a recession, which was amplified by other elements.

The most frequently cited factor of crisis in the 1990s was the freedom of capital movements on the world market. In the advanced countries this freedom radically limited the autonomy of national policies, a limitation that already constituted a serious handicap. But in the emerging countries, this capital mobility gave rise to a tremendous degree of instability. For each crisis, the imminence of recessions created the conditions in which they would deepen. This is an old phenomenon, but one that has taken on unheard-of proportions over the last ten years. The tremendous rise in capital inflow into the so-called emerging countries dates back to 1990; those flows were suddenly reversed as the crisis of 1997 approached.[6]

The problem of the free circulation of capital touches on a fundamental aspect of the functioning of capitalism, a nerve point of the neoliberal strategy to reassert the prerogatives of the proprietors of capital. The real threats do not come from this or that macroeconomic imbalance, this or that imprudent financial act, from this or that policy error, but from the degree and the ways in which this freedom is asserted.

There is no capitalism without the circulation of capital. Capital is made productive in firms through production, but there must exist agents at a higher level, capitalists, who constantly move capital among various companies and various sectors—one of the means of maximizing the rate of profit and one of the functions of finance.

The problems flow from the inevitable process of the financial mechanisms' becoming autonomous in relation to their base in production. In productive activity capital movements are slow, because part of the capital is immobilized in buildings and machines. Companies do not make strategic decisions (to develop an activity, reorganize it, or abandon it) overnight. If one commits oneself, it must be on a long-term basis; that is the price of efficiency.

Complete mobility should not be interpreted as a simple necessary appendage to the internationalization of production. It cannot be denied that the development of multinational companies required reorganizing monetary and financial operations on the world level, but the demand of total liberalization, even in a crisis situation, means that financial operations function not so much as indispensable additions to production within vast corporations, but rather as distinct and largely autonomous operations (in which the multinationals are also involved).

The financial markets have their own functioning and logic. Finance is hypersensitive to the least sign indicating possible gains or losses. When a business seems profitable, capital streams to it; when another turns out to be not too lucrative, capital flees from it. The construction, parallel to the world of production, of financial institutions that make these movements easier runs through the whole history of capitalism, as do attempts to constantly perfect these institutions' functioning—hence the equally constant necessity to regulate these operations. These mechanisms are effective in some ways in the sense that they facilitate choices. But they also have potentially devastating consequences. The history of stock market crises demonstrates this—when everyone wants to get out, stock prices collapse.

The same is true for the monetary markets. If capital holders sense that a currency will be devalued, they tend to convert their holdings into another currency. Exchange rates may be maintained thanks to purchases and sales of currencies by the central banks or by an increase in interest rates, or they may drop, confirming the negative expectations.

When we speak of financial and monetary fragility, we are speaking of all of this—of the utopia of a capitalism in which one can always be sheltered from losses, of the myth of a game where the holders of capital always win—and of all the holders of capital, fleeing, deserting before the collapse.

CHAPTER

12

Globalization under Hegemony

Neoliberalism may mean a return to the hegemony of finance in the main developed capitalist countries and on a global level, but this is no reason to neglect American preeminence. Internationalization of capital and globalization of markets are not synonyms of balanced relationships, particularly in relation to the least advanced countries. Completely to the contrary, the affirmation of neoliberalism coincided with the renewed robust hegemony of America and American finance.[1]

The United States occupies a privileged position in world finance. The financial institutions (banks, mutual funds, and so on), big multinationals (largely financialized), and rich holders of securities of the United States dominate. This domination is relayed by their state,[2] the one that tends to free itself from the old political compromises, to deregulate and to re-regulate according to their financial interests, and to favor American positions in the world, be it a question of finance, trade, or research. This situation is reinforced by the close relationship between U.S. finance and that of the United Kingdom, given the importance of the London market.

This American financial hegemony falls within a more general context: technological, military, political, and cultural.[3] On a strictly economic level, it may be recalled that in 2000, the United States was responsible for nearly one-third of the output of the thirty countries of the OECD. Despite much catching up by others, who have perhaps taken the lead in certain areas, the American economy remains the most advanced in many technologies.

The advantages the United States receives from this position can be illustrated in all the areas explored in the preceding chapters. The policy of high real interest rates caused a great deal of damage everywhere, including in the United States, but ultimately less there than elsewhere; Europe and, worse still, the peripheral countries suffered from it terribly. It was not the United States that paid for market globalization; rather, on the contrary, it was the United States that benefited from it. The status of the dollar as international currency made it possible for this country to combine high rates of consumer and housing spending with the growth of its economy. It is worth examining these points a bit more carefully (we shall leave aside the question of trade negotiations).[4]

This American hegemony sends us back first of all to Chapter 9, where we observed the negative effect of the 1979 rise in interest rates on the French economy, an American decision. French companies were financed by loans in higher proportions than companies in the United States, particularly at the beginning of the 1980s, when rates increased (Figure 9.4). As long as real interest rates were low or negative, as in the 1970s, this type of financing benefited companies, but the sudden change in rates did considerable damage to the French economy. Because of this the profit rate declined in much larger proportions there than in the United States. This shock prompted companies in both countries to attempt to reduce their debt, but this was more difficult to carry out successfully in France. This reduction in debt still remains incomplete, especially for the smallest companies, despite the fact that they have avoided borrowing during recent years. The debt burden is an essential factor in the slowness with which France has emerged from the structural crisis, and hence in the difference in growth rates registered in the 1990s in both countries.

What may be said of the peripheral countries? The 1979 coup took a brutal toll on these economies (Chapter 11). The figures are so violent that they spare us the necessity of commenting.

This toll on the peripheral countries and, to a lesser extent, the handicap that the rate hike represented for Europe and Japan were foreseeable. They should not be seen as secondary effects of a therapy that the complexity of the mechanisms made it impossible to anticipate. The United States provoked the debt of the peripheral countries in the 1970s; its policy of fighting mercilessly against inflation, which it put into practice at the end of the decade, could only lead to devastation in the countries that had taken the road toward growing indebtedness. The fact that European companies used more bank credits as financing was a well-known phenomenon. But the United States, in its triumphant arrival in the neoliberal era, could not be bothered by such trifles, all the more because the main costs would be borne elsewhere, and because the revenues of finance were at stake.

We turn now to the international monetary and financial mechanisms—in whose functioning the United States is privileged by the fact that it holds the world currency. This strategic advantage has often been discussed. In this regard, one speaks of *seignorage*, that is, of the feudal lord's privilege to coin a currency and to fix its rate.

The crisis of the dollar in the 1970s could have affected the international status of the dollar. But it was only fleetingly weakened and, after the crisis, unambiguously reasserted its position as the world currency. Admittedly the yen threatened for a while, but the Japanese economic crisis left the American currency incontestably dominant. Was the mark ever a candidate for this succession? Can the euro be a pretender?

We are emphasizing here the role of the dollar in American domination, within a world of floating exchange rates and free capital mobility—a world of market globalization. We should not hesitate to assert: if the United States had not enjoyed this dominant position, it never would have been the agent of globalization, and no other country would have replaced it as the vector of such a new financial order. In a system of free international capital mobility, all countries are exposed to fund withdrawals, but they are more so when their currency represents little in the eyes of international investors, that is, when their exchange rates may be easily destabilized. A country whose currency is placed above those of others is little exposed to the effects of open markets. An internal crisis will affect it much less than the others, because it will not be amplified by capital movements (this country might, however, suffer from the repercussions of a deep foreign crisis). For all the other countries, whose governments have, to a large extent, lost control over their own currency, both because of floating exchange rates (or rigid pegging to the dollar) and the free circulation of capital, the risks raised by globalization are permanent and considerable. These countries may profit occasionally, as long as their economic, political, and social situation appears sufficiently secure and it is possible to make large profits there, but globalization is a permanent threat to them.

To this must be added the manipulation of exchange rates, and its relationship to American domestic prosperity. Examining the evolution of exchange rates reveals the great freedom of movement enjoyed by the United States in carrying out its policy and in prioritizing its domestic problems.

Figure 12.1 describes an indicator of the evaluation of the franc and the yen in relation to the dollar (the curve for the mark is very close to that of the franc). If the variable is low, the currency is undervalued; in the opposite case, it is overvalued. In the interpretation of this variable, it is convenient to first set aside the sudden fall and recovery of the franc and yen during the mid-1980s. This movement reflects the peaking of the dollar during the 1982 recession. The crisis of the dollar, at the beginning of the 1970s, represents an abrupt change. The first thing is a change in level, which expresses the devaluation of the dollar after the crisis. For the franc,

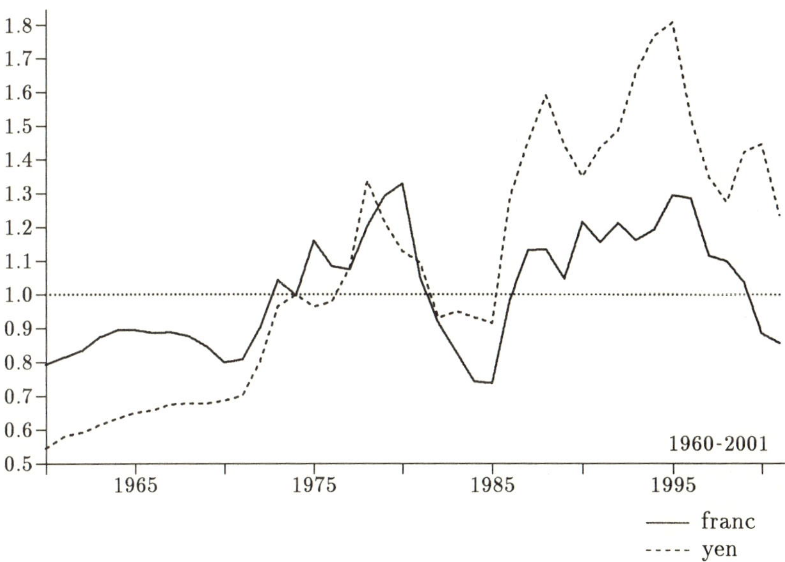

Figure 12.1 Evaluation of currencies relative to the dollar: franc and yen. The OECD calculates exchange rates, so-called purchasing power parities, which, if they prevailed, would assure the same purchasing power for a given amount in the given country and in the United States, once this amount was changed into dollars. The statistics from this figure are the ratio of the actual exchange rates to these purchasing power rates. This ratio is high for a currency overvalued in relation to the dollar and low for an undervalued currency. When the variable is below the horizontal line, the dollar is high.

aside from the slack period of the mid-1980s, the revaluation is around one-third, and is relatively stable until the late 1990s. For the yen, with the same restriction for the 1980s, there is a continual rise until 1995, which reflects American policy in relation to the threat that the Japanese manufacturing industries have represented to those of the United States, because of the progress achieved in Japan. This threat has been perceived very explicitly in the United States. By looking at these broad movements, we understand that the world monetary system that has prevailed since the crisis of the dollar has allowed the United States, and still allows it in relation to Japan, to assure not the devaluation of the American currency (a dominant currency does not devaluate!), but the revaluation of the yen as soon as, and as often as, necessary, without compromising the position of the dollar.

Currency floating is a dramatic phenomenon—instead of the slow slide of the 1960s and the beginning of the 1970s, there are very wide swings. They generally represent the effect of American decisions responding to domestic policy needs, particularly the fight against inflation. Thus the most striking event of the period under consideration was the tremendous rise of the dollar at the beginning of the 1980s, at the same time as the change in monetary policy in 1979 (this rapid rise is expressed in the figure by the broad drop of the curves). The later swings are often interpreted as a product of the United States' wielding its weapons against Japan. One observes the rise of the yen in the mid-1990s, and then its later drop—a wide swing, which played a central role in the boom of the economies of East Asia (notably the Korean industry between 1993 and 1996) and the beginning of their crisis in 1997 (Chapter 11).[5]

It is easy to understand that, in such conditions, the European countries attempted, after the crisis of the international monetary system, to reestablish more or less rigid exchange rates within the European monetary system, isolating their reciprocal relationships from these unpredictable movements. The establishment of the euro marks a stage in this attempt to assert a certain degree of autonomy, through increased international weight, which may be capable of confronting the all-mighty dollar.

Another aspect of this American hegemony is linked not to the damage caused by these policies, but to the treatment of these damages. The negative repercussions of a policy are one thing, and the capacity to handle them another. In this regard, it is interesting to compare the intervention of the American authorities during the crisis of the banks and the savings and loan associations in the 1980s, and the IMF interventions during the monetary and financial crises at the end of the 1990s.

When high real interest rates devastated a part of the American financial system, the government did not attempt to avoid the collapse of certain segments of its financial system (banks or savings and loans)—the wave of bankruptcies was enormous (Chapter 11). The concern was elsewhere—preventing the spread of the financial sector's contamination in the direction of the nonfinancial sector. The memory of the 1930s was on everyone's mind. This intervention consisted in placing the very large amount of funds required to indemnify customers at the disposal of the deposit insurance system. These funds were out of proportion to the sums previously allotted for this purpose. Without this guarantee of compensation, the bankruptcy of numerous establishments would have aroused distrust, even prompted a movement of panic, which might have destabilized other financial institutions and driven the economy toward chaos. The American government watches over its finances, its companies, and over the stability of its economy.

We have outlined a delicate combination, made up of often contradictory stakes. On the one hand, the rise in interest rates was used as a motor force in the reform of the monetary and financial system. Certain aspects of the system set up after the Great Depression were eliminated (such as the regulation of interest rates), whereas others, such as deposit insurance and controls, found themselves reinforced. It was also necessary that this cleanup not endanger the other components of the financial system and economic activity in general. Everything was accomplished with this in mind, with the support of a powerful state, and at the expense of the poor taxpayer who is so compassionately spoken of in the United States.

Such solicitude stands in stark contrast to the treatment of catastrophes that are external to the capitalist metropolis. The repercussions of the financial crises on the real economy abroad were major, whether on peripheral countries, following the rise in rates at the beginning of the 1980s, or on countries dragged into globalization crises during the following decade. Who cared about that at the center? Who, besides the officials of these countries, paid any attention to the impossibility of keeping these monetary (exchange) shocks from destabilizing their economies, leading to, or worsening, unemployment and poverty? No one—the United States, with the help of the international monetary institutions, paid attention only when the danger of repercussions at the center became too threatening and the crisis was already severe.[6]

Instead, the United States seized the opportunity to reinforce and extend the sway of the neoliberal order, in this case toward territories that were still partially outside of it. The interventions of the international bodies, the IMF and the World Bank, strived in this direction. Little was undertaken to avoid the devastating effect of the financial crises on the economies that had been directly affected, but a maximum effort was made to reinforce the U.S. hold on world finance and to defend American interests. Everything was there: overcoming the crisis and reinforcing the hegemony of American finance had to coincide. That is a remarkable aspect of this double or triple neoliberal game—to claim to guarantee to end the crisis, to end the crisis in its own way without bothering too much about the damages for everyone else, and to favor the emergence of an order that guarantees the preeminence of American, particularly financial, interests. The record at the center up to the end of the 1990s was impressive: a financialized society, increased financial revenues, a euphoric stock market, and a bonanza for the highest incomes.

One must wonder about the degree of cynicism that prevails in carrying out these policies.[7] It has already been said that the United States must have been conscious of the unbearable price that the rise in interest rates represented for the peripheral countries, and of the burden placed on the European economies. How exactly did the crisis of the dollar and the subsequent monetary and financial deregulation unfold; what was the transition between a defensive attitude and the return to an offensive one? What were the motivations of the United States when, after the 1997 crisis, it blocked the formation of a yen zone in Asia, capable of contributing to the stability of the countries of East Asia?[8] Why did the United States not oppose European economic construction and the creation of a single currency?[9] Specialists will have to analyze each stage of these events on the basis of the available archives and pursue the debate. At our level of analysis, the degree of subjectivity or of objectivity is of secondary importance. Only the result matters, and it is unequivocal.

One of the most obvious expressions of the position of the dollar as world currency is precisely the fact that, unlike other countries, the United States is not obliged to balance its foreign trade accounts; it can afford to have a trade deficit. When the United States spends more than it produces, it has no difficulty in obtaining financing from abroad. Creditors the world over have been happy until now to extend credit to it, and the increase in the foreign debt has not appeared to be a threat—which doesn't stop American authorities from periodically worrying about the extent of this deficit. Nothing forces the United States to institute a restrictive policy in order to limit its imports and to limit the structural trade deficit. The poor have to be frugal, but the rich can be extravagant. To what point such imbalances can be maintained is another question.

This absence of external constraint confers on the contemporary American economy one of its salient features: its capacity to grow and to accumulate capital, while saving little or not at all.

What does "not save" mean at the level of an entire country? Purchases of goods and services may be divided into two major components: firms' investments and all other purchases (particularly household and government consumption, household housing purchases, and government investment). We shall adopt this global point of view, calculating savings by subtracting from the total income of a country all spending other than firms' net investments, because we are interested in the capacity of an economy to make its productive apparatus grow.[10]

Figure 12.2 describes the ratios of savings, as defined above, and firms' investments to the total income of the United States. Both rates dropped together at the beginning of the 1980s. Since 1975, and especially since 1982, American companies have invested more than the country saves. How is that possible? The answer is simple: thanks to the financing ensured by foreigners (Box 12.1).

This contribution of foreigners to the current growth of the American economy travels along various roads. There is an initial channel, direct investments, which is registered in corporate accounts. These operations go both ways: either investments by Americans in other countries, or by foreigners in the United States. The term "investment" is a bit misleading here—it designates long-term financing of other companies (stock, profits that have not been repatriated, or credits); the term "direct" refers to the possession of at least 10 percent of the capital of a company in which the investment has been made.

Figure 12.3 traces the profile of direct investments of Americans abroad and of foreigners in the United States. It shows first of all that American companies are taking more and more stakes in foreign companies and vice versa.[11] These developments attest to the growing internationalization of

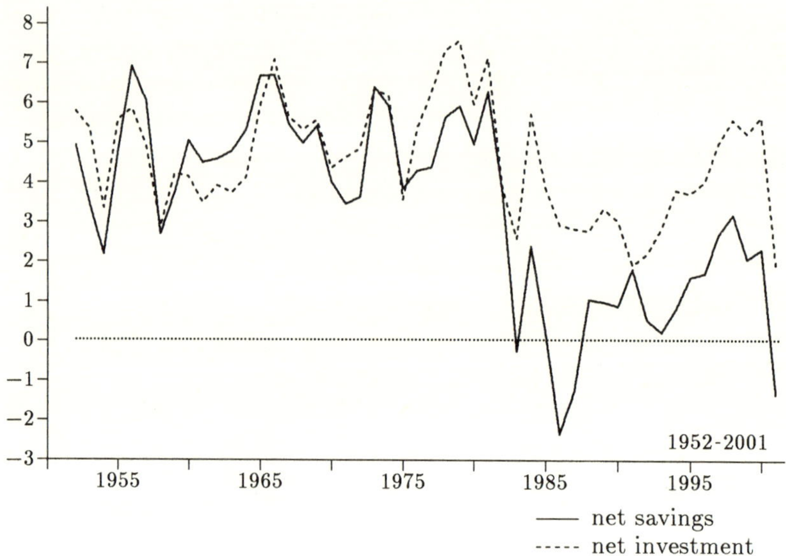

Figure 12.2 Rates of net savings and of net investment (percent): United States. "Net" here means after the depreciation of fixed capital has been deducted.

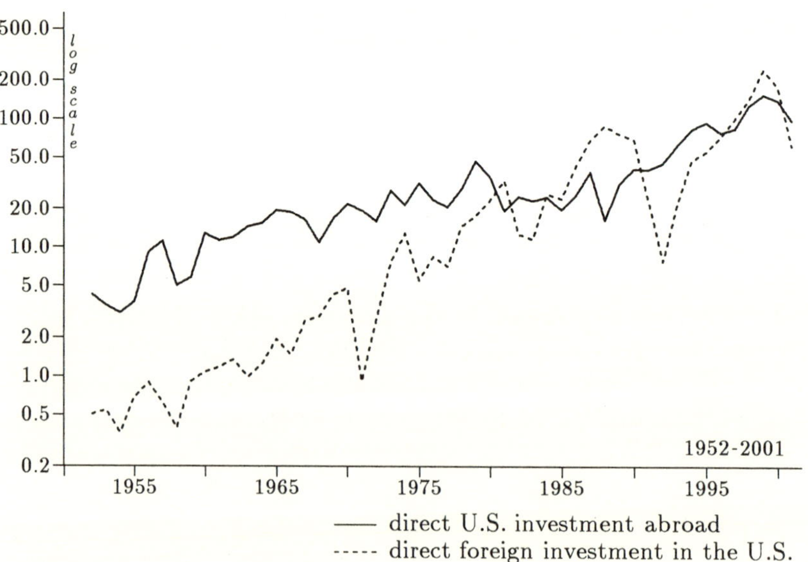

Figure 12.3 Direct U.S. investment abroad and direct foreign investment in the United States (billions of 1996 dollars): nonfinancial corporations.

Box 12.1
The imbalance of payments

The surplus of investments over savings in the United States in recent years (Figure 12.2) has led to a deficit in the American balance of payments.

The first variable to take into consideration is the balance of foreign trade (exports minus imports). Since savings, in the definition that we use, is equal to income less all spending (purchases of goods and services) other than corporate investments, it may easily be deduced that the total spending of the United States, including corporate investments, is more than the total income of the country. From the point of view of goods and services, that means that the United States is importing more than it is exporting. That is the foreign trade deficit.

Moreover, the United States must pay out certain sums to foreigners (interest, dividends, and so forth) and make certain transfers (such as military aid to other countries); symmetrically, it benefits from such flows. The import and export operations, to which these flows are added, do not balance out, and the difference is called the savings of the rest of the world in relation to the United States, or capital account balance.

A series of financial operations corresponds to these savings. When it is asserted that foreigners finance the American economy, these are the operations being referred to. Some of them are direct forms of financing, for example, the purchase of a stock share or of a U.S. Treasury security by a foreigner. Others correspond to the variations of account balances or of currency transactions, and it is because these variations in balances are included that these operations are strictly equal to the savings of the rest of the world.

the economy, an old and continuous phenomenon. The size of these capital movements in both directions is considerable. In the 1990s their size was equal to the domestic net investments of nonfinancial American corporations in the United States (in 1950, direct American investments abroad represented a tenth of these domestic investments, and direct investments by foreigners, a hundredth). The United States only remained net exporters of capital until the end of the 1970s.

The strong decrease in the gap between the flows of direct American investments abroad and the flows toward the United States is an expression of the increase in external American imbalances. Here we are putting our finger on a structural transformation that makes the United States more and more dependent on flows coming from abroad.

These direct investments do not exhaust all the financial relations between the United States and foreigners. Foreigners hold accounts in the United States, buy securities from Americans or sell them to them, and have debts and credits. These flows indirectly finance the accumulation of capital in the United States (Box 12.1).

Although the United States represents only one of the destinations of French financial operations abroad, and not the main one, it is not surprising to observe that France finds itself placed in a symmetrical situation. Since 1985, direct investments abroad have exceeded direct investments of foreigners in France. Between 1992 and the end of the 1990s, net French savings (balance of payments) were strongly positive.

There is no doubt that if these exported capital flows had been invested in France, accumulation and employment would have benefited. We noted in Chapter 9 that capital exports are a factor that likely explains the low rate of accumulation, even in relationship to the rate of retained profit (Figure 9.6). From 1970 to 1985, the balance of direct French investments abroad and from abroad to France represented only 0.2 percent of net investment, that is, practically nothing. From 1986 to 1997, however, the balance of these movements reached 25 percent of investments. This percentage is considerable. But it is impossible to globally ascribe the weakness of investment in France to capital exports, thus reducing the low level of investment to a crowding-out effect (one type of investment driving away another), because the total amount of investment both in France and abroad has declined very steeply, indicating deeper causes.

There are two ways in which to judge this situation from the point of view of a country like France—one leading to a positive assessment of the situation in the United States, the other negative. The first argument sees the United States as the locomotive of world growth. Foreigners come to invest in the United States or buy securities there because the economy of that country is dynamic and provides safer and more attractive investment opportunities (the profit rate there is high). Foreigners are willing to make loans to the companies or the government of the United States, to invest in its financial institutions, because they have confidence in the solvency of these agents and in the solidity of the currency (which is in fact the case, because of the dominant position of the United States and of the dollar). America functions like a pole of accumulation. It stimulates world demand by its foreign deficit, an expression of the strong demand prevailing in that country. The second argument affirms that the United States is living beyond its means, and that this cannot last forever. A reversal of these flows, one that could result from a strong recession, a financial crisis, or a combination of both, is possible. American domination is very strong, but not necessarily absolute; the importance of perpetuating that dominance by all means possible may be easily understood.

One of the traditional features of imperialism, as analyzed by Hilferding and Lenin, was the exporting of capital.[12] Neoliberal globalization seems to have drastically redefined the problem. One of the expressions of American domination, often put forward, is, on the contrary, the contemporary position of the United States as an importer of capital. Symmetrically, France appears as an exporter of capital. The problem is now posed in new terms, in relationship to the wave of unemployment that has developed in the structural crisis. Importing capital would be the means for a country to employ its labor force; exporting capital would prolong unemployment.

The complexity of the current configurations does not, however, refute the role of capturing surplus value on a global level. In order to show that, it is necessary to establish the record of revenue flows generated by these investments and the financial activities that accompany them.

CHAPTER

13

Financialization: Myth or Reality?

The neoliberal era is one of finance. Finance imposed its law or, more precisely, imposed it once again, after a period of relative decline. What has been the effect of this takeover, not on the economy in general, but from the simple point of view of finance? Have financial activities experienced an exceptional level of growth during these years of power, perhaps in novel configurations? These questions have often been formulated in terms of "financialization." We are said to be in a financialized economy, turned toward financial operations and institutions. This chapter will examine one by one the main aspects of this problem, adopting the point of view of various agents: the financial sector, households, and nonfinancial companies.

The most direct way to take up financialization is to examine the growth of the financial sector. Statistics for the United States distinguish actual financial companies and funds—mutual funds and (private and public) pension funds, whose purpose is to finance retirement pensions.[1] In the United States, financial corporations, in the strict sense of the term, grew strongly during the neoliberal years. Figure 13.1 traces the evolution of the ratio of the net worth of these financial corporations to that of nonfinancial corporations. The relative net worth of financial corporations decreased during the structural crisis, going from 17 percent in 1968, the maximum value prior to the crisis, then dropping to 12 percent, the minimum level, in 1982, and then going back up to 23 percent in 1999. As for the funds, their growth was, as is well known, spectacular. Figure 13.2 traces the evolution of the sums invested in them, expressed in the percentage of the net worth of nonfinancial corporations. By this measurement,

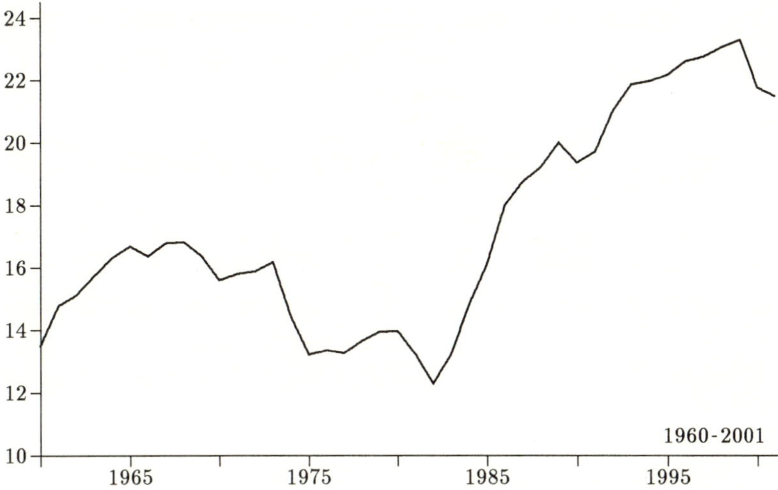

Figure 13.1 Ratio of net worth of financial corporations to that of nonfinancial corporations (percent): United States.

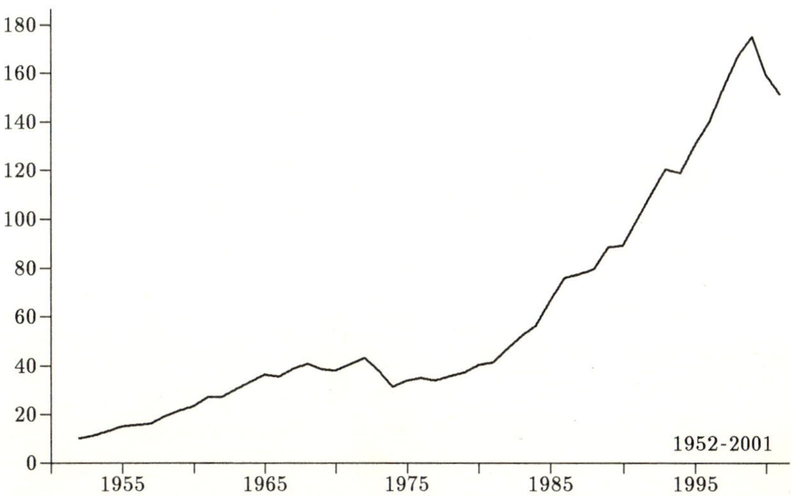

Figure 13.2 Ratio of funds held by the mutual and pension funds to net worth of nonfinancial corporations (percent): United States.

the funds were ten times smaller than the nonfinancial corporations in 1952; in 1999 they were nearly twice as large (a ratio of 1.70).[2]

The change of the 1980s was therefore particularly abrupt in the United States concerning financial corporations in the strict sense of the term, whose relative importance had diminished during the 1970s. Their subsequent comparative ascent, as documented in Figure 13.1, made it possible to attain unprecedented levels, at least since the war. On the other hand, the growth of investment funds reflects a long-term trend, which was reinforced during the neoliberal years but had already been under way for some time (the relative size of these funds in the United States had been multiplied by four between 1952 and the early 1970s). This view of the financial institutions makes it possible to ascribe to the neoliberal era the feature of increased financialization. The most important game was played out among the institutional investors.

Households are not the only ones to invest in funds, but they are the main agents concerned (in the United States they hold all the pension funds and two-thirds of the mutual funds). It is to them that we now turn.

Do households hold more and more stock, either directly or indirectly through the intermediary of institutional investors? What about their other financial assets? Figures 13.3 and 13.4 describe the evolution of the holdings of monetary and financial assets by households in France and the United States as a percentage of their income. Altogether, in 1997, French households held nearly 3 years' income in such assets, against 4.5 in the United States (it must be emphasized that these figures trace the financial holdings of households, and exclude the value of individual firms).[3] The figures break the holdings down into two elements: stock shares and other assets, that is, other securities and liquidity.

The growth of corporate shares held by French households, in Figure 13.3, seems to be very strong.[4] Contrary to appearances, this increase does not testify to a rapid financialization in the 1980s. The increase results from superimposing a progressive, increasing trend and a broad fluctuation. The trend reflects the increase in stock-owned corporations in relation to individual firms (which are directly owned by households): households possess more and more stock because the status of firms has been modified, which mirrors a structural change in property forms. The scope of this relative development of corporations is considerable. In 1970, the first year in Figure 13.3, the ratio of fixed capital (aside from housing) of individual firms to that of nonfinancial corporations was approximately

1—both capital masses were equal. In 1997, this ratio had fallen to 0.27. The broad fluctuation around the trend is the image of the successively low levels of the stock market during the 1970s, and their subsequent rise.

The apparent profile in the United States (Figure 13.4), still for corporate shares, is fairly different, because the increase in corporations there was moderate over that period. This transformation had been largely accomplished before World War II (the difference in the expansion of corporations in relation to individual firms in part explains, by the way, why Americans possess more stock than do the French—and, therefore, more financial assets). We observe in the United States a large oscillation similar to that in France, but horizontal for the reason just indicated, showing sharp growth during the very last years prior to the collapse. These fluctuations reflect those of stock prices.[5] An important change is not visible in this figure—the transfer of stock held directly to the institutional investors.

At the end of the period, households in both countries possess more in liquidity or in securities other than stock than during earlier years—this has been true since the second half of the 1980s in the United States and since the mid-1990s in France. This increase expresses the reinforcement of the creditor role of a segment of households in relation to other households, the state, or companies. This polarization is specific to the neoliberal era.

Seen from the point of view of households, financialization therefore appears to be moderate and rather dated. In France especially, the change in the form of company ownership (individual firms becoming corporations) has been reflected in the growth of the number of corporate shares. Besides the increased transfer to institutional investors, which has been gradually under way in the United States for many years, only the increase in stock prices in the second half of the 1990s appears to be characteristic of neoliberalism. However, other investments have grown since the 1980s, that is, what are essentially credits (they are held either directly or through funds). Globally, it is difficult to find in households' increased holding of monetary and financial assets a salient feature of neoliberalism (Box 13.1).

In this study of the financialization of economies, we must also consider nonfinancial firms. Were they subject to a similar transformation? Can one speak of a growing involvement of these nonfinancial firms in financial activities?

There is no doubt that French firms increased their financial invest-

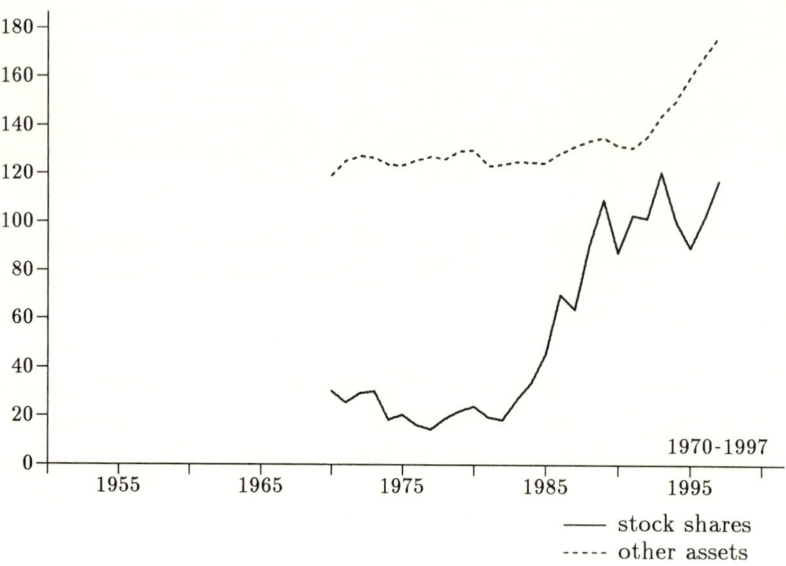

Figure 13.3 Ratio of monetary and financial assets of households to their disposable income (percent): France. Disposable income is income, increased by social benefits, less social and other taxes (as well as paid interest for France). Stock shares and other assets may be held directly by households or by investment funds.

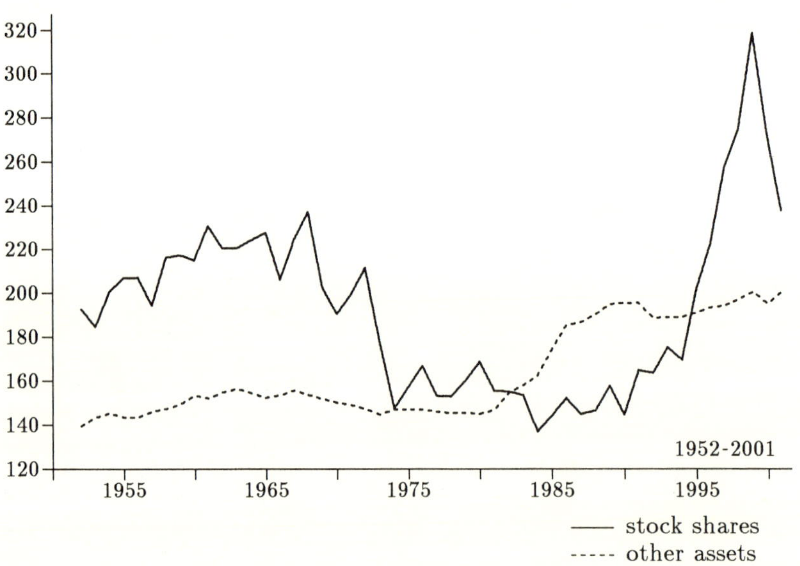

Figure 13.4 Ratio of monetary and financial assets of households to their disposable income (percent): United States.

Box 13.1
A regime of financialized accumulation?

The possible effect of holding securities on household consumption or investment is difficult to establish. Households do not hold more and more stock, but one could imagine that the variation of prices would contribute to such a "wealth effect"—certain households feeling richer would spend more. This did not seem to be the case before 1995: "[Empirical tests] find little evidence of an important wealth effect of share prices on consumption. The strong positive correlation between consumption growth and lagged stock market returns, therefore, appears to be primarily due to the leading indicator feature of stock price movements [stock prices drop before recessions]."[a]

The possible effect of the very strong increase in prices between 1995 and 2000, and of the subsequent drop, remains to be analyzed.

All this does not suffice to constitute a new regime, where demand is determined by the stock market and no longer by the "salaried relationship."[b] However, concern over how to slow down a collapse of stock prices has certainly become a crucial element of monetary policy.[c] The drop in stock prices deeply affects the economy, particularly the financial institutions and the nonfinancial companies, which hold big stock portfolios and the corresponding "goodwill." The two ideas should not be confused: a regime of accumulation where demand would be supported by the proliferation of and rise in the prices of financial assets, and the capacity of a drop in prices to destabilize the real economy. The first is doubtful; the second is probable.

---

a. J. Poterba and A. Samwick, "Stock Ownership Patterns, Stock Market Fluctuations, and Consumption," *Brookings Papers on Economic Activity,* 2 (1995): 297.

b. M. Aglietta, *Le capitalisme de demain,* Notes de la Fondation Saint-Simon, no. 101, Paris, 1998.

c. F. Lordon, "Le nouvel agenda de la politique économique en régime d'accumulation financiarisé," in G. Duménil and D. Lévy, eds., *Le triangle infernal: Crise, mondialisation, financiarisiation* (Paris: Presses Universitaires de France, 1999), pp. 227–247.

ments during the neoliberal years, and the increase was brutal. Each year these firms added to their fixed capital; their investment (net of the depreciation of this capital) provided a means to measure this, but they also acquired financial assets, particularly stock. Figure 13.5 traces the evolution of the relationship of the stock purchases to net investment. These purchases were practically negligible until the beginning of the 1980s. In 1997, in what can be termed an explosion, they were three times more than net investment. Firms now hold big blocks of shares (at market rates they are equivalent to 200 percent of their fixed capital, in 1997, as against 32 percent in 1970). Other financial assets increased as well, but at about the same rate as fixed capital and are not evidence of a shift toward finance. The possession of this stock had the effect of strongly increasing the flow of dividends received. In 1970, they represented 3 percent of profits (before taxes on profits and interest payments); in 1997, this rate reached 43 percent.

The increase in the acquisition of stock by firms expresses a growing process of mutual ownership, because other French nonfinancial companies issue a large part of these acquired shares. They may represent the stock of subsidiaries held by parent companies, or be simple investments; nonfinancial companies can also hold stock in financial or foreign companies. This development in France since the mid-1980s has led to small businesses either being taken over or organizing themselves within groups.[6] The tremendous growth in the acquisition of stock shares must also be related to that of direct investments abroad since 1985. The notion of financialization takes on here a very particular sense—the construction of a network of interdependence among national and international firms, which seems quite characteristic of the neoliberal era, even though it is not possible to separate out genuine holdings and simple investments.

It is hard to believe that a similar phenomenon did not take place in the United States, perhaps on an even wider scale. But the national statistics do not make it possible to identify it, because shares of nonfinancial corporations held within the same sector are canceled out in the accounts.[7] Unlike French companies, American nonfinancial corporations increased their other financial assets. Figure 13.6 traces the evolution of the ratio of financial assets (which do not, therefore, include shares issued by the sector and held by other corporations of the sector, but do include the corresponding "goodwill") of American nonfinancial corporations in relation to their real assets. A clear trend toward an increase is apparent, from a rate of 40 percent to roughly 90 percent. The second curve of Figure 13.6 describes the debt of firms, still related to their real assets. We can see more or less the same profile taking shape, despite the trend to reduction in net debt (measured by the gap between the two curves already evident in Figure 9.4). We again see that, since 1998, debt is less than financial assets, as the crossing of the two curves shows. The mass of debt and of monetary and

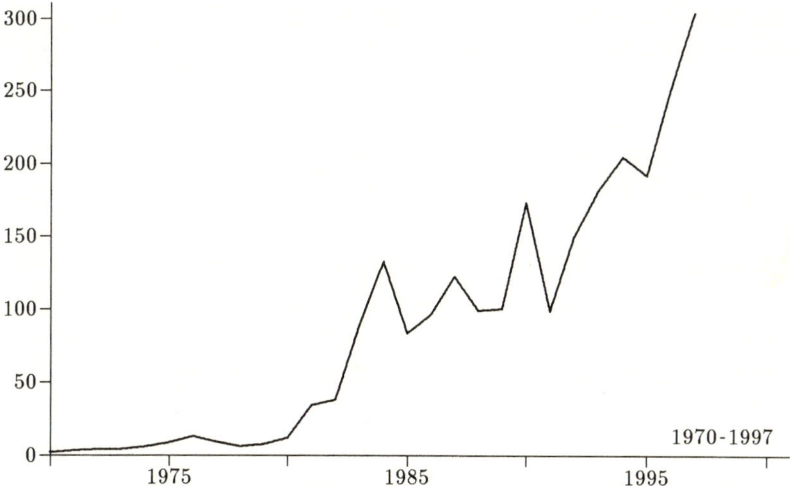

Figure 13.5 Ratio of the purchases of shares to net investment in fixed capital (percent): France, nonfinancial corporations.

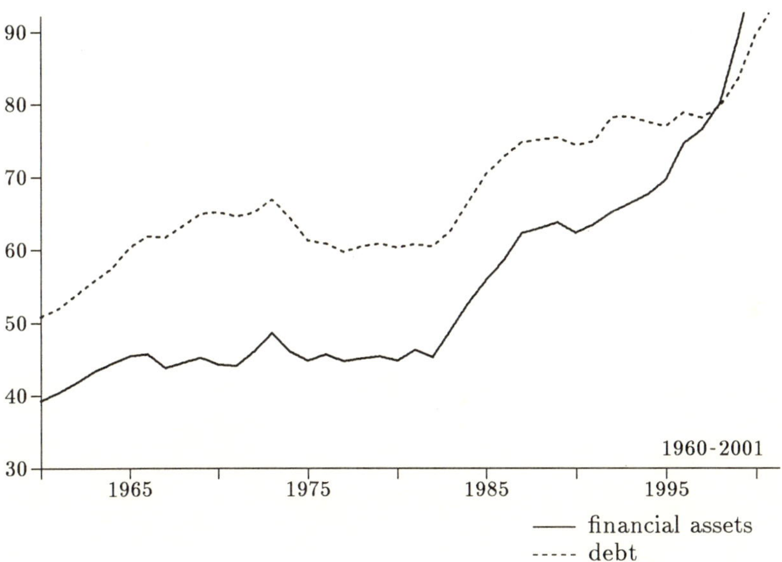

Figure 13.6 Ratio of financial assets and debt to real assets (percent): United States, nonfinancial corporations.

financial assets has thus increased in the same fashion in the United States, in very significant proportions—the purpose obviously being to make a profit in this way.[8] These increases are related to the transformation of some nonfinancial firms into genuine financial intermediaries for part of their activity, borrowing and investing simultaneously.[9]

These analyses lead to a definition of the financialization of the economy, which is not a myth, but has its ambiguities. It is first necessary to distinguish the long-term structural developments from elements specific to the neoliberal era. In the first category, it must be emphasized that in France, and to a lesser extent in the United States, the growth of financial portfolios reflects the relative development of corporations in relation to individual firms, and hence the multiplication of shares—a long-term historical movement. Moreover, in both countries a progressive institutionalization of investments is under way—financial portfolios are being transferred to institutional investors. This trend is also an old one, but was strengthened since 1980. Other transformations are specific to the 1980s and 1990s. First of all, we see an increase in activities by credit—households hold more credit (in the United States, households and firms simultaneously borrow and loan more than before). To that must be added in France, and certainly in the United States, the extraordinary growth in purchases and possession of stock by firms, denoting the establishment of a network of intercompany financial relations. This latter development is expressed by strong increases in financial revenues in relation to revenues linked to the main activity of firms. In this way, the traditional frontier between financial and nonfinancial firms tends to become blurred.

CHAPTER

14

Does Finance Feed the Economy?

Is it possible to associate with financialization, whose contours we defined in the preceding chapter, specific financing channels? What have been the effects on the real, that is, the nonfinancial, economy? More precisely, does finance contribute to investment?

These questions suggest a further exploration of whether the financial configuration associated with neoliberalism is useful or harmful as far as growth is concerned. Two types of answers are advanced. It goes without saying that the champions of the benefits of financial activities belong to the neoliberal camp. Their arguments are simple; the primary role of finance is, as its name indicates, to finance the economy, and it does that brilliantly, as the appetite of investors for risk capital shows (as in the famous start-ups). If these advocates are to be believed, in the best of worlds, profits should not stay in companies, but retrieve their autonomy by being transferred to stockholders or creditors, either individuals or financial companies, in order to be redistributed to firms in the most efficient manner. In this way a certain discipline can be imposed on managers; high interest rates and big dividends are thus factors of progress; a powerful financial sector is beneficial for the entire economy. The critics of neoliberalism argue, on the contrary, that financial activity diverts capital holders from productive investment: financial investment is a substitute for real investment and is harmful to it.

We already know the answer to these questions. It flows from a simple comparison of the rate of profit and the rate of accumulation, and refutes the neoliberal arguments. First, the rate of profit before the paying of interest and dividends has significantly recovered since the beginning of the 1980s, without capital accumulation's reaching corresponding rates. Second, the rate of capital accumulation does correspond to the rate of retained profit, that is, the rate of profit after payment of interest and dividends. (This analysis refers to Figures 3.1, 3.2, and 9.6.) These observations imply that profits distributed in the form of interest and dividend payments do not flow back to the nonfinancial sector to contribute to investments.

A company's funds can have two uses, investments in fixed capital and financial investments. But it is possible to distinguish three origins for them (Box 14.1). The provisions for the depreciation of fixed capital remain in the hands of companies, as do the retained profits, that is, profits that are realized and not distributed (the sum is the cash flow). Corporations can collect capital by issuing stock; they can borrow. How does this work in neoliberalism?

The curves of Figure 14.1 measure the relative importance of the three sources of funding that contributed to increasing the holdings of nonfinancial French corporations. The mid-1980s clearly marked the end of an era. During the 1970s, companies obtained financing in a very regular way, 55 percent by borrowing, 39 percent by self-financing (using their cash flow), and the remaining 6 percent by issuing stock. The neoliberal years have appeared turbulent, but things stabilized at the end of a transition period, in very different proportions than before—for the last three years in the figure (1995–1997), an increase in self-financing to 65 percent, an increase in the issuing of stock to 23 percent, and a drop in the level of borrowing to 12 percent.

One feature of the neoliberal period is thus the flight from borrowing, which is hardly surprising, given the rise in interest rates. We have already noted this decline (Figure 9.4); we now learn that it led to an increase in self-financing. To that is added a growth in the issuance of stock, which was multiplied by about four.

What is this financing used for? Does it contribute to productive investment? When companies issue and purchase stock simultaneously or borrow and make loans, they are not financing their real activity—only what remains after these purchases and loans can be used to invest with. Figure 14.2 describes the composition of these sources of financing of just the gross investments for French nonfinancial corporations: gross retained profits, stock issuances less stock acquisitions, and net debt (the difference in debt minus financial assets outside of stock).

As in the analysis of the global financing of all assets, a structure of sta-

Box 14.1
The sources of company financing: Comments on Figures 14.1, 14.2, and 14.3

A company's holdings are calculated in its annual report by adding together everything it possesses—real capital (factories, machines, and product inventories) and monetary and financial assets (securities, liquidity, and credits). All these elements constitute assets. Once debt has been subtracted, we obtain the net worth, that is, capital that is not borrowed.

Two types of financing can be distinguished. *Internal financing* (gross retained profits or cash flow) itself has two components, provisions for capital depreciation and profits that have not been distributed to stockholders. Its extent depends on profitability and on what portion of the profits are distributed to stockholders. *External financing* also possesses two components: borrowing (once reimbursements have been made) and stock issuances (once buybacks of its own stock by the sector have been subtracted). These diverse sources of funding finance investment (adding to real capital) and the growth of monetary and financial assets (including the purchase of stock).

In analyzing financing, one can also have a *net* point of view. From stock issuances the purchases of stock from other agents (households or funds) are subtracted;[a] from borrowing, the purchases of financial assets, other than stock, are subtracted.

Figure 14.1 focuses on the total financing of all components of company assets. For France the three sources of financing are taken into consideration globally—gross retained profits, stock issues, and borrowing. These sources finance gross investment and the increase of monetary and financial assets, including the possession of shares.

Figures 14.2 and 14.3 focus on financing the gross investment of companies by gross retained profits, stock issuances minus stock acquisitions, and the net debt (that is, borrowing, minus the increase in monetary and financial assets other than stock).

---

a. When a household or an investment fund purchases a share from another household or another fund, or a company does so from another company, no amount has been shifted to companies, considered globally, nor has any amount left them.

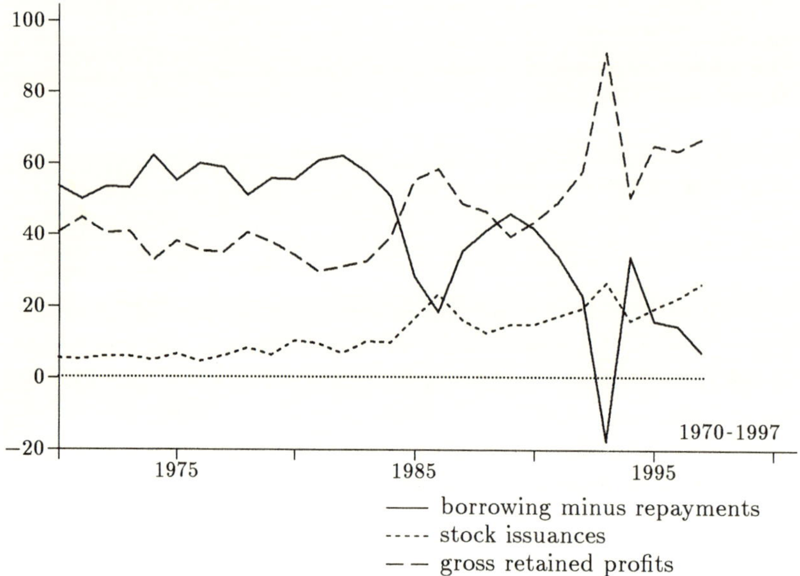

Figure 14.1 Composition of the sources of financing of all assets (percent of the total): France, nonfinancial corporations.

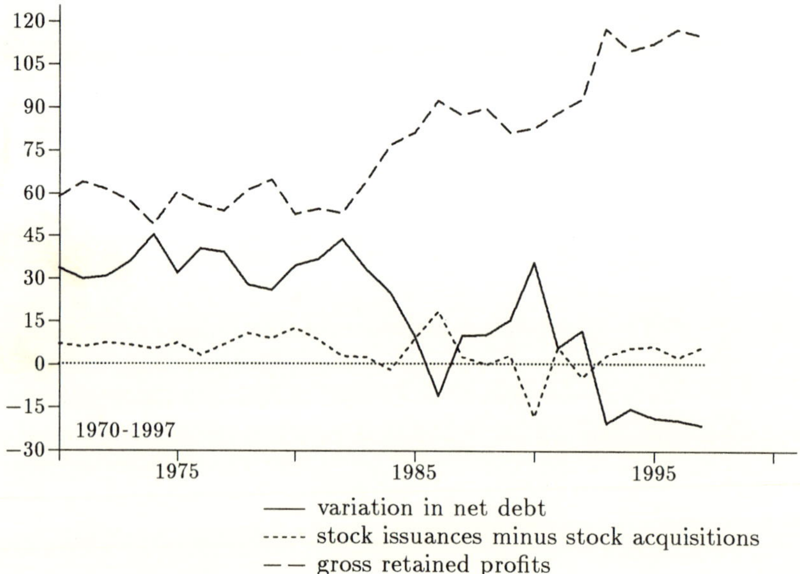

Figure 14.2 Composition of the sources of financing of gross investment (percent of the total): France, nonfinancial corporations.

ble financing of investment is obvious before the 1980s. From this second point of view, self-financing is more important than debt (59 percent, as against 34 percent). The change was, as before, sudden. We observe once again that borrowing gave way to self-financing, but the apparent configuration for the last three years (1995–1997) is very strange. It is so puzzling that it is hard to imagine that it can continue in this excessive form. Self-financing provides more than the funds necessary for investment, or 115 percent of investment. The contribution of loans is negative: companies use their internal funds to reduce debt instead of investing.

Contrary to what neoliberal propaganda would have us believe, the net contribution of the stock market to investment is very low—stock issuances finance only 5 percent of investment. More and more shares are issued, but companies buy more and more shares of other companies. These issuances and acquisitions tend to cancel each other out, so well that the recourse to the stock market does not finance real activities. In other words: corporations issue stock in order to buy stock, in the logic of financialization.

It may be thought that this configuration is specific to France, and that it cannot characterize the fortress of neoliberalism, the United States. There is nothing to this view. Figure 14.3 analyzes the financing of gross investment for the United States in the same terms as the preceding figure. From a comparison of Figures 14.2 and 14.3, an initial difference stands out: the amount of self-financing in the United States. But the contribution of the stock market proves to be, as in France, very limited. No rise in the net issuance of stock has appeared since the beginning of the 1980s, and the percentages noted are similar, or even inferior, to those that prevailed in the period preceding neoliberalism.

Although the scale of Figure 14.3 minimizes their importance, it is possible to note large fluctuations in stock issuances and in borrowing during the 1980s, and at the beginning of the 1990s, and in particular to note the negative level of net stock issuances during the second half of the 1980s. Many nonfinancial companies purchased shares from other agents between 1984 and 1990. In a symmetrical way they resorted to borrowing in order to finance it. During this time, investment remained self-financed. These purchases of stock by the American nonfinancial companies from other agents, particularly from households, involve various phenomena: a company buying back its own shares, the purchase of shares during a merger or an acquisition, or simple investments. National accounting data

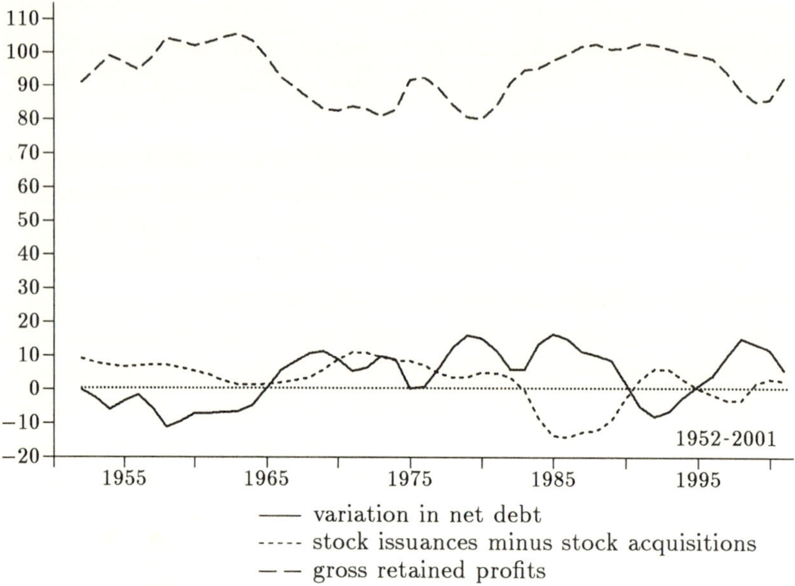

Figure 14.3 Composition of the sources of financing of gross investment (percent of the total): United States, nonfinancial corporations.

do not make it possible to determine their relative proportions, but whatever their purpose, these massive purchases indicate that the neoliberal years saw a great restructuring of financial relations, which should be tied to the financial crisis of the 1980s, but without a globally notable contribution of the stock market to growth.

There does therefore exist a financial configuration specific to neoliberalism. It is disconcerting. It would have been natural to imagine that, faced with the rise in interest rates and attempts to reduce debt, a transition toward channels of financing investment where stock issuances play a central role would take place. This did not occur. Without oversimplifying, it may be asserted that finance finances itself, but does not finance investment. More than ever growth goes through company self-financing—a process that one would have thought characteristic of the 1960s. The funds that leave companies in the form of interest payments, dividends, or share buybacks very seldom return—or rather, if they do return, they have destinations other than investment.[1]

What becomes of these amounts that leave the nonfinancial companies and don't return? An initial answer refers us to the fact that these revenues finance purchases of goods and services through agents other than the companies. Households that receive interest payments and dividends can use them for consumption or housing. Another portion of these funds is not spent by those who receive them, but invested financially. Correlatively, other agents borrow—households (especially in the United States), the state in order to finance its deficit, and foreigners (which corresponds to capital being exported)—or, in the case of financial institutions, issue securities (as the extraordinary growth of their net worth attests).[2]

It should be emphasized that the mass of funds that is directed to the capital markets or to the monetary institutions does not determine the volume of credits in an economy.[3] It is up to monetary policy, via interest rates, to control total credit, with the main goal being everywhere and as never before to watch the general level of prices—to fight inflation. To this should be added, for all countries except the United States, the necessity of balancing the balance of trade, which reinforces the severity of neoliberal monetary policy.

In this analysis, the difference between a dominated country, like France, subject to strong external constraints, and the dominating country, the United States, must be well understood. In Chapter 12 we contrasted the American balance-of-payments deficit to the French surplus. In the United States, the deficit may be linked to more credit for households, stimulating their purchases. The fact that the additional demand is directed to imports seems to moderate its inflationist character. In France, the decline in investment credits was not compensated by an increase in household and government borrowing—hence the surplus.

From our examination of the situation in the United States, it is clear that neoliberalism has simultaneously freed finance from financing company investments and favored households' and the state's negative savings—an unusual situation, a product of two hegemonies, that of finance, and, on the international level, that of the dollar. We thus end up in this American-style neoliberal configuration: on the average, the households of the country whose financial sector is the most powerful, the country of pension funds (Box 14.2), spend more and save little—which does not prevent accumulation.

Finance functions according to its own rules. In the neoliberal era, not only has it ballooned, but it has been redeployed. Financial capital has put itself in the most advantageous positions, within a complex network, structured by the pursuit of maximum profitability. While doing this,

Box 14.2
Opening new ways of financing? The paradox of employee savings

The fact that the country of mutual and pension funds—the United States—saves very little may be called the "paradox of employee savings." Neoliberal society, especially American society, has clearly not opened up promising roads in these areas. The most acceptable argument in favor of pension funds is the idea that the levies future retirees will make on future producers should be routed through the current accumulation of a productive potential that their savings finance today.[a] By building up its pension funds, America was supposed to be stimulating its savings. However, the rate of savings is lamentably low in the United States. Many are convinced of this initiative's success, although the American experience demonstrates the opposite.

The real challenge posed by the question of how to finance retirement is growth—and that is an intuitive idea.[b] It is not necessary to appeal to the Marxist labor theory of value to grasp the fact that the goods and services consumed by retirees will be produced by those who work.

Behind this discussion stands another, perhaps more decisive than the preceding one in the choice of strategies by governments. The American funds involve only a fraction of the population.[c] Optional, complementary funds, such as they might be conceived in France, would have this same feature. In practical terms, what is at stake is setting up dual, very unequal, systems of retirement pensions.

---

a. Such is, for example, the thesis supported by Michel Aglietta (*Le capitalisme de demain,* Notes de la Fondation Saint-Simon, no. 101, Paris, 1998, "Le choc démographique et les systèmes de retraites").

b. This requirement is coupled with another one, which, in a certain way, takes away from the centrality of the first—increasing productivity.

c. In 1998 only 48.8 percent of U.S. households had holdings in pension funds, following a very clear hierarchy: 6.4 percent of households earning less than $10,000 per year, as against 88.6 percent of those which earned over $100,000 (A. Kennickell, M. Starr-McCluer, and B. Surette, "Recent Changes in U.S. Family Finance: Results from the 1998 Survey of Consumer Finances," *Federal Reserve Bulletin* 86 (2000): 1–29).

finance has not financed the real economy, but has led companies to refocus on self-financing, while finance decreased the mass of available funds through interest payments and massive dividend distributions. In this general framework the dominant country, the United States, has placed itself in a particular, more favorable configuration, to which it has exclusive rights—and which cannot be exported.

CHAPTER

15

Who Benefits from the Crime?

As preceding chapters have indicated, the response of finance to the structural crises of the 1970s was particularly negative. True, this judgment deserves to be qualified, and we shall return to that. For the time being, two primary categories of criticism are evident. First, the benefit of the rise in profit rates, which wage concessions played a prime role in, was siphoned off by the holders of capital through the rise in real interest rates and massive dividend distributions; these levies did not stimulate savings and especially not the accumulation of capital; far from returning to the production system, the amounts that were siphoned off reinforced the transfer of wealth to finance. This action extended the crisis and unemployment. Second, the vast series of crises in the countries of the center and the periphery, whose consequences were often dramatic, should be counted among the negative effects of neoliberalism.

The extension of the negative effects of the structural crisis and the financial crises cannot be purely and simply ascribed to the 1979 rise in interest rates. Numerous other aspects of neoliberalism, such as the currency fluctuations and the free circulation of capital of the period, have been called into question. In any case, the problems cannot be reduced to so-called market mechanisms (for the rise in rates) or inevitable structural developments (for the circulation of capital). A more general and deliberate offensive was involved. These harsh judgments justify the term "crime" employed in the title of this chapter.

Behind this balance sheet various controversies stand out, having to do with the usefulness or parasitic character of finance. Does it produce or create income, or does it only appropriate it? These questions are political, and the answers given refer us back, implicitly or explicitly, to a small number of accounting and theoretical frameworks, references that are nearly inevitable (Box 15.1).

We have already answered the question raised—who benefited from the crime? Finance benefited. This chapter therefore seeks more to explain this answer than to reveal it. Benefited in what ways? By which means? It was above all a question of the transfer of revenues, and of the consequences of these transfers in terms of unequal treatment.

Chapters 9 and 10 have already emphasized the considerable burden that interest payments represented for nonfinancial companies, households, and the state. But this initial investigation left aside the other aspect of these operations: these operations benefited some agents. The full network of interrelations—for example, to which agents did the state pay interest, or how much did each sector pay to finance—is impossible to decipher. The statistics describing these flows do not permit us to follow them from one end of the chain to the other, but we know the total amounts paid out and received.

Figure 15.1 traces the evolution of net flows (interest received less interest paid) of interest payments in France, given the transfers due to inflation, for the various agents: nonfinancial corporations, public administrations (the government and the entire social security system, which covers health insurance, pensions, unemployment benefits, and "family" payments), the financial sector, and households (including self-employed persons). These flows are expressed in percentages of total French output.

This record obviously hides enormous heterogeneity. For example, large differences exist among households—some are in debt and pay interest, others have monetary holdings (bank and savings accounts and so on) and securities (treasury and other bonds), and receive interest payments. Altogether, households possess more monetary holdings and claims on the other agents than they themselves receive in loans. They are, therefore, globally creditors, and potential victims of inflation. Moreover, interest rates on their investments are, on the average, lower than on the loans they are granted. Although they are creditors, they pay out more interest than they collect.

The contrast in Figure 15.1 between the period prior to the rise in rates at the beginning of the 1980s and the subsequent period is striking. Financial corporations (including insurance companies) benefited from positive flows during the entire first period. Inflation was reducing creditors' revenues, but interest payments (received minus those paid out) always com-

Box 15.1
Does finance create revenue? Value? Is it useful?

Much confusion surrounds the nature of financial mechanisms. Finance itself contends that it creates wealth. What is the reality?

This book makes considerable use of national accounting records, which distinguish, on the one hand, the financial sector's providing a service, which is billed to its beneficiary (such as the cost of establishing an application for a loan or purchasing another currency), and, on the other hand, its receiving interest payments or dividends. According to the practices of national accountants, only the first are treated as production and create income. As for an interest payment or a dividend, the income is counted as a "transfer" to the creditor or to the stockholder.

There is nothing wrong with this logic of transfer. When a bank makes a loan to a company, it charges interest, that is, it transfers profit.[a] Nothing is created in this operation. Loan capital links up with the capital of nonfinancial companies and thus appropriates part of the latter's profits. The proliferation of credit operations of this kind adds nothing to production and revenue; it redistributes (even if this loan makes increased output possible). When a financial company makes a loan to another one, the profits pass from hand to hand within the financial system.

Lenders also go to seek their income beyond companies by giving credit to the state and to households. The levy is then made through taxes and household incomes. We therefore should not limit ourselves to the idea that financial income is the exclusive result of direct transfers of profits already made by a company. To the extent that taxes have been paid by companies, state creditors indirectly appropriate these profits; to the extent that taxes are paid by households, on wages, for example, this represents the levying of a new surplus.

In a period of low profitability of capital, these other types of levies took on considerable importance. Taxation appeared to be quite lucrative, and household loans made it possible for holders of capital to seek out profits that the production system had not made.

Like national accounting records, Marxist theory treats interest and dividends as revenue transfers, while production holds a very special status. It is linked to productive labor, work that produces goods or provides services to people, which alone creates value. Marxist theory notes other types of work, such as factory surveillance or all the commercial activities, that don't enter into the category of productive labor. These are costs required by production or by the circulation of capital. They are far from being useless; their function

(continued)

(continued)

is to maximize the profit rate. They correspond to "management" tasks in a very broad sense of the term.

In this theoretical framework, all financial activities are part of these unproductive tasks; finance does not create value; its profits result from the redistribution of surplus value created elsewhere. Unfortunately, national accounting records do not make it possible to reconstitute the separation, which is distinctive to Marxist theory, between work that creates value, on the one hand, and activities used to maximize the profit rate, on the other—a very pertinent analytical distinction.

In the same way that nonproductive work is not useless according to Marx's theory, finance is not, by nature, parasitic. It assumes a certain number of functions in monetary and financial transactions (what Marx called the "capital of the money trade"); it contributes to the circulation of capital between different firms and sectors; it organizes company restructuring and contributes to their financing. However, Marx often denounced, in vigorous and colorful language, the parasitic aspect of financial activities.

---

a. Because of inflation, this operation is combined with another transfer, the devaluation of debt—that is, the devaluation of principal—which the borrowing firm benefits from, thereby decreasing the amount charged. Nevertheless, the overall transfer generally profits finance, provided that the real interest rate is positive.

pensated for this effect and more. In the opposite case it would have been preferable that this sector cease its activity. The effect of the change in policy at the beginning of the 1980s appears in a very obvious way. Starting in the mid-1980s the financial sector siphoned off tremendous masses of interest. Interest paid to financial corporations had represented around 2.5 percent of French output before 1980; this rate reached 7.5 percent in 1992, and was still at nearly 5 percent in 1999.

Before the 1980s net interest flows of nonfinancial corporations and public administrations remained low, and households were the main source of interest payments to the financial sector. From the 1980s, nonfinancial corporations and the public administrations had to pay large amounts of net interest. The extent of the levy on public finances appears particularly clear—the rise in rates having simultaneously created the deficit and constituted the corresponding revenue for finance. Non-

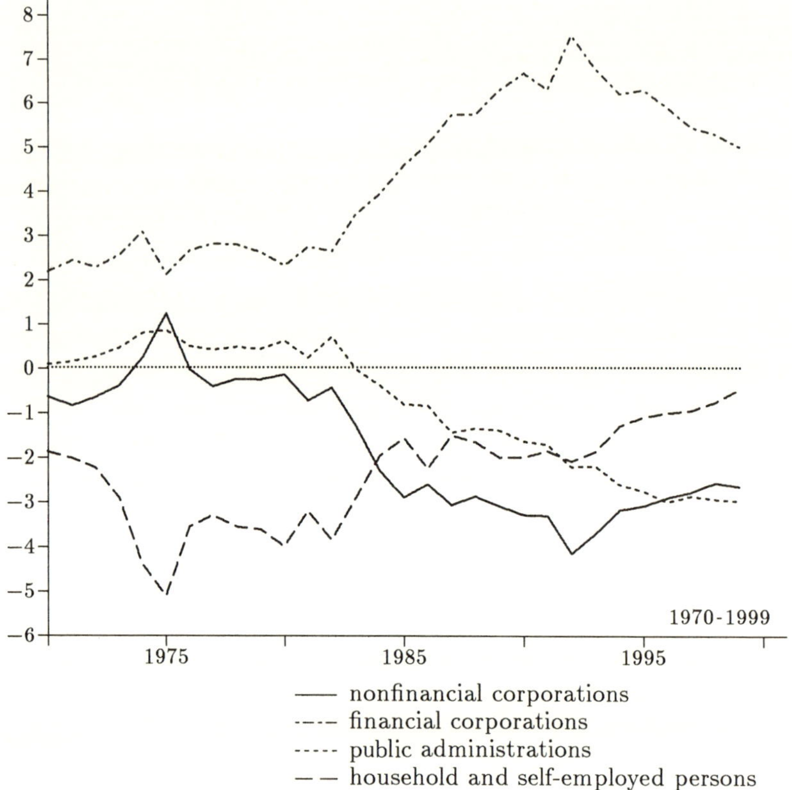

Figure 15.1 Net flows of real interest (received minus that paid out) (percent of total output): France. In order to simplify, we leave aside the always positive but low-level flow of interest received by the rest of the world.

financial corporations that were already heavily in debt prior to 1979 (Figure 9.4) suffered from the rise in real interest rates; only in the late 1990s did they begin to reduce their debt. The interest payments made at the end of the period decreased, but remain weighty.

It is easy to guess that neoliberalism had, on the whole, very positive effects on the profitability of the financial sector, both in the absolute and in comparison with other sectors of the economy. Figure 15.2 traces the evolution of the profitability of financial corporations in France and compares it with that of other corporations. The first curve reproduces the profit rate of nonfinancial corporations, which was introduced in Figure 9.2; we find there the drop in the profit rate, then its rebound and its stabilization. The contrast with the profit rate of the financial sector is striking. The inflation of the 1970s and the corresponding very low or negative real interest rates expressed themselves through *low* profitability in the financial sector, even negative rates in the measurement presented in the figure. It should be recalled that a large number of these financial institutions belonged to the public sector. The deployment of a configuration specific to the neoliberal years is, once again, clearly apparent in Figure 9.2 at the beginning of the 1980s. As has been shown, the increase in real interest rates transferred a large portion of nonfinancial corporation profits, which were increasing, toward finance, and in particular toward the financial sector, which thus granted itself a considerable increase in profitability. To this was added the drain on the resources of the state and indebted households.

The rise in interest rates, however, had negative as well as positive effects on the financial sector. We have already suggested the idea of the countercoup of 1979—the backlash of the 1979 coup (Chapter 11). Its negative consequences on the nonfinancial economy (company bankruptcies, excessive debt in some households, peripheral countries incapable of paying their debts) provoked a wave of nonpayments, destabilizing part of the financial sector itself, which was dragged into the crisis.

Figure 15.3 provides the same information as Figure 15.2 for the United States—a comparison of the profitability of financial and nonfinancial corporations. The American situation appears to be less unbalanced than that of France during the 1970s. But the recovery of the relative profitability of financial corporations is also very marked. It came later than in France, a fact that is related to the financial crisis that ravaged the United States during the 1980s (Figure 11.3). The ample fluctuation during the 1990s in the profit rate of U.S. financial corporations in Figure 15.3 reflects the effects of capital gains during most of the decade, and then capital losses.

Despite temporary problems, neoliberal policies during the 1980s and most of the 1990s thus unequivocally benefited financial corporations, whose situation strongly improved in both countries. In the 1990s their profit rate was higher than that of other corporations.

Among the advantages that finance derived from neoliberalism, one should not omit the one that constitutes its emblematic symbol—the rise in stock prices. In Figure 15.4, the stock index is divided in each country by the price index, in order to express constant purchasing power (to correct for inflation). The parallel nature of the two countries' evolutions is strik-

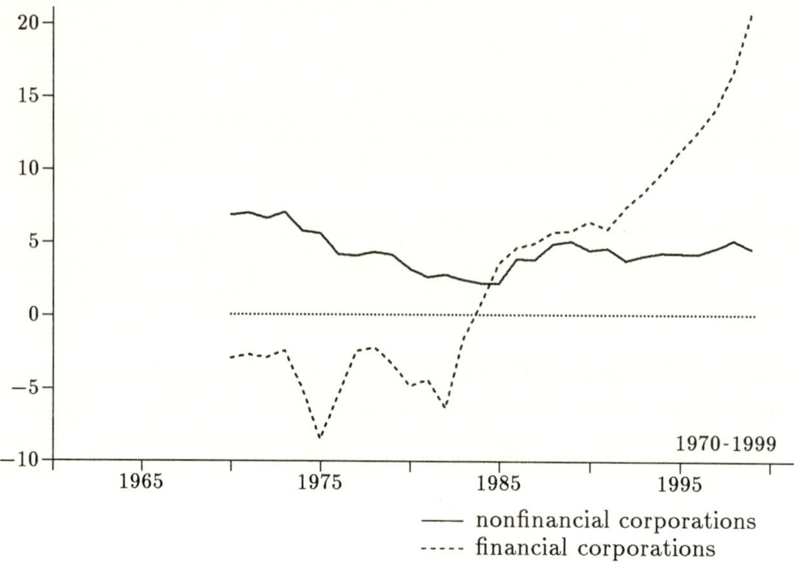

Figure 15.2 Rate of profit (percent): France, nonfinancial and financial corporations. The profit rates of nonfinancial corporations are identical to those of Figures 9.2 and 9.3. In both this figure and Figure 15.3 the profit rates of the financial sector include capital gains, which fluctuate a great deal, and have been slightly smoothed out.

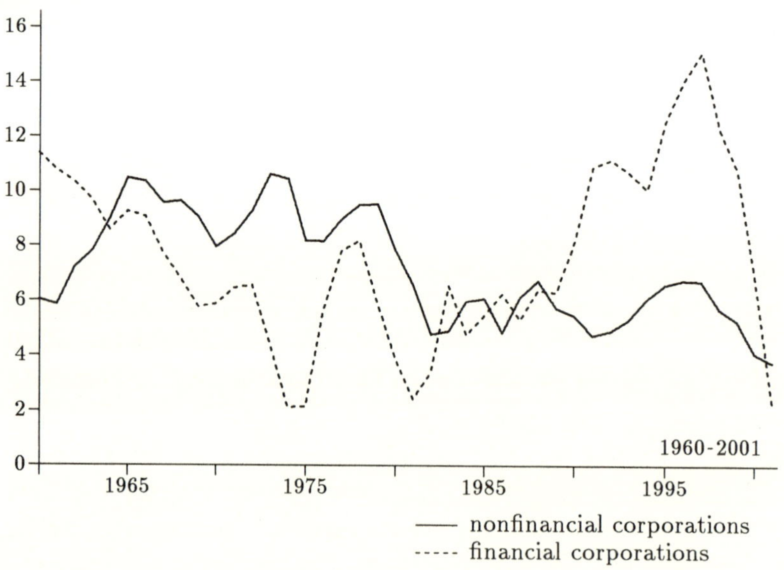

Figure 15.3 Rate of profit (percent): United States, nonfinancial and financial corporations.

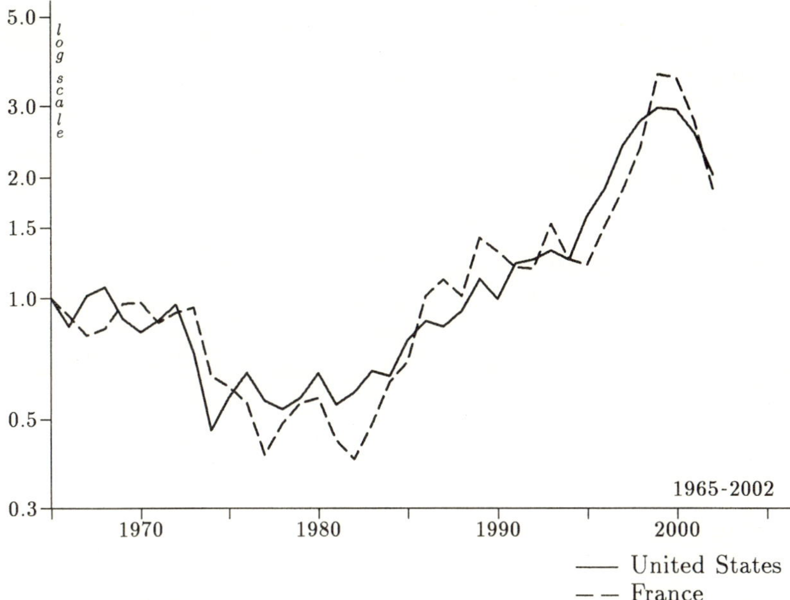

Figure 15.4 Stock prices (1965 = 1): United States and France. The prices have been deflated by the price index of each country.

ing. Starting with the 1965 level, we can appreciate the large-scale drop during the crisis years, with prices being divided by two in the United States and more still in France. The rise was stunning at the beginning of the 1980s, and the 1965 level was reached in the second half of that decade. After a gradual rise over ten years, prices exploded in the mid-1990s and culminated, in 2000, in levels three times higher than prior to the crisis of the 1970s. After 2000, prices began to fall. The last observation, the average price for the year 2002, remains fairly high.

How solid is this edifice? For the time being we shall limit ourselves to wonderment, leaving the discussion on the possible fragility of this monument that finance has built for itself to the comparison with the Great Depression in Chapter 20.

The scope of what neoliberalism brought the holders of capital—interest payments, dividends, and the rise in stock prices—is clearly revealed by an analysis of household financial income, which is worth scrutinizing.

Institutions are only intermediaries. Who, in the last analysis, benefits from the crime?—those who live off of financial revenues, under these circumstances, perpetuate and increase their holdings. One can imagine that the 1980s and 1990s marked a strong improvement in their position—besides the financial sector, and also through it, the wealthy constituted the most favored layer that benefited from the neoliberal order.

Since, in national statistics, it is impossible to separate the wealthiest households from the others, we shall take into consideration here the totality of financial revenues. The variations of these total revenues are a good indicator of the evolution of the incomes of households whose holdings incorporate sizable financial assets. Figure 15.5 describes the ratio of financial gains (or losses)—interest and dividends received, to which the increase in stock prices is added and from which the depreciation of all monetary and financial assets through inflation is subtracted—to total household income.

In France before 1980, the effect of inflation canceled out these financial gains, and transformed them into an average annual loss of nearly 7 per-

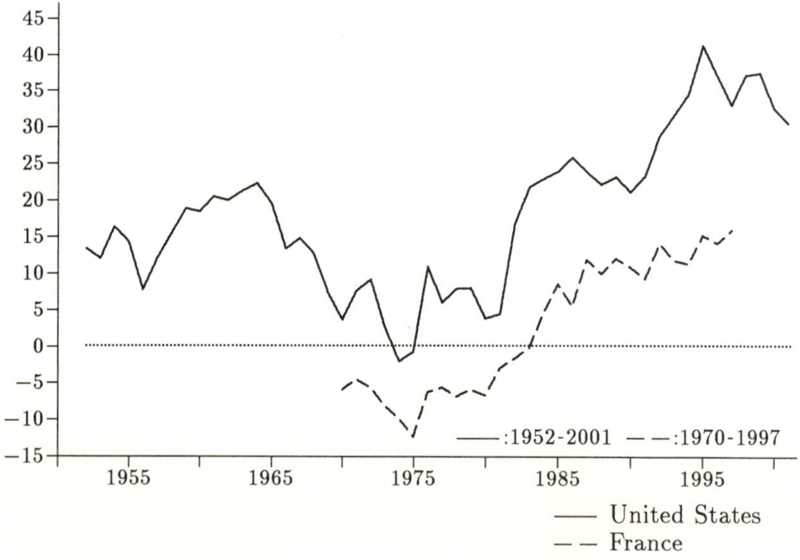

Figure 15.5 Ratio of financial gains (or losses) to disposable income (percent): United States and France, households. The financial gains include, first of all, interest payments and dividends received by households. Potential gains from increases in the stock market are added. The decline in value of monetary and financial assets due to inflation is subtracted. Gains due to the variation of stock prices, which fluctuate greatly, have been smoothed out in order to make the figure easier to read.

cent of total available household income (between 1970 and 1980). The effect of the change in monetary policy, of the fight against inflation at the beginning of the 1980s, and of the rise in the stock market is then visible. The variable becomes positive in 1984, remaining around 12 percent of household income over the 1988–1998 decade, with a slight tendency to increase.[1] In the 1990s it became very advantageous to have monetary and financial holdings.

The profile obtained for the United States confirms the decline in income linked to holding monetary and financial assets during the 1970s and the rebound in the 1980s. These gains are higher than in France, because American households hold more monetary and financial assets (especially stock),[2] but up until the mid-1990s the profile is comparatively low as in France. After this date financial income took off prodigiously.

As may be imagined, these developments in the 1980s led to a stark increase in social inequalities: a multifaceted process affecting incomes, holdings, status (particularly in relation to work), health, knowledge, culture. Such social inequalities are a fundamental feature of capitalism generally, and their reproduction is part of the logic of this system. They naturally tend to perpetuate themselves and to spread—those who possess more have access to the real means of getting richer. No one will therefore be surprised to observe that neoliberalism, which reinforces many capitalist features of the center and the peripheral countries, added even more to this propensity to reproduce and widen inequalities and injustices.

In Chapter 1 we emphasized the considerable inequalities in the development among countries, gaps ranging from 1 to 74, after substantial widening during recent decades. Within most countries, the inequalities in income between different layers of the population also increased. The report from which we extracted these comparisons between countries draws up a balance sheet of these internal inequalities for a group of nineteen advanced countries.[3] During the 1980s, the first neoliberal decade, the inequalities in the (available) income of households decreased in only one country, Italy; they changed little in eight countries, and they increased in ten. At the head of the list of increases in inequalities came the United Kingdom, followed by the United States and Sweden (which started at a very low level, given its social-democratic orientations). The study of salaries in Chapter 6 noted the reduction in the rate of wage increases in the United States and the decline, in absolute terms, of weekly earnings of production workers (Figures 6.1 and 6.2). Both these developments emphasize the increase in inequalities between workers, especially the least favored, and households living off financial income.

We shall now look at the holdings of the richest. These holdings are always the least well known, more for social and political than for technical reasons—a recurring theme in investigative studies.[4] Here only a portion is identified.

In a series of studies whose interest is their synthetic and retrospective character, Edward Wolff analyzes the chronological evolution of inequalities in the United States, beginning with data available from the period 1922–1998.[5] From these studies emerge trends, which tally well with the general accounting that we have presented.

One of the most revealing variables is the portion of assets belonging to the richest 1 percent of households. By "assets" we mean the total amount of real assets (real estate assets and durable consumption goods) and monetary and financial assets, minus debt. The movement of this variable forms the profile that is familiar to us (Figure 15.6). From the 1950s to the 1970s, the richest 1 percent of households possessed from 30 to 35 percent of all assets. This percentage then dropped to 22 percent, attesting to the pressure placed on financial revenues in the first phase of the crisis. The neoliberal turn put a halt to this deterioration, and the rate of 35 percent was again reached in 1986, then passed. Wolff's work also emphasizes the increased link between wealth and the financial sector. In 1983, 22 percent of rich families, according to the criteria of the study, declared that they worked in this sector (finance, insurance, and real estate); by 1992, this rate had reached 36 percent.[6]

The studies available suggest a similar development in France. In 1992 the richest 1 percent of households held 20 percent of all assets. But this figure is strongly influenced by the fact that large layers of the population own their primary residence. The same 1 percent held 40 percent of securities (stock, bonds, and mutual funds).[7] These studies, however, provide us with little information concerning chronological evolutions. A study by the French Research Center for the Study and Observation of the Conditions of Life (CREDOC) has developed a balance sheet of the variation of inequalities in France from 1980 to 1994 on the basis of an overall indicator, which includes income, assets, how well the household is equipped, cultural heritage, unemployment, and subjective indicators.[8] It concludes that there has been an increase in the gap between the groups at the two

Figure 15.6 Portion of assets held by the richest one percent of households (percent): United States. Assets include real estate assets, securities and monetary holdings, and durable consumption goods.

ends (the 10 percent best-off and the 10 percent worst-off). Securities have weighed heavily in widening this gap.[9]

What these analyses teach us about the concentration of fortunes is simple. It may be summed up in two propositions—relative deterioration of the holdings of the best-off layers in the first phase of the crisis, and restoration and more under the neoliberal banner.

More generally, this chapter completes the description of this genuine tour de force accomplished by the dominant classes through neoliberalism—restoring their revenues and assets, both in the absolute and relative to the other classes of the population. By draining profits (which had, moreover, declined) toward the financial sector, expanding the levy made through taxation, and increasing interest payments and dividends, these classes restored their income, although the rate of profit had not yet rebounded. It sufficed to levy proportionately more, and that is what was done.

PART

IV

The Lessons of History

In order to properly grasp the import of the events recounted in the preceding chapters—the structural crisis begun in the 1970s and the installation of a neoliberal order under the aegis of finance—it is useful to place them in historical perspective, and that is the purpose of Part IV. Do the opinions that we have expressed on the real, monetary, and financial aspects of the neoliberal period take us back to other, earlier, historical situations?

The examination in Part II of the evolution of the main variables that describe technology, distribution, and employment during the period after World War II made it possible for us to formulate a diagnosis. The disappearance of the relatively efficient forms of technological progress that had prevailed until the mid-1960s was the source of a movement of decline of the profitability of capital, slowing of growth, and unemployment. This development was followed by vigorous efforts to get wages under control. Under the pressure of the crisis, a certain level of technological progress was restored beginning in the mid-1980s, creating the conditions for a rebound in the profit rate.

Similar patterns prevailed at the end of the nineteenth century and at the beginning of the twentieth—a decline in the rate of profit, a structural crisis, a rebound of the profit rate, and an end to the crisis. This precedent sheds light on some contemporary transformations as expressions of an end to the crisis.

Part III then revealed that the potential advantages of this improvement in profitability had been largely confiscated by finance, thanks to neoliberal macroeconomic policies—mainly the increase of real interest rates and the increased distribution of dividends. Finance thus prolonged the effects of the crisis. In doing so, it enriched itself tremendously, reasserted its hegemony over the production system, and imposed its rules—its deregulation and its new rules—with their accompanying monetary and financial crises and the explosion of stock prices. Is this apotheosis of finance dangerous, as suggested by the fall of the stock market and the recession that began in 2000? It is easy here to evoke the Great Depression. The similarity is striking, and similar conditions do indeed exist. Should we expect the same kind of outcome?

But there is a third historical parallel, which has now, in a bout of collective amnesia, retreated to the background because of the so-called triumph of the market and the "new economy." What was the formula for postwar prosperity? Has it now become out-dated?

By placing developments in historical perspective, we shall finally be able to define more precisely this slightly mysterious agent that we have been constantly putting on stage—*finance.* Stifled after World War II, finance is what we have seen reassert its preeminence in neoliberalism.

CHAPTER

16

Historical Precedent: The Crisis at the End of the Nineteenth Century

The decades that we have just lived through and the trends that emerge recall the crisis that struck the main capitalist countries a century ago and the way in which it was overcome. The underlying circumstances for the emergence of these two structural crises are very similar. The last decades of the nineteenth century were marked by a development of technology and distribution à la Marx, with a decline in the profit rate similar to the one preceding the structural crisis of the 1970s. At the root of this movement are the rates and forms of technological change. Such change has a particular feature, linked to mechanization, which is central in Marx's analysis: the resorting to very large investments in big masses of fixed capital, buildings, and machines (Chapter 4). In such a context, the savings on labor required by production, that is, the rise in labor productivity, demand ever-increasing masses of capital—far more machines, or more expensive machines, for less labor. This road to technological change is expressed through the progressive increase of fixed capital, both in relation to employed labor and in relation to the output obtained. This latter result is measured by the ratio of one year's output to the stock of fixed capital invested in companies, termed capital productivity. This ratio unfortunately often tends to decline, which means that more and more capital is employed for the same result: far from saving capital, more is used.

Figure 16.1 traces the evolution of the productivity of capital since 1870 for the entire American private sector. Declines both at the end of the nineteenth century and in the second half of the twentieth century are

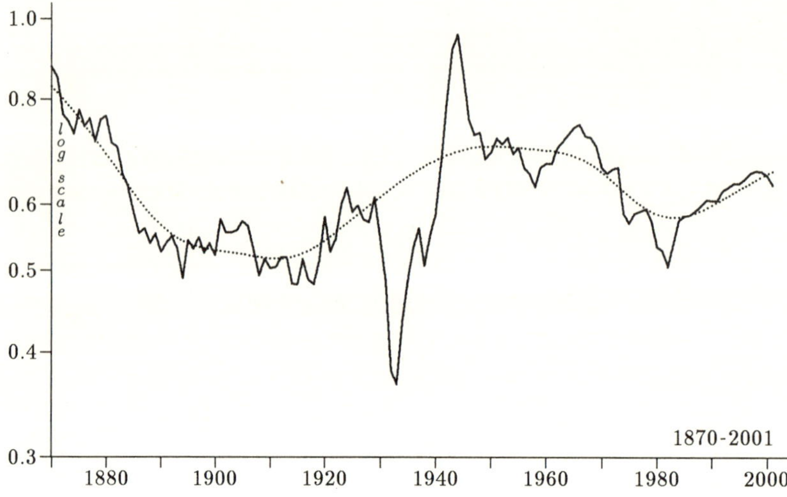

Figure 16.1 Long-term profile of capital productivity and its trend: United States.

clearly apparent. The dotted line suggests the general direction of the movement. The similarity between the first and third period is obvious.

This profile à la Marx of technological change at the end of the nineteenth century was coupled with a decline in the profit rate. By one measurement, comparable to that used in Part II (and which does not subtract interest payments and taxes from profits), the profit rate reached 26 percent during the decade of the 1870s; in the 1890s, it had decreased to only 13 percent.[1]

This trajectory à la Marx was a factor of instability. In the American case, economic activity contracted twice between the Civil War and the end of the century (in the 1870s and 1890s). The first instance combined the effects of this unfavorable trajectory with the monetary consequences of the Civil War. The crisis of the 1890s, designated a "great depression," was deep and long lasting. The unemployment rate reached 18 percent during this period, an exceptional figure, exceeded only during the depression of the 1930s. It had been preceded by economic activity that suddenly overheated in 1880, after the crisis of the 1870s. This high degree of economic instability, following a drop in the rate of profit, recalls—in an obviously different institutional context—that of the 1970s and 1980s. The same causes produced effects that, while not identical, were at least similar. The monetary and financial frameworks were significantly different—no equivalent to the big wave of inflation, like that of the 1970s, or to the reprieve that it made possible for the nonfinancial sector, were to be found at the end of the nineteenth century in the United States.

One of the specific features of the crisis of the end of the nineteenth century was that it was coupled with a crisis of competition. Companies facing a lowering of their profitability sought salvation through reciprocal agreements, whose purpose was to protect them from the hardships of competition. This approach was all the more natural in that the drop in the profit rate had been combined with an increase in the size of production units, linked to the new features of technology and to the progress made by transportation in creating larger markets. Both of these developments effectively made competition a major issue. Some companies agreed to fix minimal prices with each other or to share markets and profits (as in pools). The end of the nineteenth century is thus known as the era of cartels and trusts: capitalism of the monopolies.

This movement ran into very strong opposition from small companies, workers, and those left out of this modernization, especially farmers. This crisis of competition led to the famous Sherman Antitrust Act in 1890, the first federal legislation aimed at guaranteeing free competition.

The game being played out behind this crisis of competition was of another nature. The real stake was the constitution of the modern institutions of capitalism—big finance, on the one hand, and big corporations, on the other—and the link that now tied them together.[2] The "old finance" banks of the nineteenth century had facilitated firms' operations and contributed to financing their transactions (the highest tier of these banks was turned toward financing government spending); from this point on, finance headed up, so to speak, the big business system. The emergence of these new forms of organization placed the traditional sector in danger, hence the tensions—the small against the big.

There is something disconcerting in the events that took place at the turn of the century. The antitrust legislation had all the appearances of an offensive against the invasion of the giants of big business. But simultaneously another legal framework was adopted, encouraging the development of stock-owned companies (corporations) and of holdings, that is, big groups organized under the leadership of finance. This meant giving big business its legal foundations. So was it a question of fighting or of encouraging the formation of big companies?

This was only a surface contradiction. The antitrust legislation had two types of consequences. First, in keeping with its declared goal, it offered some protection to small businesses, allowing them to survive. But by prohibiting agreements in which each company preserved its autonomy and its own organization, it reinforced the formation of big companies and groups, that is, it encouraged genuine mergers, which was all that corporate legislation authorized at the time of the antitrust laws. Rather than impeding the formation of large entities, these laws encouraged concentration. In a few years, just at the turn of the century, an extraordinary wave of mergers arose, for which finance provided the leverage.[3]

Popular struggles played an essential role in these transformations. Unions expanded rapidly during this period, and a socialist party was created. Workers waged hard-fought struggles. These events should not, by the way, be isolated from their world context, that of the rise of the labor movement and revolutionary struggles. In the United States, the outcome of these struggles was reformist in nature. The pacifist leanings that revealed themselves during World War I were used as a pretext for strong repression, and contributed to the reformist outcome.

This labor agitation became part of confrontations between business leaders—those from firms that had preserved the old form of organization and its technologies, and those from corporations of the rising generation tied to finance. The result of these confrontations was a compromise, guaranteeing the traditional sector and the labor movement certain protections, but not impeding the forward march of capitalist institutions (Box 16.1).

The large companies were the scene of a tremendous technological and organizational revolution, known in the United States as the managerial revolution. Its two main aspects were, on the one hand, the emergence of vast general staffs of executives and employees, forming a pyramid-shaped hierarchy, and on the other hand, the transformations that took place on the shop floor involving Taylorism and the assembly line. In fact, the sudden emergence of executives and employees made possible a genuine revolution in all aspects of management, in the broad sense that the managerial revolution suggests—on the shop floor, through the control of inventories and the conduct of commercial transactions, as well as in financial management (of liquidity and financing). These transformations first affected the railroads and telecommunications, and were then, over the course of several decades, gradually extended to industry, to commerce (to the new forms of mass marketing), and to finance.[4]

Box 16.1
Class struggle and compromise at the turn of the nineteenth century

The end of the nineteenth century and the beginning of the twentieth were a time of particularly violent class confrontations, when working-class struggles became linked to rivalries between different factions of the ruling classes.[a]

At the end of the century, strong tensions existed between the owners of traditional firms and workers, because these owners dealt with their workers with an iron hand and vigorously opposed the growth of the union movement. In this context, they deliberately encouraged workers' animosity toward the trusts, stigmatized as being responsible for the low purchasing power of wage workers, because of the excessive prices they charged. The opposition of the agricultural world only added to this hostility. Faced with these attacks, the leaders of the big corporations, supported by finance and enjoying much higher profitability, engaged in a conciliatory policy at the beginning of the century.[b]

The most advanced leaders of these big corporations opened their doors to unions and to collective bargaining; they set up insurance and retirement systems. This tactic bore fruit, and these leaders, helped by the dynamism of their companies and this new political posture, turned the situation around to their advantage, serving as representatives of a modern approach. At a higher political level, they exercised their influence on the legislative and executive powers in order to consolidate their position. Concessions and repression were skillfully combined. The labor movement won a better level of purchasing power and some adjustments in its conditions, but lost its revolutionary potential. From these class struggles came the social configuration of modern, American-style capitalism, with the domination of finance and big corporations and its compromises in relation to the traditional sector and to labor.

---

a. On these questions, see J. Weinstein, *The Corporate Ideal in the Liberal State, 1900–1918* (Boston: Beacon Press, 1968); L. Galambos, *The Public Image of Big Business in America, 1880–1940: A Quantitative Study in Social Change* (Baltimore: Johns Hopkins University Press, 1975).

b. However, certain financiers, such as John D. Rockefeller, opposed these concessions through genuine class wars.

What interests us here is that this technological and managerial revolution led to extraordinary gains of efficiency. The example of the assembly line is the most striking. It may be seen as the height of mechanization, but, compared with prior innovations, the assembly line possessed two specific features. The first is that, thanks to the continuous use of all its elements, and thanks to the speed it imposes, the assembly line employs labor extremely intensely; it consumes labor greedily. This aspect of assembly-line labor has been caricatured many times. The second is that the assembly line is very productive—it generates a continuous flow of products at a previously inconceivable rate. Setting it up means obtaining the advantages of mechanization without its disadvantages. Mechanization no longer entailed an excessive growth of the stock of capital in relation to labor, nor a relative growth of the stock of capital in relation to production; nor was it any longer coupled with a rapid increase in the capital-labor ratio, nor with a decline in the productivity of capital. On the shop floor, as in the rest of the company, the improvement in management meant saving both on costs (of production and circulation) and on capital invested, with a better result. In these improvements of management and organization should be seen the countertrend par excellence of the decline in the rate of profit.

The advantages gained from these improvements were enormous, as may be judged from Figure 16.1. Between the beginning of the century and the 1950s capital productivity increased, instead of declining as during the preceding and subsequent periods. This favorable development made the increase in the rate of profit possible, although the rate of growth of real wages was relatively high.

The initial method of ending the crisis thus consisted in increasing the profit rate—a preferred, almost royal road, but long, and one that implied considerable upheavals. The American economy took this road at the beginning of the century, but its effects were only felt progressively. The somewhat mysterious notion of the end to a structural crisis finds here its initial content: modifying on a long-term basis the unfavorable trends concerning the historical trends of technology and distribution. Because of its gradual character, the process was difficult to identify at the time, but it affected the course of developments in depth. An examination of aggregate indicators, such as the productivity of capital, reveals no abrupt change, because such evolutions are necessarily very progressive (institutional changes, like the wave of mergers, are easier to identify).

The crisis at the end of the nineteenth century thus has several major features. This crisis followed a trajectory à la Marx; ending the crisis required turning these trends around; reversing the trends was the labor of the technological and organizational revolution, that is, the managerial revolution; these transformations at the beginning of the century took place within an intense climate of class struggle.

CHAPTER

17

The End of the Structural Crises: Does the Twentieth Century Resemble the Nineteenth?

The similarities between the crises at the end of the nineteenth and the twentieth centuries are so strong that it seems superfluous to go back over them. Like its ancestor, the crisis at the end of the twentieth century followed a trajectory à la Marx; the end of such a trajectory would also be a prime factor in ending the crisis.[1] We note, however, a crucial difference: whereas the end of the nineteenth century and the beginning of the twentieth were periods of increasing social struggle and of the organization of labor, the last decades of the twentieth century were marked by important defeats, which led to the stagnation of both real wages and social protection.

The first indication of the end to the more recent crisis is the rise in the profit rate (Chapters 3 and 8). Note here the combined effect of the stagnation of wage costs and the increase in the productivity of capital, which together promote a movement toward saving on fixed capital (buildings and machines). This latter element is the most remarkable and testifies to a new road, a countertrend to the decline in the profit rate. The previous decline in the productivity of capital has now been interrupted and has turned into an increase. The latest observations confirm the theory of a rebound.[2]

In Europe the growth of labor productivity is lower than during the three decades that followed World War II, but remains significantly stronger than in the United States. Since the increase in wage costs is also limited, the share of profits has increased more in Europe than in the United States. The productivity of capital is growing at a similar pace. The form of technological progress is thus somewhat different, but the increase in the profit rate, its financial determinants left aside, is considerable. However significant these developments may be, it should be emphasized that they still are limited and express, to some extent, an intensification of the utilization of capital, which is made possible by the flexibility of the workweek and the intensification of labor itself.[3] These regressive transformations are coupled with a managerial revolution—of the organization of labor and production, of corporate structures and intercompany relations—without it always being possible to separate these elements.

How did capitalism find the road to technological progress while simultaneously saving on labor and capital? Through an extraordinary effort of research and development (Box 17.1)? Were the mechanisms the same as at the beginning of the century? If it is possible to speak of progress in management, organization, and technology, was the same true for social relations and the institutions of capitalism?

It is difficult to form a precise opinion concerning the objective transformations of management. This is a recurring theme in management, but not easily quantifiable. In spite of the bursting of the stock market bubble,

Box 17.1
Research and development

The partial turnaround of the course of technological change cannot be separated from so-called research and development spending, that is, costs incurred by companies in order to innovate. Although they are difficult to isolate, it is worth examining the few global sets of statistics available. We find that this spending has greatly increased in France. It would be tempting to interpret this growth as the expression of efforts stimulated by the crisis, thus attempting to put an end to the crisis. It is also possible to associate the particularly low figures for France from the 1960s and 1970s with a period in which the main concern was to make up for a less advanced technological level through a process of "imitation," rather than through investment in research. When it nears the technological frontiers, French spending reaches levels similar to those of the United States. The curve for the United States reveals a high degree of instability in this spending since World War II, interrupted by a low point corresponding to the years of structural crisis. Research and development spending greatly increased during the 1980s, but the higher level in the 1990s may be interpreted as returning to previous levels. The first postwar decades had been years of great innovation.

our discussion focuses, above all, on the role of information and communication—the new economy.

The databases used in this book provide an unequivocal indication of these transformations. An analysis of the content of investment in the United States shows that the 1980s and 1990s were marked by a tremendous transformation of the composition of investment.

Two major components can be perceived in investment—equipment (machines, vehicles, and so forth) and structures. It is *equipment* that was the subject of this transformation. American statistics track four relevant categories of investments: data processing (communication and computers) and programs, industrial equipment, transportation equipment, and a miscellaneous category. As Figure 17.1 shows, in 1946 the last three categories shared about 90 percent of total investment, 30 percent each, and communications (computers did not yet exist) not more than 12 percent. By 2001 the situation had changed. Each of the last three categories represented between 15 and 20 percent, whereas communications and computers made up almost 50 percent. That means that around half of the dollars

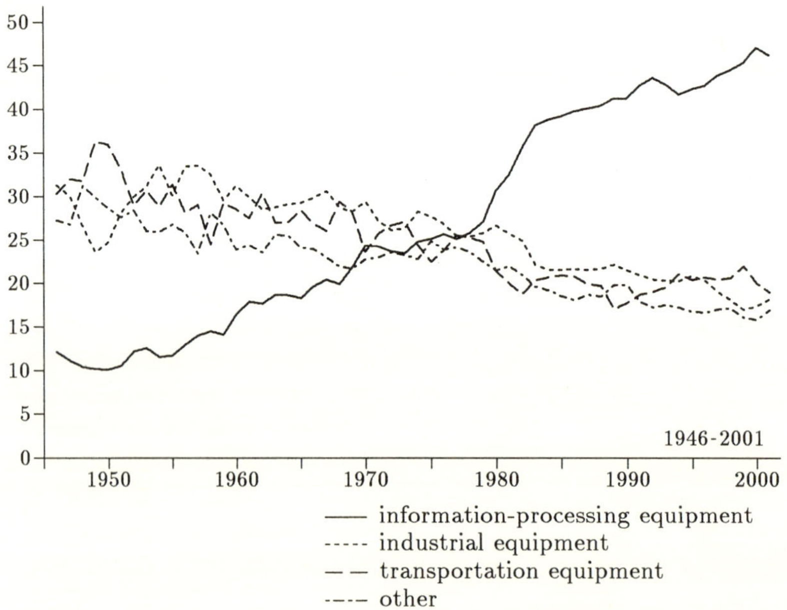

Figure 17.1 Components of fixed investments in equipment (percent of total): United States.

currently invested in the United States in all types of equipment are invested in communication or computing materials or software. This rise has been continuous, with a leap at the beginning of the 1980s—by 1970 the postwar period's 12 percent had already been doubled, but the real surge took place between 1978 and 1983, that is, during the worst of the structural crisis. It is interesting to note that the investment in software was, in 2001, greater than the total investment in transportation equipment (cars, trucks, airplanes, and so on).

How should these changes be viewed? Can they be compared to the great organizational innovations of the beginning of the century? Should we speak of a new managerial revolution? One fact seems established—the 1980s and 1990s were not characterized by the emergence of big staffs of managers as during the first decades of the twentieth century. This was rather a period when staffs were being reduced.

We interpret the information revolution as a component of an internal management revolution—in the broad sense of the term "management," which was introduced in the preceding chapter. Communications and information are the technologies of organization, of management, par excellence. Managers and employees collect information, treat it, and communicate among themselves at unprecedented rates and in unprecedented proportions. As long as the price of equipment remained high, its use required substantial training, and it was not very mobile, its potential remained hidden. Jobs that were difficult to do before became possible, but the difficulties and costs involved limited the positive effects. The revolutionary thrust of this equipment was only gradually revealed as its cost decreased and it became simpler to use.

Robert Solow, the Nobel Prize–winning economist, observed that the progress ascribed to the use of computers is not evident, given the still low growth rate of labor productivity.[4] There is an error concerning the variable—computers are above all found in the profile of the productivity of capital, rather than labor. They can be detected in the rise of the total productivity of the factors, which is an average of both productivity rates.

If our interpretation of the current trends of capitalism is justified, the ends to both the earlier and the later structural crises take the shape of one and the same process, in two stages. During the first end to the crisis, at the beginning of the last century, the production system underwent an initial upheaval, the managerial revolution. It established technology and organization in their mutual relationships and radically transformed the workshop and production, but its scope was even more widespread, affecting all aspects of corporate life. That is why we use the term "managerial." In the last decades of the twentieth century a development was initiated whose effects, from the point of view of the main variables (productivity rates, capital-labor ratio), are similar. Once again its nature concerns progress in management, now linked to the maturing of procedures founded on the technologies of communication and information. This progress combines increased efficiency in the capacity to organize production, distribution, and financial operations and to reduce costs—management that improves its own management, applies its principles to itself, and improves its performances.

One may wonder about the consequences of these transformations concerning relations between different categories of salaried workers (production workers, employees, and managers), the hierarchy, and the division of labor. Doesn't computerization reinforce the polarization of jobs between conception, management, and execution? Doesn't it lead to new armies of employees just as dependent in relation to computers as production workers are in relation to their machines?[5] These questions warrant further investigation.

Of course, it is not simply computers and their software that are behind the current revolution in management. In present-day capitalism, improved performances—always measured by the yardstick of the profit rate—necessitate bettering the efficiency of the managers. The whole problem is there: how can efficiency be pursued against the natural bureaucratic trends inherent in the growth of managerial general staffs? How can hierarchy and initiative be combined? How can order and creativity be put together? The solutions doubtless require the development of horizontal relations and the reduction of cumbersome hierarchies. The new methods of organization and management are confronted with this challenge.

In ending the crisis, both the earlier and the later periods also have in common a radical modification of policies concerning competition, in the broad sense of the term. In the same way that the development of stock-owned companies and mergers was made possible by a change in legislation at the end of the nineteenth century, the affirmation of neoliberalism has coincided with a change in attitude toward mergers, both in the law and, above all, in its application.

After much hesitation, relatively restrictive legislation concerning mergers was adopted at the end of the depression of the 1930s. It encouraged a very particular kind of concentration, whose center was situated in the big nonfinancial companies, relatively independent of the large financial institutions. This concentration led to the formation of conglomerates, which led to a diversification of business, echoing the increased autonomy of corporate managers.[6] But things changed radically with neoliberalism.

In order to understand the favorable disposition toward concentration at the beginning of the 1980s, it must be viewed in a more general economic context. The slowdown in the growth of labor productivity, generally recognized on an absolute level and especially in relation to Japan, created a psychosis of efficiency in the United States. The new theories (relayed by the Chicago School) rapidly gained headway in this atmosphere. The internationalization of capitalism raised the problem of competition, now on a world scale. Somehow the law had to make it possible for large American firms to acquire the needed dimensions. Any sector remaining outside these transformations had to adapt. This change in course reflected the reality of internationalization, but it also demonstrated the return of the hegemony of finance. During the 1980s finance more directly took back the initiative concerning competition, renewing ties to the great tradition of the beginning of the century, giving rise to a vast movement of restructuring of the production system, of concentration, of takeovers, and, in a more general way, of strengthening the property networks. This transformation took place, and continues to take place, under the aegis of the bank holding companies in a context of great permissiveness on the part of the judicial system.[7]

The record of contemporary mergers and acquisitions is a disputed one. Some of these combined operations have ended in failure. A theory is arising that the development of agreements or understandings between companies constitutes at least as important an element of renewal as the new favorable attitude toward concentration.

The consequences for the social structures of this second stage of the managerial revolution seem less than those of the first stage. At least they are of a different nature. Managers and employees already constitute important social layers; property is already separate from management; productive labor is already supervised to the highest degree. These transformations, now complete, no longer need to be accomplished. We can instead expect quantitative modifications or modifications of forms, such as those that are taking shape today.

CHAPTER

18

Two Periods of Financial Hegemony: The Beginning and the End of the Twentieth Century

The dominant role of finance in neoliberalism is not without precedent in the history of capitalism. The period that covers the end of the nineteenth century to the Great Depression corresponded to the first period of hegemony of modern finance, which had just arisen. This situation was disturbed by the depression of the 1930s and by World War II. For this reason, neoliberalism may be described as the reestablishment of the domination of finance after a period of retreat.

The comparison between the two periods of finance's domination—from the end of the nineteenth century until 1933, and since the 1980s—is full of lessons. It makes it possible to better grasp the very notion of financial hegemony and the risks associated with such a situation. What are the areas within which this power was exercised and with which tools? What are the particularities of each of these two periods? What was the nature of the intermediate period separating them? When finance was forced to retreat on certain fronts, what changes were made? How may the institutions that were set up be characterized? Were they less capitalist? Pursuing the answers to these questions would involve a vast program of research. In this chapter we shall focus on the problems linked to the macroeconomic policies and the institutional frameworks (policy goals such as the determination of the general level of economic activity and its stability, as well as the control of the monetary and financial institutions).

At the end of the nineteenth century, finance created its own institutional universe for itself, accompanying the development of large stock-owned companies and the managerial revolution—holding companies and financial company networks, the central role of the stock market, a credit system turned toward stockholders, and so on. It ruled according to its criteria and interests.

Parallel to this proliferation of financial institutions at the turn of the century was a prodigious growth of monetary mechanisms. The amount of money grew in large proportions. Between 1880 and World War I, the quantity of money (bills and coin and bank accounts) increased much more quickly than output. It represented less than a third of output in 1880 and more than two-thirds in the 1920s (it has remained at approximately the same level since that time). A salient feature of this development was the increase in bank accounts. In 1880, the balances of these accounts represented twice the amount of liquid assets; in 1921, eight times; in 1929, eleven times. Correlatively, we can easily imagine what the rate of growth of the credit system was. The witnesses to these transformations (practitioners, professors, economists, politicians) took time to assimilate them, and continued to call only cash "money." The development of the financial system echoed these monetary transformations. The stock market played a key role in financing companies, and banks made more loans to stock investors (households and financial institutions) than to the nonfinancial companies themselves, in order to facilitate selling the securities that had been issued or conducting transactions in securities already in circulation.

There were obvious risks to this monetary and financial structure. The power of its mechanisms was increased, but the tools of centralized control had been little developed. Throughout this period, private finance kept control of monetary creation, which it managed in accordance with its views, virtually unchallenged (Box 18.1). The creation of money through credit was closely linked to market operations, whose volatility is well known. The development of large corporations and of finance certainly entailed a metamorphosis of the monetary and financial processes, but the means of ensuring their stability were insufficient.

The crisis of 1907 was a financial crisis of unusual scope and led to a significant reduction of economic activity. The Treasury Department made timid interventions in addition to interventions by the banking system, but the measures taken did not prevent the suspension of payments at bank windows. The crisis was seen as a failure of the traditional, private, decentralized procedures, and led to the setting up of the Federal Reserve in 1913. This institution, however, was dominated by private finance and

Box 18.1
The American monetary and financial system before the Great Depression

Gold played a central role in the monetary systems at the end of nineteenth century and the beginning of the twentieth, both on a domestic and on an international level, justifying the expression "gold standard." Some transactions, particularly international ones, were paid in gold. Bank bills issued (by all banks) were convertible between each other (with a commission), both in gold and at a fixed rate. Convertibility could be suspended for periods, sometimes long (as in the United States at the beginning of the Civil War in 1861, until 1879), or during crises. On top of bank bills were bills issued by the Treasury during the Civil War, the famous "greenbacks," whose removal from the economy was undertaken but turned out to be difficult to achieve. The mass of bills and the balances of bank accounts considerably exceeded the stock of gold and varied according to the credits that were allotted. Inflation was feared, because it threatened the convertibility of fiduciary money into a given quantity of gold. The volume of credits was regulated by mechanisms related to what might be called a self-disciplined hierarchy—a discipline that the system imposed on itself, but in which the most powerful banks played a preponderant role.

The system established in the United States after the Civil War, and which was perpetuated until the creation of a central bank (the Federal Reserve, in 1913), is known as the National Banking System. This was a private system, where requirements for certain percentages of assets were imposed upon banks by law and by practice, and in which a strong hierarchy existed among banks—the big banks of New York played the role of reserve bank for the rest of the system. These New York banks reacted to imbalances—not so much macroeconomic imbalances (economic activity and price fluctuations), as in our day, but mainly those internal to the financial system (for example, movements of funds between reserve and local banks). Thus it was not possible to speak of monetary policy in the current sense.

In crises, the banking system organized itself in order to avoid its own collapse, or to limit the scope of the crisis. Shutting down banks was obviously the event to be avoided, in the same way that it was necessary to attempt to remedy any destabilization of the stock market. The clearinghouses set up exceptional credit procedures in order to help make it possible to stay in business. When a closing was inevitable, it took place under their control, in order to limit the panic and to maintain certain transactions. Globally the system was characterized by the hegemony of the largest banks, essentially from New York.

continued to be subordinated to the prior goals of finance—preserving the convertibility of the currency into gold at a fixed rate and, during the crises, maintaining the normal functioning of banks. What had to be avoided above all was the suspension of payments at bank windows, which had marked previous crises. Concerns relative to economic activity and employment were secondary and indirect. They were taken into account only to the extent that any disruption of the production system might, as an indirect consequence, destabilize the financial system.

The tool should therefore not be confused with the use that was made of it. The leaders of the Federal Reserve progressively modified their conceptions during the 1920s, but the notion of stabilizing economic activity was never really established as a direct goal. Finance remained caught in a too slow process of adaptation, made necessary by its own brazenness.

Thus despite the creation of the Federal Reserve, the period extending from the end of the nineteenth century to the Great Depression may be considered globally. Its main features were: an explosion of the quantity of money and of the monetary and financial institutions, the hegemony of private finance concerning controls, and the slowness with which the procedures required by the situation, deriving from the very actions of finance, were set up.

The Great Depression destabilized this edifice. We shall not take up here the narration of the first years of the crisis (Chapter 19). Beginning in 1933, the New Deal prompted the massive intervention of the state in financial and macroeconomic mechanisms. This intervention was extended through the setting up of a legislative and regulatory structure that significantly limited the powers of finance and constituted a major feature of the post–World War II period (Box 18.2). The term "financial repression" is sometimes used.[1]

It was in such a situation that the relations between the state and the business world were transformed, raising state economic intervention to a higher level. The monopoly on the control of monetary creation was lost by finance, and capitalism set up the institutions necessary for its survival under modern conditions. The activity of the central banks targeted distinct tasks of wider scope than the traditional goals of finance. The adoption by Congress in 1946 of the Employment Act, defining economic growth and particularly the fight against unemployment as governmental responsibilities, even duties, introduced this new course of events, at least symbolically. These policies were to culminate in the 1960s.

Box 18.2
The limitations of the power of finance: The New Deal heritage

The new framework resulting from the Great Depression was defined by a series of laws: the Banking Acts of 1933 and 1935, the Security and Exchange Act of 1934, and various new versions of the Federal Reserve Act. This legislation, broadening the responsibilities of the Federal Reserve, sought more stability for the financial system. The new acts mainly affected banks, but also nonbanking financial institutions, and introduced sharp divisions within the financial system.

Six primary measures may be noted: (1) the Q regulation placed limits on interest rates for deposits in order to limit competition between banks (it was also thought that this would reduce loan rates); (2) restrictions were placed on holdings of assets by banks, particularly securities labeled as speculative, like stock shares, and credits for acquiring securities were required to respect limits on margins fixed by the Federal Reserve; (3) the Federal Deposit Insurance Corporation was created in order to insure deposits; (4) this institution and the Comptroller of the Currency, a federal official named by the government, were invested with increased powers in order to guarantee that banks were managed prudently, to control new entries in this sector, and to limit competition; (5) all agents issuing stock or bonds on the markets were compelled to make their financial situation public; and (6) the Glass-Steagall Act of 1933 forbade deposit banks from underwriting and placing corporate stock shares and bonds, that is, from acting as intermediaries in the issuance of these securities—this activity was reserved for business banks.[a]

---

a. See T. F. Cargill, *Money, the Financial System, and Monetary Policy* (Englewood Cliffs, N.J.: Prentice-Hall, 1991).

But these transformations also had an international side. The roles played by the Englishman John Maynard Keynes and the American Harry Dexter White in the birth of the accords signed in 1944 at Bretton Woods —which led to the creation of the International Monetary Fund (IMF) and the World Bank—have been described many times. There were several aspects to this plan: exchange rates established between currencies, and rules fixed for changing them; credits for countries having unfavorable balances of payments; control over the international mobility of capital; and so on. The plan made it possible to set up restrictions of movements of funds in the case of a crisis; the collaboration of various states, both victims and beneficiaries of these transfers, was even envisaged. However, it is necessary to distinguish between the accords and the use that was made of them (Box 18.3).

Finance was violently opposed to this plan, which encroached on its prerogatives.[2] In a context in which the activities of the central banks were no longer the private domain of finance, it was clear that the same would be true of the international institutions deliberately conceived in order to extend onto the international level the new functions of these central banks.

The setback to the hegemony of finance, following the great depression and World War II, was very real, but its import should not be exaggerated. Capitalist logic (particularly maximizing the profit rate) was obviously preserved, and finance remained powerful, as further events were to prove. The fight continued, both on a national and on an international level. Even within the United States, an active Keynesian policy of long-term support was little used during the 1950s by the conservative Eisenhower administration. It was not applied until the early 1960s. When John Kennedy's counselors felt that the end to the 1958 recession had led to insufficient economic activity, they vigorously stimulated the economy by lowering taxes, aiming to create something of a budget deficit and relaunch the economy. This episode was brilliant, but relatively brief. It was followed by similar interventions, although the structural crisis had already begun and inflation was rearing its head, whatever the causal relationship involved.

On the international level, finance did not resign itself to being thwarted and was quick to join in the IMF structures and to save its preferred institution, the Bank for International Settlements.[3] It was precisely on this international level that the gradual movement that was to lead to restoring the hegemony of finance via neoliberalism began.

The Euromarkets, that is, the activity of banks (genuinely or fictitiously) outside of their own countries that effectively avoids the controls of the national central banks, provided a favorable terrain for this rebound of finance (Box 18.4). The decisive blow was, however, the crisis of the dollar in August 1971, when enormous transfers of funds from the United States to Western Europe led the United States to suspend the convertibility of the dollar and forced the Europeans and Japanese to allow their currency to float. During 1971–1973, the countries of Western Europe resisted American pressure, reinforcing their control of exchange rates, in order to avoid a forced revaluation of their currencies. The failure of these measures finally compelled them to resort to floating. This meant the end of

Box 18.3
The framework of Bretton Woods and its dissolution

The three pillars of the Bretton Woods system were fixed exchange rates, the creation of world monetary institutions capable of granting credits to countries that needed them, and limits set on the mobility of capital. The agreement defined the principle of fixed exchange rates between currencies (with a small margin of fluctuation), but adjustments were allowed within certain limits, upon consultation with and agreement from the IMF. It could intervene in order to temporarily support countries in difficulty through credits granted in certain currencies that were considered to be "as good as gold." Article 6-3 of the agreement authorized restrictions on the international circulation of capital (exchange controls), at least in crisis situations. The meticulousness in the definition of rules and their constant adjustment expressed the difficulty of separating good capital movements from bad, a distinction often expressed nowadays, in a more or less appropriate manner, by referring to the terms of the investments: long-term (good investments) and short-term (bad ones). This ambiguity expressed the rather futile hope that capital would come in and not flee in case of a crisis.

Up until the first difficulties, which foreshadowed the world monetary crisis at the end of the 1960s, it was the European countries and Japan that made use of the dual possibility that was open to them—readjusting their exchange rate combined with limitations on the international mobility of capital (the numerous forms of exchange controls). When it could be seen that a currency was overvalued because of an inflation differential (through the widening of balance of payments deficits and the lowering of currency reserves), holders of capital would sense the imminence of a devaluation and would tend to convert their holdings into another currency, even if this meant jumping back into the first currency as soon as the readjustment was made. Thus the adjustment of exchange rates was coupled with a strengthening of exchange controls, which were later loosened up.

The position of the United States, the incontestable dominant power after World War II, was singular from the beginning. The clause stipulating that IMF credits could be granted in a currency as good as gold, endowed the dollar, the currency of the dominant country, with a central role, establishing it for all practical purposes as the international currency. American finance's room to maneuver may have been reduced, but the hegemony of the United States was consolidated. The United States did not use the opportunity to readjust the rate of its currency. Either it didn't need to, or this practice would have been in flagrant contradiction with the status of the dollar (when a

(continued)

(continued)

readjustment became inevitable in the 1970s, the United States preferred to destroy the system). It did not resort to controls until the world monetary crisis was approaching, when its commercial preeminence was weakened at the end of the 1960s.

Abandoning fixed exchange rates and going over to floating rates was initially forced and temporary, then made official in 1973. This was a first step toward the new monetary and financial order, followed by others indicating the advent of neoliberalism. Limits on the circulation of capital were lifted in the United States in 1974. This initiative was followed by the United Kingdom in 1979, and then by the rest of Europe (the Single European Act of 1986, the decision of the European Commission and of the Council of Ministers in 1988) and by the countries of the OECD (adoption by all the OECD countries in the Code of Liberalization in 1989).

The destruction of the framework of Bretton Woods may be analyzed as a scuttling ordered by the United States. Since the dollar had asserted itself as the international currency, despite the development of special drawing rights (as the IMF currency), the system did not survive the reduction of American supremacy. What the world economy was lacking was a genuine international monetary institution capable of creating and guaranteeing a world currency, sufficiently autonomous from the dollar, in conformity with the initial project.[a] The world monetary crisis of the 1970s could have been seen as an opportunity to create such a system, but, on the contrary, it led to the installation of rules that once again consecrated the preeminence of the dollar and the projects of finance, led by American finance. It was not globalization that deprived economies of their autonomy concerning economic policy, but the neoliberal trajectory of globalization.

a. Keynes wanted to call this world currency "bancor."

Bretton Woods and of state control over parities and capital movements (Box 18.3).

The United States found itself at the center of this crisis. The Bretton Woods system, as it had been applied in practice, had consecrated the primacy of the dollar within a situation where it dominated the world economy. Until the beginning of the 1970s, the rate of American inflation had remained below that of the levels reached by most of its partners, and the readjustments of exchange rates were traditionally made by these coun-

Box 18.4
Restoring the hegemony of finance: The role of the Euromarkets

The initial stages of the constitution of Euromarkets came at the end of the 1950s, during the international payment crisis of 1957.[a] At the beginning of the 1960s, these markets were located mainly in London, and received at first the blessing of the English and American authorities. The advantage of the London financial market in this activity is fairly easy to grasp. The American attitude was more surprising, and derived from two concerns. First, finance, or more precisely the New York bankers, discovered that it was in their interest to shift their activities to London, thus escaping the heritage of the New Deal, particularly the required reserve level and the interest rate limits.[b] Second, the accumulation of dollars abroad let hang a threat of conversion, and put into question the status of the dollar as an international currency. The dollar became the currency of the Euromarkets. Whether right or wrong, the American government saw in them a means of stabilizing this liquidity. Finally, this system made it possible for companies whose business had expanded on the world level to enjoy considerable leeway in shifting funds around. At the same time that the production system was becoming internationalized, international finance naturally grew up. It largely eluded the traditional national regulations.

---

a. Concerning the technical aspects, see G. Dufey and I. Giddy, *The International Money Market* (Englewood Cliffs, N.J.: Prentice-Hall, 1994).

b. "During the domestic credit squeeze of 1966 and 1969–1970, for example, domestic financial business was 'roundtripped' through the Euromarket to avoid interest rate ceilings." E. Helleiner, *States and the Reemergence of Global Finance: From Bretton Woods to the 1990s* (Ithaca, N.Y.: Cornell University Press, 1994), p. 88.

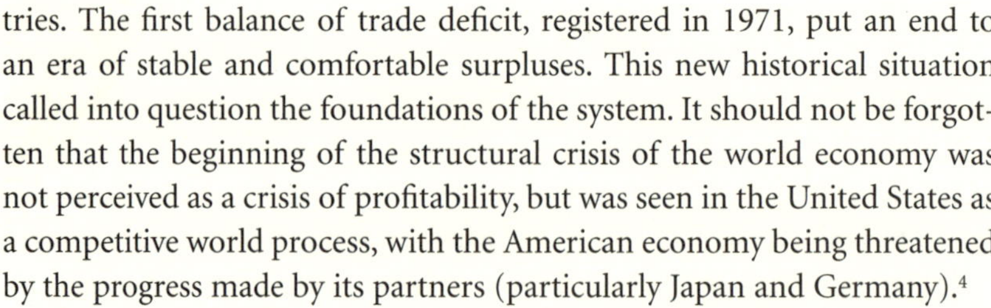
tries. The first balance of trade deficit, registered in 1971, put an end to an era of stable and comfortable surpluses. This new historical situation called into question the foundations of the system. It should not be forgotten that the beginning of the structural crisis of the world economy was not perceived as a crisis of profitability, but was seen in the United States as a competitive world process, with the American economy being threatened by the progress made by its partners (particularly Japan and Germany).[4]

The relation of these events to the reassertion of the power of finance is easy to grasp when they are viewed in the context of earlier conflicts. The continuity with the negotiations that had preceded Bretton Woods was striking—it seemed that the same discussion was being resumed. However, the positions had evolved. The United States, seeing its domination threatened, made an about-face, now opposing the exchange controls accepted at Bretton Woods and championing the sacrosanct market. Its position was exposed in the Economic Report of the President of early 1973 (which is supposed to have been dictated by Milton Friedman): the free international mobility of capital should be treated on an equal footing with free trade in goods and services, and controls should be suppressed. This meant giving power to the markets, alias finance. The international aspect of the Keynesian system, particularly the possibility of temporarily opposing capital movements in crisis situations, disappeared. The Federal Reserve, because it perceived the possibility of a weakening of its position, indicated a certain degree of opposition, but this attitude remained isolated and fleeting.

Beginning with the 1970 recession (the first period of stagflation), the 1970s and the beginning of the 1980s were very unstable. On a national level, the crisis of the 1970s initially led to the usual resort to Keynesian stimulation. For a few years, policies supporting economic activity extended prosperity in an inflationary Keynesian reprieve. These policies delayed the effective appearance of the trends in the nonfinancial companies, but could not find a remedy for them. Inflation placed the weight of the crisis on the creditors, that is, on finance, making it possible for the profit rates of the nonfinancial companies to remain relatively high during the 1970s (Chapters 9 and 15). When inflation took off, that sounded the death knell for Keynesian policies.[5] The monetarists in England and the United States, defending the interests of the creditors in the most direct way, designated inflation as public enemy number one.[6] In addition, the dollar had depreciated since the crisis of the beginning of the 1970s (Figure 12.1), which was disapproved of by finance. These events concluded with the nomination of Paul Volcker as head of the Federal Reserve, leading to the major change in monetary policy in 1979—the 1979 coup—which favored restoring price stability whatever the cost and introduced the high real interest rates specific to neoliberalism. More generally, a legislative framework was set up (Box 18.5).

Finance, with the aid of the Federal Reserve, now under its sway, took back the control of monetary creation and imposed a policy and a course of events similar to those observed before the Great Depression. The cen-

Box 18.5
The financial system of the 1980s in the United States: Deregulation–new regulation

The American monetary and financial system is not of one piece, and general interests may come into conflict with certain special interests. Finance set great store in relaxing regulations in the 1980s, but it wanted to vigorously fight inflation, which required fairly rigid rules and structures.

Certain measures were already made public in October 1979, when interest rates were increased, but the Deregulation and Monetary Control Act dates from 1980. It is especially known for having worked to restore competitive conditions (deregulation), but it also increased the power of the Federal Reserve (monetary control).

The law of 1980 organized the gradual elimination of the Q regulation. New accounts were authorized; savings institutions saw their range of activities broadened. A 1982 law extended these reforms concerning the collection and utilization of funds in relation to the first crisis of the savings and loan associations. In 1988 a law abrogated the Glass-Steagall Act. These measures represented a considerable loosening up of the rules to which the financial system had been subjected, especially those inherited from the New Deal (Box 18.2).

There were two obstacles to the strengthening of monetary policy required in order to fight inflation: certain weaknesses of the American financial institutions, and the existence of the Euromarkets, which were a source of capital flight.

Concerning American institutions, the law strengthened the prerogatives of the Federal Reserve. Joining the system had remained optional, and the number of members was decreasing; the law made membership obligatory for all institutions accepting deposits (including nonbanking institutions). The Federal Reserve had always asked for such measures, but had run into the opposition of Congress and the administration, which favored maintaining an autonomous component of the banking system. The monetary and financial system was thus more strongly supervised, which did not go in the direction of the deregulationist creed, but was the price to pay in order to regain price stability, a prime goal of finance.

The Euromarkets, which had been looked upon favorably in the 1960s, now appeared as potential obstacles in the fight against inflation. In 1979 the United States requested that, under the aegis of the Bank for International

(continued)

(continued)

Settlements, the central banks of the other member countries study measures making it possible to control Eurobanking activities. These attempts met with strong opposition from international (especially English) finance, and the restrictive measures were rejected. Not able to regulate the Euromarkets, the Americans introduced them in the United States, creating the international banking facilities (IBFs), located mainly in New York.

tral bank could fulfill its role in the United States of guaranteeing price stability—and even do it with great efficiency—as long as it cooperated with the markets. The juxtaposition of strict monetary policies and this power of the markets is one of the most subtle expressions of the hegemony of finance in neoliberalism, which combines great efficiency in carrying out American monetary policy with factors of national and international instability, such as the free international mobility of capital.

The similarity between the early-twentieth and late-twentieth-century periods of hegemony on the part of finance is considerable, but not complete. Two aspects of it should be distinguished, one related to price stability and the other to the freedom of maneuver of the financial institutions.

At the beginning of the last century the institutional system, both national and international, and the way it was controlled by private high finance guaranteed price stability.[7] Only World War I imposed a high rate of inflation. Once finance was back in power in the 1980s, its first concern was to regain this stability. It accomplished this, on a national level, by quietly establishing itself within the Keynesian institutions. With great efficiency, it diverted their tools and methods to its advantage. Despite all the talk, the American state, the Federal Reserve, and monetary policies are more powerful than ever.

Moreover, finance granted itself an extremely dangerous freedom of action, which directly recalled in some of its aspects the decades prior to the Great Depression. This freedom allowed tremendous instability to ferment on the national and especially the international levels: a dramatic increase in financial activities, the unpredictable fluctuation of currencies, and reckless capital movements. Thus capitalism revived some of its prior aberrations, which it was believed to have outgrown in the 1960s—the national and international financial crises and the stock market craze.

CHAPTER

19

Inherent Risks: The 1929 Precedent

The analogy between the crisis at the end of the nineteenth century and the structural crisis of the 1970s is very strong. Some will find this observation encouraging. The crisis has a precedent; this precedent found a way out; why shouldn't it be the same this time? An analysis of the neoliberal society the crisis has taken the world into, however, suggests a moderation of this enthusiasm. The end of the crisis is not rosy for everyone; it prepares a future for us that many will want to refuse.

But isn't this still being too optimistic? Following the analogy between the two periods quickly gives one the shudders, because, as we know, the end to the crisis of the end of the nineteenth century led in a few decades to the Great Depression. The possibility of such a catastrophe may amuse, but many economists have pursued the comparison. Is such a risk hanging over our heads? This is the question to which this chapter and the following one are devoted. Before we directly take up this comparison, it is, however, necessary to examine the circumstances that led to the Great Depression.

Up until now, we have essentially spoken well of the end to the structural crisis of the nineteenth century, in its economic aspects. There was a genuine revolution in corporate technology and organization; this managerial revolution was expressed by a profound reorientation of the course of the principal variables concerning technology and distribution, a far-reaching countertrend to the decline of the profit rate. The Great Depression thus had a paradoxical character.[1] Why did such a favorable course lead to such a catastrophe? In this analysis, we shall again favor the example of the United States.

The end of the crisis of the late nineteenth century hid certain weaknesses, of which two main categories can be distinguished. The first concerned the uneven impact of technological change on the various components of the production system; the second had to do with monetary and financial institutions and policies.

An initial element of fragility of the American economy was the strong heterogeneity of its production system. Naturally not all companies could be equally advanced in the technological, organizational, and managerial transformations at the beginning of the century. But there was more to the fragility than that. It was possible to distinguish two components within the production system, one deeply implicated in these transformations and going rapidly forward, and the other practically foreign to this movement, incapable of taking advantage of it.

The formation of such a dual economy was a risk intrinsic to the modalities of the managerial revolution, and almost preprogrammed. This revolution was the affair of certain large companies; it took place under the aegis of finance. Major financiers, who manipulated enormous masses of capital, took control of companies that already existed and created others. Starting with transportation and communication, this movement progressively spread to industry and to distribution. Although these companies were called monopolies at the time because of their imposing size, they did not occupy the totality of each sector. A considerable mass of traditional, smaller companies survived next to them. These companies never acquired the size necessary to reform their management and to adopt more effective technologies; they were never chaperoned by finance—and both elements are linked. The term "heterogeneity" refers to this phenomenon. The American economy was characterized at the beginning of the twentieth century by the coexistence in the main sectors of both major new companies and older firms whose organization and technology remained traditional.

Automobile manufacturing in the 1920s provides an excellent illustration of this duality.[2] Contrary to what might be imagined, numerous small production units, using obsolete methods, survived next to the giants (Ford and General Motors). The latest advances of technology and organization remained foreign to these smaller producers.

One has to wonder about the conditions in which two unevenly developed and unevenly performing sectors coexisted. How could the small companies hold on in such circumstances? As has been shown, antitrust legislation had not hindered the development of large companies, but had obtained a certain level of protection for the older sector. Moreover, the price structure seems to have been gradually modified, preserving a certain degree of profitability for the backward sector, which leaves to one's imagination the size of profits for the big companies. The backward sector was doomed to disappear, but as long as business was prosperous, during the 1920s, this sector held on as well as it could (tending to go further into debt). When the economy entered into a significant recession in 1929, which still wasn't at all a depression, the survival of this sector was in question. Bankruptcies increased; debts remained unpaid; the banking system was shaken, which in turn undermined the production system, and so on.

The second element of instability had to do with the monetary and financial institutions and policies. The first period of the hegemony of finance was characterized both by a fragile financial setup and by considerable delay in installing macroeconomic control procedures (Chapter 18).

The Great Depression resulted from the cumulative effect of these two factors, an underlying threat linked to the backwardness of a still important sector of the production system, and a currency and a financial system that was out of control. The 1929 recession was thus transformed into a depression.[3]

It is impossible to go into the details here. Everything began in mid-1929 as in a normal recession. Industrial production reached its maximum level in February 1929; in September it had dropped 26 percent.[4] The stock market, which had risen fantastically, collapsed in October. The central bank and the banking system came to the aid of stock investors and rapidly stabilized the indexes, just as they had done in prior panics. The market crisis did not cause either the recession or the depression. At the beginning of 1930, economic activity seemed to stabilize, no longer declining, but there was no genuine rebound. At the beginning of 1932 the crisis took a particularly sharp turn, which would continue until the low point of 1933 with its business and price collapses and banking crises. Whereas the economy continued to need credit, the increase in the number of suspensions of loan payments led the banking system to practically abandon its function of creditor. It sought refuge by investing in government securities—holding them was not very risky, but not very lucrative. The banking crisis, that is, bank bankruptcies, raged again in early 1933. The very evening that power was transferred from Hoover to Roosevelt, the closing of the banking system was proclaimed on a national level.

This decision to declare a bank holiday, the first action taken by the

Roosevelt presidency, put an end to the disastrous management of the crisis by finance in the name of the sacrosanct principles of monetary orthodoxy, and kicked off the New Deal.

The banks that were considered to be viable were quickly reopened. The system set up in this moment of panic–the so-called first New Deal—was extraordinary. The various sectors of the production system were organized into commissions, employers and unions brought together under the aegis of the administration. The purpose of these measures was to interrupt what was called at the time cutthroat competition, by adopting agreements concerning market sharing. These measures tended to interrupt deflation by fixing minimal prices and salaries. After the storm, this system was declared to be unconstitutional. The dollar was devalued, with the purpose of stopping prices from collapsing (by raising the cost of imported raw materials). The government remained committed to the necessity of balancing the budget, but initiated a works program that was supposed to "prime the pump," as the expression went at the time. Against *laissez-faire,* the two dominant economic ideas of the time were, on the one hand, the necessity of generating sufficient demand by increasing workers' purchasing power and, on the other hand, regulating the activities of finance, which was felt to be responsible for the cataclysm. At the same time the government gave finance the means to get back on its feet by taking over bad credit, and by regulating the functioning of the monetary and financial system (Box 18.2).

Despite these Draconian measures the weeding out of the production system continued, with its share of closings and layoffs. Output, still low, but rising since 1933, dropped again in 1937, which is supposed to have converted Roosevelt to the necessity of having a budget deficit and have converted a significant segment of America to Keynesian economics.[5] In fact it was the beginning of the war that got the American economy out of the crisis, by means of a forceful intervention under state control, pushing economic activity to the limits of the productive potential.

In this summary of events, we have left aside the international dimension of the crisis, which did have its importance. The United States found itself at the center of the world crisis because it was further along the road of the transformations that were at the origin of the crisis. The heterogeneity of the production system and the scope of the monetary and financial innovations were farther ranging there. The relations between the United States and the rest of the world worked in both directions. The collapse of the American economy destabilized world trade and finance. In return, the stability of the international monetary and financial mechanisms had also been weakened by attempts to return to the procedures of the gold standard, particularly in France, which only added to the general deflation. The international dimension that the crisis took on should have led to measures in each of the main developed countries as well as international cooperation. No international institution was capable of orchestrating the recovery. The financial markets of London and New York were competing. This dual leadership within the world monetary system has often been presented as a major cause of the crisis,[6] but the contrary could be just as well argued.[7] Whatever the case, agents determined to do everything possible to build international financial institutions equal to the task were not in command in any country. An important feature of the period, which distinguishes it strongly from the contemporary era, was the commitment to traditional principles of monetary orthodoxy and the gold standard, with potentially catastrophic deflationary effects.

Was the Great Depression avoidable or inevitable? Could other policies have stopped the catastrophe? These questions raise a series of problems.

First, we must ask when the best time would have been for a vigorous intervention: in 1932, when the crisis within the crisis occurred; in early 1929, when the overheating of the economy suggested an imminent recession; in 1913, when the central bank was conceived and its missions defined; at the turn of the century, when the monetary and financial mechanisms were booming; or at the end of the nineteenth century, when the conditions of the duality of the American economy became perceptible?

Other questions must start with the degree of freedom we can allow ourselves retrospectively in the conception of alternative policies. In rewriting history, do we permit ourselves to reform the institutions, or should we limit ourselves to conceiving alternative policies without touching the institutional framework of the time? It seems obvious that we must begin by placing ourselves within the American monetary system and its problems at the time. But it is nevertheless also clear that vigorous intervention was necessary, which in turn implies an overhaul of the institutions.

The crisis was not, as has been written, the consequence of an error of economic policy clearly situated in time.[8] But one cannot therefore conclude that errors were not made. There were underlying conditions for the Great Depression that put the economy at considerable risk and forced it to face unprecedented situations. Never had the American economy harbored such elements that fermented instability—the heterogeneity of the production system and the exceptional growth of monetary and financial mechanisms. The economic officials did not take leave of their senses in 1929. At first they perpetuated old attitudes, the principles of good finance, whose effects were disastrous, given the acute and unique nature of the problems. The extraordinary situation, however, does not take away from the warranted criticism of these orthodox principles—they embodied the interests of the ruling classes, and of certain factions of these classes, with a whole gradation of attitudes, from the most backward to the most innovative. Under the successive blows of preceding crises, most recently the 1907 financial panic and the crisis of 1921, finance had made the institutional and political frameworks evolve, but always with reticence and delay. This evolution was not sufficient to deal with the problems that were now encountered. It is this responsibility which is in question, that of a ruling class in given historical circumstances. The conditions of the Great Depression took this ruling class by surprise, through its lack of experience in similar conditions and its absorption in protecting its privileges.

If we sweep away the shackles of historical and social conditions, of powers, of learning processes, it is possible to assert that the crisis was avoidable. What should have been done? Action could have been taken on two levels. First, with regard to the underlying conditions for the crisis, two types of interventions were necessary. On the one hand, the backward sector should not have been allowed to benefit from passive protection, but should have been helped to transform itself; otherwise it had to disappear. On the other hand, the development of monetary and financial mechanisms should have been accompanied by the definition of a centralized, state framework of control of the stability of the macroeconomy, largely autonomous from private finance. This would mean the establishment of the institutions required by a true monetary policy, targeted to economic activity instead of to the narrow interests of finance (its banks and stock market). Second, in the crisis itself, business should have been strongly supported and on a lasting basis through credits as well as through public demand (deficits)—and all the more so if, prior to that, the backward sector had not successfully disappeared.

One grasps how naive it would be to reproach the officials of the time with not having carried out such procedures. Ruling classes do not innovate in this way. They do not act on the basis of knowledge and the anticipation of events and in contradiction with what they perceive to be their own immediate interests. Only the violence of the crisis could produce such transformations.

What is the most striking in the analysis of the Great Depression is that it is possible to see in it the crisis of the end to the structural crisis of the final years of the nineteenth century. The crisis at the end of the century had led to the development of a new configuration of the production system, that of big joint-stock companies, with unprecedented efficiency; it had prompted the rise of a financial system far different from the preceding one, and strongly tied to the production system. These movements had found their natural extension in the emergence of a monetary and financial system corresponding to these transformations; but these evolutions were not coupled with appropriate procedures of macroeconomic control. In spite of the pronounced heterogeneity of the production system, this period was characterized by the particularly favorable evolution of the major variables involved in the description of technological progress (labor and capital productivity), which extended to equally favorable movements concerning distribution, wages, and the profit rate. The Great Depression intervened in this context in disconcerting fashion—favorable developments on the one hand, depression on the other. But this paradox is only apparent—that is what is expressed in the notion of crisis of the end of the crisis.

CHAPTER

20

Capital Mobility and Stock Market Fever

The analogy between the conditions presiding over the Great Depression and the current situation of the main developed capitalist countries is very strong. At the most general level, both periods may be characterized as the ends to structural crises. Twenty years following the crisis at the end of the nineteenth century, capitalism was already far along on the road toward a profound transformation, leading to a wave of technological progress. What is emerging today does not have the same social depth, but progress in organization and technology, in management in a broad sense, seems to be leading to a new course for the major variables accounting for technological change—especially capital productivity, which favors capital profitability.

What the analysis of the Great Depression teaches us, and what throws a shadow over the current period, is that such an end to the crisis carries certain dangers—and all the more so when the transformations specific to companies are coupled with monetary and financial innovations, without control of the system's overall stability being reinforced through adequate policies and institutions.

The more we get into the details, the more the resemblance is striking—feature by feature. Since the 1980s, as in the 1920s, the wave of technological change affects companies unevenly (the multinationals get by, but numerous small and mid-size national companies have delayed reducing their debt and have had a harder time tackling the new technologies); the financial innovations have been considerable; the stock market has skyrocketed upward and then collapsed after 2000; and financial scandals, banking crises, and bankruptcies of other financial institutions are on the rise. Everything seems to indicate the possibility of a crisis similar to that of the 1930s.

The analysis of the early decades of the twentieth century shows that the threat represented by the heterogeneity of companies, in terms of technology and organization, was first made concrete during the depression of the 1930s in the collapse of businesses and prices following the recession begun in 1929. The heterogeneity of the production system since the mid-1980s should therefore be interpreted as a source of potential fragility, whose effects could be felt during a strong recession such as that of 2000 (possibly linked to the drop in stock prices).

What kind of danger do the soaring stock prices over the last decades of the twentieth century and their drop since 2000 represent? The collapse of the market in October 1929 is on everyone's mind, and it's most often in these terms that the parallel between the current situation and the Great Depression is taken up. Besides the effect of a drop in stock prices, one can imagine a banking crisis (a cumulative movement of bankruptcies like those occurring between 1930 and 1933), convulsive movements in currency exchange rates that destabilize economies, or private or government debt insolvency. There is an overabundance of mechanisms and forms.

In the late 1990s the possibility of a serious stock market and even broader financial crisis was not merely formed in the mind of a few radical critics of neoliberalism. The possibility was largely recognized by officials of the Federal Reserve and the major international monetary institutions, where it was the subject of constantly repeated declarations. Of course these confessions struck a skillful balance between assurances, concerns, and warnings, but their content was unequivocal—the world economy was threatened by a financial crisis.

Why such lucidity? The way in which this reality has asserted itself is simple to grasp. The repetition of international monetary and financial crises around the globe had convinced the officials of the world's financial institutions of the reality of the risk incurred. The 1987 crash was still on everyone's mind, and some markets, like those of Tokyo and the countries hit by financial and monetary crises in recent years, had undergone harsh turnarounds. Many experts agreed that stock prices were significantly overvalued in the advanced capitalist countries before the readjustment now under way asserted itself.

The rise in stock prices was tremendous (Figure 15.4) in France as well as in the United States (the markets of Germany and the United Kingdom experienced similar growth). In the United States, between 1982 and 2000, stock prices corrected for inflation were multiplied five times. The level reached in 2000 was 2.9 times that of 1965, which had been maintained until the drop of 1974. What can be said about such levels? We shall take up here two traditional ratios, which emphasize how high the 2000 levels were in the United States and show the extent of the adjustment under way.

The first rate frequently employed in measuring stock prices is the ratio of the value of market capitalization, that is, of the number of shares multiplied by their price, in relation to companies' net worth (Appendix B). The market capitalization is the price the market accords to companies; accounting provides another estimate. The variable considered is the ratio of these two estimations. It is known as Tobin's *q* coefficient.

Figure 20.1 describes the evolution of this ratio in the United States (in quarterly data). Between 1952 and 1963, it rose from around 0.5 to 1, a reassuring value. It then increased to a high of roughly 1.3 in 1968. As with stock prices, it then dropped drastically during the structural crisis of the 1970s (this similarity to stock prices is not surprising; since the evolution of corporate net worth is fairly regular, it is the stock prices that are reflected in sudden movements of the ratio). This ratio was divided by three. It progressively rose again to 1 in 1995. It was only at this point that it bounded ahead, reaching 1.8 during the first quarter of 2000, pulverizing the record of the 1960s—a movement characteristic of the second half of the 1990s. The decline was then rapid, reaching 0.83 in the fourth quarter of 2002.

Securities corresponding to the new economy were in the forefront of this movement. In this sector, the ratios between corporate net worth and the evaluation given by the market reached fantastic levels, which were reflected in the dramatic rise of the NASDAQ. The inordinate growth of the NASDAQ dates to between August 1999 and March 2000. It increased by 110 percent, whereas the Standard & Poor 500 index remained almost constant. Previously the NASDAQ had evolved like the Standard & Poor 500, and thus it is possible to interpret its growth as a general explanation of the dramatic rise in prices only since 1999, not since 1995.

One may also observe stock prices from the point of view of yields. Corporate stock capitalization is presented in this case as a multiple, either of total corporate profits (the ratio of price to earnings) or of distributed dividends. These two ratios are presented in Figure 20.2 for the United States

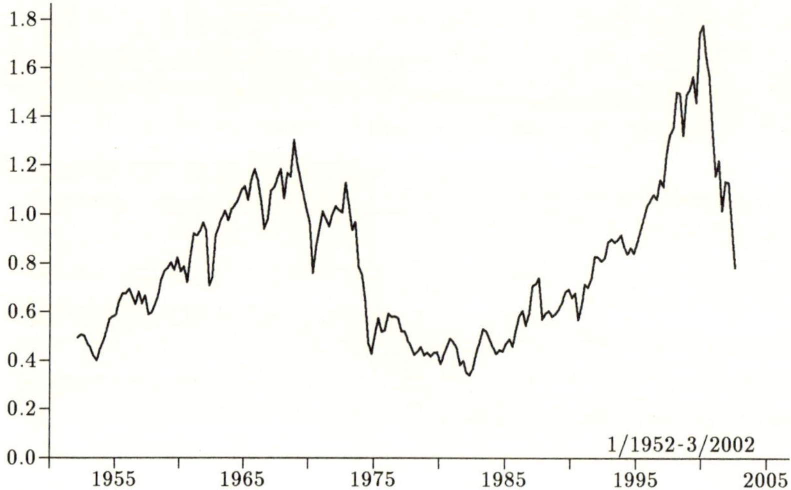

Figure 20.1 Ratio of the value of market capitalization to net worth (Tobin's q): United States, nonfinancial corporations.

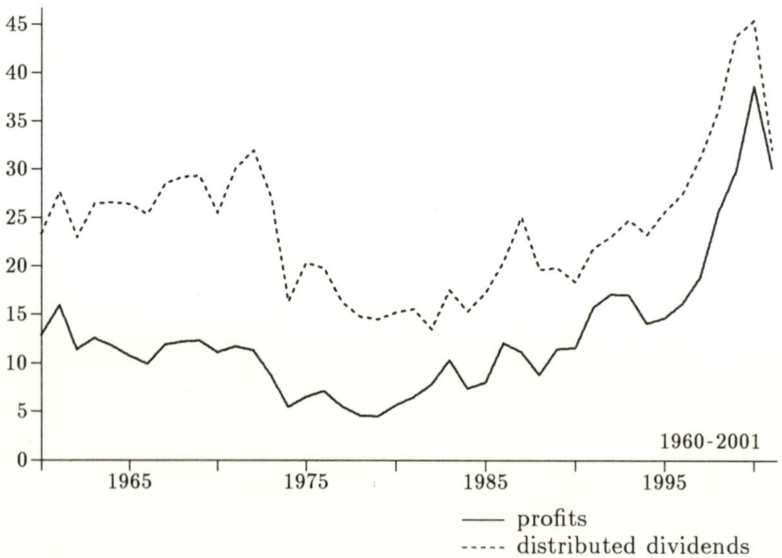

Figure 20.2 Ratios of market capitalization to profits and to distributed dividends: United States, nonfinancial corporations.

(the ratio of capitalization to dividends is obviously higher than that of capitalization to profits, because only a fraction of profits are distributed).

The profile of the ratio of capitalization to profits in Figure 20.2 confirms the diagnosis suggested by Figure 20.1, of a brazen rise of stock prices in the second half of the 1990s. Between 1960 and 1972, capitalization represented between 10 and 16 times profits; the ratio declined thereafter, to under 5, because of the drop in stock prices, overreacting to the decline in the profitability of companies. The levels of the second half of the 1980s were approximately those of the stage prior to the crisis; the final dramatic rise took this ratio up to 39 times profits in 2000.

The second curve, relative to the ratio of capitalization to distributed dividends, reveals a similar profile: an initial plateau, a decline during the structural crisis, and a rise after. It is the percentage of profits distributed to stockholders (Figure 9.5) that explains the gap between the two curves. The lowering of dividends during the crisis explains why this variable declined proportionately less than the preceding one. Despite the later increase, we find not a rapid return to the precrisis level, but rather a progressive increase since 1985. The rate of 2000 is thus significantly higher than prior to the structural crisis. Therefore stock prices relative to dividends appear to be high, but proportionately less so than relative to profits, because of the increase in dividend distribution characteristic of neoliberalism.

It may be more intuitive to look at the reverse ratios: profits or dividends divided by market capitalization. Table 20.1 gives the corresponding values, with the same conclusions.[1] One may observe in particular the low level of the yield rates in 2000 in relation to the values prior to the crisis (between 1960 and 1973): 2.6 percent, instead of 8.7 percent for the ratio of profits to capitalization, and 2.2 percent, instead of 3.7 percent, for the

Table 20.1 Yields on stocks (in percent)

	1960–1973	1974–1985	1986–1995	2000
Profits/market capitalization	8.6	15.9	7.7	2.6
Dividends/market capitalization	3.7	6.2	4.6	2.2

ratio of dividends to capitalization—the smaller decline in dividend yields reflecting increased distribution.

It is tempting to speculate—we mean intellectually—about the level of market prices, and the stakes for the future of neoliberalism are considerable. However, one should remain cautious—there is no established theory for these prices. We shall not take up here theories of speculative bubbles or mimicry. At the level of the very general analysis we are pursuing, the prices seem to respond to a dual logic. First, companies have a certain value as areas of potential financial investment for other companies, alternative to internal growth. Second, holding stock guarantees its owners a certain income, the flow of dividends. These logics are the subject of complex movements of anticipation. Neoliberalism drives its prices higher in both these ways—the wave of mergers and, more generally, the development of the network of interdependence among companies (Chapter 13) that it prompted, and dividend distributions at rates unprecedented since at least World War II. Leaving aside the absence of theoretical foundations, this analysis finds its limits in the global character of the variables considered—the very strong degree of heterogeneity between sectors and companies is not taken into account.

Prior to the collapse, the rise in stock prices was sometimes interpreted in relation to the extraordinary growth of mutual and pension funds in the United States (Figure 13.2). This interpretation was far from obvious. As we have shown, the growth of the funds is only an expression of the transfer of securities, previously held directly by households, toward the funds. Altogether, with or without the funds, households do not hold more stock than before (figure 13.4). It is thus impossible to argue that it is the demand for stock by the funds that made prices rise, without adding other elements to the analysis.

If we take seriously these fundamental indicators, despite their rudimentary character, they point to speculative excess. They suggest a staggering level of pricing—prices had doubled when the high point was reached in 2000, and are now coming back down, as could be expected.

The parallel with the Great Depression is very marked here. Both periods of financial hegemony risked producing the same effects. However, one should recall that, according to our analysis, the drop in Wall Street prices was not a fundamental cause of the depression in the 1930s. It contributed to the first phase of the crisis, which ran from 1929 to 1931. But the Federal Reserve quickly lowered interest rates, so that the financial institutions linked to the market could obtain new financing, in order to avoid massive sales of stock. This vigorous intervention rapidly halted the fall.

Independent of market speculation, one of the major aspects of the current situation is the international monetary and financial instability, which was discussed in relation to the epidemic of financial crises in Chapter 11. The widespread fear of seeing the crises of certain countries destabilize the economies of other countries, especially those of the center, is permanent. It is important to note that this is a difference with the first hegemonic period of finance. In the 1920s, though already mitigated by currency reserves, the international monetary regime was that of the gold standard.[2] Currency parities were defined in relation to gold. Capital circulated around the world, but these flows did not have the vigor of the movements within neoliberalism. Countries controlled the flow of gold, and thus capital flows. Here we touch on an element of instability that is specific to neoliberalism.

In terms of international monetary and financial processes, finance has created for itself a difficult challenge—reconciling the freedom of movement of capital with financial stability without going too far along the road to centralism, which it fears. Beyond the self-discipline of prudential regulations and permanent pressure, its main approach remains the largely after-the-fact intervention of the central national and international monetary institutions. Private capital is free; the institutions discipline it somewhat by imposing norms and supervising practices, and they intervene suddenly in crises, pretending to contribute to a return to prosperity. This situation is all the more surprising in that finance could encourage the international organizations to evolve into genuine central world banks, while still keeping control over them—which could be done in the future, but probably only under the constraint of events. The parallel with the history of national monetary institutions would then be complete (Chapter 18).

How can the strengths and the weaknesses of the neoliberal world, led by the United States, be balanced? Will the neoliberal world plunge further into this crisis of the end of the crisis? Will history repeat itself with such regularity?

It seems clear that the conditions capable of provoking a new major crisis exist, but the fact that an adjustment is necessary does not imply that the change will necessarily be catastrophic. The least advanced parts of the production sector still functioning will have to adapt or be eliminated (the strongest tensions will follow the beginning of a recession, or several beginnings of recessions, acting as a trigger). Stock prices will have to be adjusted, whatever the scope and rapidity of the movement. The fluctuations of currency rates and the excessive movements of capital will have to be regulated. The internal and external disequilibria of the U.S. economy, the growing indebtedness, will have to be curbed, and this might well be the most difficult aspect of the adjustment. But while the necessity of an adjustment is beyond doubt, the methods are still to be determined. Will those responsible for world affairs know how to lead this transition while limiting its potential damage? Is that compatible with neoliberal options?

Finance currently has the Great Depression in mind. It suffices to read statements by officials to become convinced of that. Finance knows that it can, during such catastrophes, lose a great deal of money and, even more seriously, compromise its supremacy. However, an important element for making an evaluation is the fact that the depression of the 1930s has already taken place. Any disturbance of some import to the center would prompt a burst of state intervention—which doesn't mean that this action would be able to turn the situation around. We can state that there will be no repeat of the laissez-faire of 1929–1933. Either finance will take the situation in hand, introducing a new, more centralized phase of neoliberalism, or it will pass, taking us beyond neoliberalism. This option does not depend only on finance—it is not the only social force.

The fall in the rate of growth of the U.S. economy in 2000 and the manifestation of a new recession make the parallel with 1929 very topical. Stock prices are being adjusted. It is clear that macroeconomic stabilization appears to be difficult during a period where the market is declining. It is necessary to simultaneously control the market's soft landing and stimulate the economy. The market depreciation is capable of destabilizing the financial system, an indispensable transmission belt for carrying out monetary policies. Part of the road has been traveled, but more remains. The events of September 2001 stimulated public spending and can only reinforce the determination of the U.S. government to bolster economic activity. It should not be forgotten that the U.S. economy ended the depression of the 1930s via World War II. Much will be done to avoid a further fall in activity and the occurrence of a more serious crisis, not only by lowering interest rates, but by stimulating economic activity more directly through public spending.

Neoliberalism, under U.S. hegemony, must, however, face up to a major contradiction, which counterposes its determination to protect its financial institutions and stability with its exploitation of the financial crises of the peripheral countries. Until now the repercussions of these crises on the U.S. economy have been contained, but the risk of their spread throughout the world is obviously real.

Should we speak of a revival of Keynesian policies, given the recession begun in 2000? As we have pointed out, neoliberalism did not lead to the waning of policies aimed at stabilization in the main capitalist countries, much to the contrary. The instruments are there; it is the policy goals that have changed. This is true of monetary policy as well as budgetary policy.[3] The question in the fall of 2001 was not whether to stimulate the economy, but how. Very simply, besides monetary policy, the choice was whether to increase spending, such as unemployment allocations (which would benefit the layers least privileged and most affected by the crisis), or to increase revenue by lowering the highest tax brackets (which would benefit the highest incomes). This debate followed the traditional party lines that divide Democrats and Republicans.

CHAPTER

21

Between Two Periods of Financial Hegemony: Thirty Years of Prosperity

The most ardent advocates of neoliberalism are ill at ease when confronted with the performances of the developed capitalist economies from the end of World War II until the 1970s, particularly in Europe and Japan—the famous "thirty glorious years." The neoliberals' defense is built around the necessarily fleeting nature of the kind of growth and progress thus registered—what is unhealthy ends up going bad. In their view, the crisis begun in the 1970s demonstrates that. On the left, some continue to deny that these three decades were prosperous, basing their arguments on the most shocking forms of exploitation that it did not eliminate—and which did, moreover, stimulate this progress. But nostalgia is at the heart of the perspective of the great majority.

The prosperity of the first decades following World War II had two pillars—exceptionally favorable conditions for technological progress and for institutions turned toward development, on the one hand, and policies that are commonly called Keynesian, on the other. In Europe and Japan labor productivity increased rapidly and the rise in the capital-labor ratio indicated that the main developed countries were quickly catching up to the American economy. As in the United States, capital productivity was high. These happy developments made it possible for social struggles to obtain a substantial increase in workers' purchasing power, coupled with a system of social protection.[1] In some countries, the state also embarked on industrial policies aimed at developing the national production system. Sometimes the state directly took charge of fundamental components of the production system via national companies, especially certain basic industries and public services. The Bretton Woods agreement authorized foreign investments, but, in practical terms, allowed each state to control its exchange rate and the possibility of temporarily restricting capital movements whenever it felt parity readjustments necessary (Box 18.3). Policies were put into place to stabilize economic activity and stimulate growth, as well as to promote full employment. Inflation was tolerated and real interest rates were maintained at low levels, ensuring income transfers that were more favorable to agents investing, such as companies, or to certain households that were purchasing their homes.

The link between the course of technological change, on the one hand, and institutions and policies, on the other, was so strong that, when favorable conditions for technological progress disappeared and the next structural crisis asserted itself, the attempts to pursue the former policies failed. Postwar prosperity was not founded on formulas that could be generalized for all contexts, at least not without being modified. Nevertheless, its lessons should not be neglected.

This chapter limits itself to an examination of three major aspects of the decades of prosperity following World War II: corporate management, the role of the state, and the methods of the internationalization of capital.

One of the aspects of the decline of the power of finance after World War II was the greater autonomy of managers in relation to owners. We are not familiar with any study that makes it possible to draw a quantitative balance sheet of this development in the 1960s and 1970s. However, numerous analysts, both in the United States and in France, have unambiguously recognized the fact itself. There exist a good number of studies, particularly in the United States, regarding managerial capitalism, that is, a capitalism in which the wage-earning managerial personnel manage and exercise their resulting power in a relatively autonomous manner.[2]

The debate between owners and managers over the question of power in companies is reminiscent of the response earlier in the century to the transfer of the power of the owners (the shareholders) to the managers.[3] The expression "corporate governance" is often used to describe the discipline finance imposed on companies under neoliberalism. Finance demands that the power of the owners be restored and the managers subordinated to the shareholders' interests. It does not demand that the owners directly manage the company.

Different, more or less technocratic, or pluralistic variants of managerial power have been suggested. Some, like John Kenneth Galbraith, extending theories dating from the beginning of the twentieth century, have seen in managerial personnel, particularly engineers, corporate leaders who have won a large degree of autonomy in relation to stockholders, and whose goals have been not so much profitability as growth and technological progress.[4] The firm was understood as an arena of compromise between various participants—owners, managers, wage earners and unions, and the public authorities. François Bloch-Lainé presented France as it was in the 1960s in these terms and argued in favor of a new "corporate governance."[5] He detected in this a developing socialization, an alternative to collectivism. These authors, like the original advocates of managerial theories at the beginning of the twentieth century, saw managerial personnel as enlightened leaders.

Whatever terminology is used, and whatever may be the rules of this kind of capitalism,[6] it should be emphasized that not only did it work, but it was effective from the point of view of both technology and growth. During the decades of postwar prosperity, the power of stockholders was largely held in check without progress grinding to a halt.

The economic role of the state since World War II is now a widely debated issue. We shall not emphasize here either macroeconomic policies or the development of social protection systems. The involvement of the state in leading the economy was much farther reaching—everywhere, in the United States and in the other more advanced countries of Europe and Japan.

The state played a key role in research and technological progress and, more generally, in the development of industry. The United States was not an exception to the rule with its weapons, space research, electronics, and so on. Government orders placed with private industry stimulated business activity and the new technologies. The countries of Europe, Japan, and other countries such as Korea founded their development on research that was largely financed by the state and industrial policies.

The case of the Japanese MITI (Ministry of International Trade and Industry) has often been analyzed.[7] Before the Japanese crisis of the 1990s, the phenomenal ability of this country to catch up and compete with the American economy fascinated many—all the more so because this development strategy was turned toward exports. MITI was created in 1925. As in the first American New Deal (Chapter 19), the role of the state and technical and managerial personnel (often called bureaucrats) was central. MITI's activities were oriented toward growth and technological progress in a very pragmatic fashion. It counted simultaneously on large private firms and a strong level of state intervention. When required by a crisis, MITI had to protect small and mid-sized companies; but the same body also took action to encourage concentration. Protectionism was a crucial element. Sometimes the activity of MITI is described as conducting a gigantic world marketing study, recalling certain aspects of French-style planning, but this study was complemented by a certain number of incentives, or even constraints. The development of Korea proceeded along similar lines.[8] Neoliberalism was introduced later in these countries than in Europe and only partially imposed. In this respect we can speak of a "second neoliberal shock" (Box 21.1).

Sweden provides another interesting example. The Swedish social democratic government, supported by a trade union, found itself confronted after the war with the necessity of modernizing the economy. It placed the Rehn-Meidner model of 1951 at the center of the system—an incomes policy which regulated wage increases, but whose goals were also industrial. In order to ensure workers' unity, uniform salaries were guaranteed for the same work. In their determination, the social democrats did not adapt to the uneven performances of companies—wages were set at a level that allowed the most advanced companies to achieve profitability. Technological and organizational inadequacies were not supposed to be made up for by an inferior level of wages. The less advanced sector would thus have to modernize or disappear. At the same time, the most successful businesses were assured of a certain degree of profitability. Layoffs were inevitable, but policies encouraging investments were intended to contribute to keeping job levels up, and this macroeconomic vigilance was coupled with funds to help orient and retrain workers who had lost their jobs. In addition to these policies, demand was held in check in order to prevent inflation from getting out of control.[9]

We cannot explain here the diversity of these hybrid relationships of production, still capitalist, but bearers of transformation and the corresponding power configurations. These relationships illustrate the potential contained in a vast alliance between the managerial personnel of the state apparatus, workers and unions, and some company officials, both managers and owners, in the context of a much broader degree of financial repression than what the Keynesian compromise contained. It is possible to see here policies that go far beyond Keynesian theory. Finance feared such policies in the 1970s, before it took the situation back in hand. What forces

Box 21.1
Challenging a development model: Japan and the second neoliberal shock

Even more than France, Japan financed the growth of its nonfinancial companies through bank credit. It did so in a very particular institutional framework, under privileged conditions, and at favorable interest rates (negative real interest rates).[a] This system was the source of a significant transfer of resources between the banking system and companies, favorable to the latter. With the 1979 coup, the interest rates prevailing on the Japanese capital market increased, as in the United States, but this increase only partially affected nonfinancial companies, because the banks did not apply these rates. The transfer, which had been very favorable up to the beginning of the 1980s, was considerably reduced, but continued to operate until the beginning of the 1990s. In this manner Japan strongly resisted the first neoliberal shock.

It was the second neoliberal shock that cut into Japan's exceptional capacity to grow. This took place between 1985 and 1990, when the structure of corporate financing was transformed from bank financing to typical neoliberal sources of the capital markets.[b] This is shown in Figure 21.1. The variables represented there are new banking credits and the demands on the capital markets (stocks, bonds, and commercial paper). These sums are divided by the total of monetary and financial assets.[c] The figure makes it possible to evaluate simultaneously the amount of funds collected and the relative value of both flows. In 1960, new bank loans were high and completely dominated the other component. With the crisis of the 1970s and the concomitant lowering of the rate of profit, capital accumulation declined and so also did the demand for bank loans. But this source of financing remained clearly predominant.

As we have said, it was between 1985 and 1990 that demand for financing in the capital market took off, corresponding to the flow of new banking credits. These five years were precisely the years of the financial bubble, which was prompted by this movement. Stock prices went sky-high, reaching in 1990 a level approximately five times higher than the one prevailing previously, when the market had been playing a minor role. During these five years the banks turned to the real estate sector, feeding the speculative rise that we are familiar with. This second shock prompted the crisis of the Japanese economy of the 1990s—near stagnation. As is clear in Figure 21.1, the demand for both sources of financing dropped in concert. At the same time the nonfinancial corporations ceased investing and the banking system, shaken by the deflation of the bubble (a drop of approximately 75 percent), no longer played its role of transmission belt for monetary policy (meanwhile households, having bor-

(continued)

(continued)

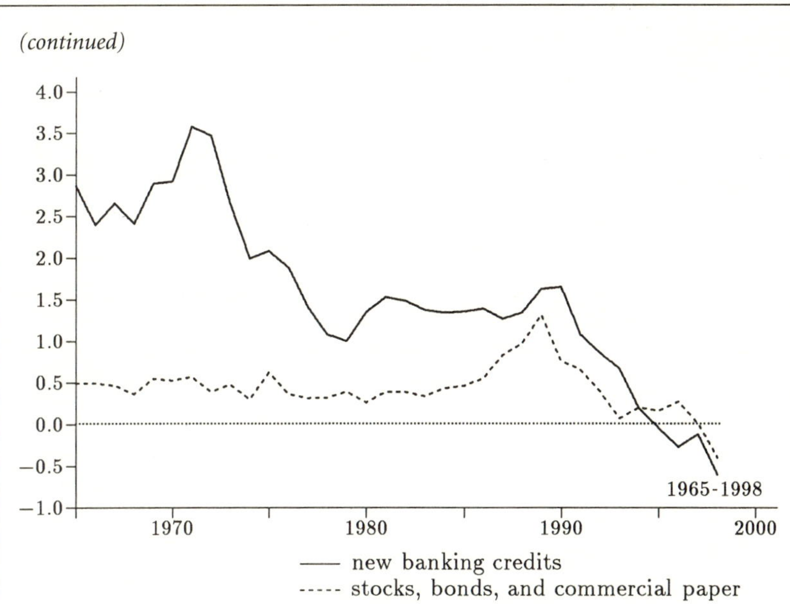

Figure 21.1 External sources of financing for nonfinancial Japanese corporations (ratio to the total of financial and monetary assets, in percent)

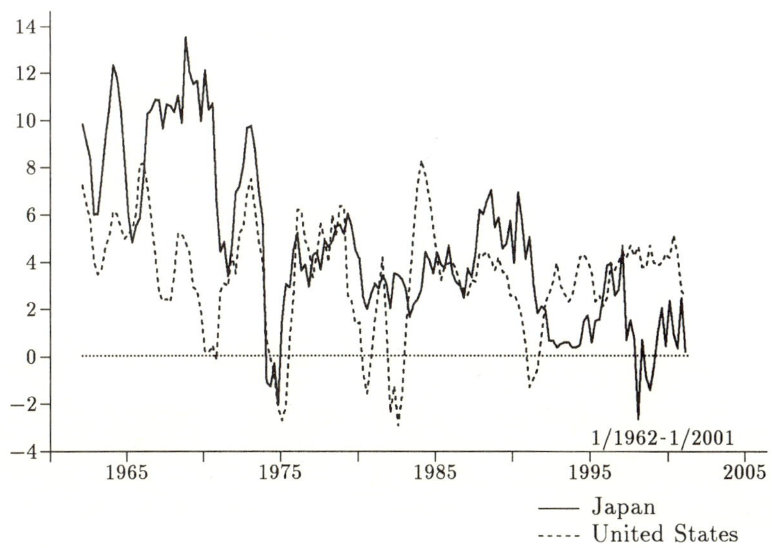

Figure 21.2 Rate of annual growth for each quarter (percent): Japan and the United States. The variable represented is the rate of growth of each quarter in relation to the same quarter of the previous year.

(continued)

(continued)

rowed heavily to purchase their homes, struggled under the weight of unbearable debt).

Figure 21.2 compares the variation of growth rates for Japan and the United States. Here we can see that rates were initially very high (around 10 percent) during the 1960s. Like the U.S. and European economies, Japan was hit by the crisis of the 1970s, but its growth rates remained relatively high until 1991, and references to a structural crisis were less common for Japan than for Europe. The second neoliberal shock was coupled with an increase in growth rates in the second half of the 1980s. These were the years when the Japanese model was described as opening new roads for the future, and it was said that the American economy had lost its preeminence. The party was short-lived and quickly led to the stagnation of the Japanese economy in the 1990s. Although Japan had been able to protect itself from the first neoliberal shock, the second one prevailed over the Japanese model.

Two aspects of this—still very partial—adjustment of the Japanese economy to the neoliberal model should be noted. The domination of finance implies both the free mobility of capital and the constitution of a profitable financial sector, turned toward itself and not toward the financing of the activities of nonfinancial companies. Both of these characteristics involve expanding the hunting grounds and eliminating restrictions and traditional privileges.

A more complete analysis would require, among other things, examining technological and distribution trends in Japan. The available data indicate that a steep drop in the profit rate does not seem to have been reversed during the 1980s. Did the Japanese model make it possible to continue accumulation, despite the drop in profitability? Was it incapable of provoking a turnaround in trends that were unfavorable to technological change? Will these trends be reversed? What role will neoliberal discipline play? What will it cost the Japanese economy? What are the chances for an alternative?

---

a. K. Miyashita and D. W. Russell, *Keiretsu: Inside the Hidden Japanese Conglomerates* (New York: McGraw-Hill, 1994).

b. T. F. Cargill, "Central Banking, Financial and Regulatory Change in Japan," in M. Blomström, B. Gangnes, and S. La Croix, eds., *Japan's New Economy: Continuity and Change in the Twenty-First Century* (Oxford: Oxford University Press, 2001), pp. 145–161.

c. It would have been preferable to take the total of fixed capital and inventories, as we did for the United States and France in Chapter 13, but this variable is not available.

made it impossible to renew and extend such experiences? Why, in particular, were the Swedish social democrats unable to conceive other policies than lower wage increases? Why did the Japanese economy open itself to the new neoliberal currents? In the meantime world finance, under American hegemony, had gotten the situation back under its control.

Laying aside the current, fermenting financial instability, finance prides itself on having been at the origin of the current course of the world economy—of the encouraging development of technology, profitability, and supposedly growth—through the role that it played in restructuring and concentration. It is supposed to be at the origin, not only of wage freezes, which is a fact, but of the increase in capital productivity, which determines the increase in the profit rate. The newfound efficiency is supposed to be due to finance.

This is a difficult question. Although the transformations involved with the end to the crisis of the 1970s touch on technology and organization, which are the responsibility of managerial personnel, they have been of such scope that they could not have been accomplished independently of the agents that ordered the major restructuring of the production system. To the extent that finance occupied this central position, it was at the heart of this development. The parallel with the conclusion to the crisis at the end of the nineteenth century is striking (Chapter 17).

Finance can claim responsibility for at least three kinds of actions. First, it played a major role in the creation of vast units of management, in the very large companies, through its attitude toward mergers and through its role in their organization and financing. Second, although neoliberalism is globally—that is, when all companies are considered—characterized by self-financing (Chapter 13), finance played a crucial role in allocating capital toward the sector of new technologies. Finally, through the new system of corporate governance, finance imposed a strong obligation of profitability (demanding high profit rates), making increased efficiency a necessity. In these different areas, one easily recognizes the features of neoliberalism —its objectives, its disdain for what costs are borne by dominated social classes and countries, and the risks of financial instability that distinguish it—all things that define it as an aggressive and violent form of capitalism, searching for efficiency from an appetite for profit.

For the question, Can finance claim to have contributed to the positive features of the new phase of capitalism by having played a role in restructuring?, another one should be substituted—Could a radical alternative, one that would have affected the private ownership of the means of production more deeply than Keynesian policies, have made it possible to do without finance? Without such an alternative, it is not surprising that finance was involved in activities that it monopolized. But the postwar period of prosperity teaches us that, with regard to technological change and restructuring, things could have gone just as fast without finance in control, because an enormous amount was accomplished during these years.

One of the reasons given for the failure of Keynesian policies or any other alternative policy is globalization. We are caught in an international system where every government's freedom of movement is limited. This is a fact. It is well known that fund transfers capable of destabilizing exchange rates follow any anticipation of an interest rate or currency fluctuation. Currencies and credits are constantly negotiated and renegotiated on the markets. For certain agents, the problem is one of taking precautions against exchange risks or benefiting from more advantageous loan conditions; for others, the problem is to profit from these transactions. These mechanisms limit, even make impossible, independent policies. Was it possible to conceive a different globalization than neoliberal globalization?

The institutions of Bretton Woods, as they were conceived at the end of World War II, and the use made of them after the war should not be confused with the current role of the International Monetary Fund (IMF). These institutions played a central role in postwar prosperity and the development of Europe and Japan (Box 18.3). There was no need to abandon fixed exchange rates or limits on capital mobility, unless they were required in order to restore American preeminence. The crisis of the dollar should logically have led to reinforcing world institutions, governed by international bodies that were more independent from private interests. But the opposite policy was followed. Institutions of the type created at Bretton Woods, reformed when necessary, would not have made impossible capital mobility and particularly direct investment abroad (just think of the influx of American capital in Europe between the end of World War II and the crisis, particularly in France at the beginning of the Fifth Republic). The development of multinationals was not incompatible with national development policies, as, for example, the prodigious progress made by the Japanese and Korean economies attested.

Indeed, the social and economic framework characteristic of the first decades following World War II was unable to prevent the occurrence of the structural crises of the 1970s, just as it proved unable to remedy the crisis when it materialized. Inflation became cumulative at the end of the decade. This does not prove that alternatives could not have been devised along the principles that had contributed so well to the prosperity of the postwar decades, only that they were not found. Obviously the problem was not the intellectual capacity to conceive of such alternatives, but rather the social and political conditions bearing witness to the internal contradictions of the Keynesian compromise, given the violence of the struggle by finance to reestablish its hegemony.

PART

V

History on the March

The functioning of capitalism and its historical transformations can be evaluated in several ways. The Keynesian interpretation emphasizes the absence of mechanisms under capitalism that are capable of spontaneously guaranteeing full employment and financial stability (Chapter 22). According to this point of view, these deficiencies can be remedied; the system can be reformed. In order to do this, a collective commitment to maintain full employment and control private finance is necessary, and these responsibilities fall on the state. Beyond this the capitalist mode of production is deemed efficient, and reforms will be sufficient to guarantee more social justice, to eliminate the world hegemony of this or that power, and to replace it with a system of planetary economic justice, thus taking on the appearance of an acceptable system, perhaps the least bad.

The analysis we have made tends to prove that this diagnosis indeed puts its finger on one of the central problems of capitalism, but remains limited. The limited nature of the Keynesian perspective is manifest in at least two ways.

First, capitalism contains a series of historical trends, which lead to deep, long-lasting, structural crises. Macroeconomic policies do not suffice to prevent or remedy them. Institutions and policies that are effective in certain situations cease to be effective in others; deeper transformations of the system become necessary. Unemployment, which Keynes wanted to rid capitalism of, is not only a symptom of an economy in which the use made of the productive potential and accumulation is poorly controlled. It is also an effect of technological change specific to capitalism and one of its regulating mechanisms. Is its elimination possible and desired under all circumstances?

Second, behind these processes—trends, crises, and policies—the powers and riches of the privileged classes, domination, and exploitation are at issue. It is within this framework of social conflict that both the financial repression of the first postwar decades and the hegemony of finance in neoliberalism should be understood.

The limitations of the Keynesian perspective have important practical consequences. Control of the macroeconomy is not sufficient in the long run. A combination of economic and political circumstances will repeatedly destabilize Keynesian policy frameworks. For example, macroeconomic policies cannot remedy the effects of a crisis in profitability. The failure of policies to restore prosperity creates the conditions for a transformation of the prevailing political compromises and configurations. But the analysis in this book also emphasizes the dependence of such options on political configurations and underlying economic trends, from which their fundamental precariousness and potential fleeting character derive.

These limitations of the Keynesian perspective underline the necessity for a broader understanding of the dynamics of capitalism, which we draw from our interpretation of Marx's analysis of capitalism. It encompasses both the economic and the political aspects. This will be the topic of Chapter 23. Its purpose remains analytical; the definition of a new alternative course for the evolution of human societies lies beyond our scope here.

CHAPTER

22

A Keynesian Interpretation

A Keynesian interpretation can be made of the picture of capitalism drawn in this book, particularly in Part III, devoted to the law of finance. The criticism of capitalism made by Keynes, at least in what has survived of his message, does not deal with all of its aspects. What Keynes neglects is enormous (peripheral countries, inequalities, the environment, and the long term and so on), but he puts his finger on a crucial point. In summary, capitalism works well as long as private finance is not left in control of macroeconomic processes, that is, the general level of economic activity and employment, to which we may add financial stability. Those are public, centralized, general interest responsibilities. This interpretation makes a lot of sense, and is worth examining. The purpose of this chapter is not to analyze the theoretical tools specific to Keynesian analysis, but to examine the features of the general vision of capitalism underlying it.

The Keynesian diagnosis flowed from observation of the bleak situation of England in the 1920s and in the Great Depression. Besides monetary and budgetary policies, Keynes envisaged an ambitious program aimed at developing England in the direction of an advanced social economy, which would mean substantially isolating the country from the rest of the world.[1]

Despite the violence of the world depression, the old dogmas were hard to challenge. For those ready to free themselves from the rules of monetary orthodoxy, many analyses were available at the time, more or less radical critiques of capitalism leading to potentially ambitious reforms. But after World War II, it was Keynesian macroeconomics that emerged, to the point where it became established as an alternative orthodoxy, without, however, ever eliminating its rival, neoclassical theory. At the beginning of the twenty-first century, academic Keynesian theory has lost ground, but is still alive.

Why did this theory emerge? Why did it survive against the neoliberal invasion? On an academic level, there was, above all, the obvious necessity of centralized interventions under government control. But the theory's vitality originates to a large extent in its more general political content. Contrary to the message delivered by the dominant theory, the sum of individual interests is not, according to Keynes, identical to the general interest.[2] The interests of private finance, in particular, lead to macroeconomic instability and insufficient global demand. Keynesian theory underlines the need for a strongly centralized economic power in the hands of the state and with particular goals.

Every economic theory is deeply rooted within social relationships, reflecting the questions of power at stake therein, but what is particular to Keynesian theory is that it was the expression of a compromise not only between diverse segments of the dominant classes, but between these segments and the dominated classes within the context of a relationship favoring the popular movement. It moderated capitalist rule by eliminating some of its most shocking expressions.

This relation to social structures is so strong that it ultimately obscures the very definition of Keynesian policy. The social context, which Keynesian policy was part of, made possible the development of systems of social protection that went beyond the limits of Keynesian macroeconomics. This stretch was greatly facilitated by the favorable evolution of technology, which made possible a more harmonious development of incomes (increase in the rate of profit despite an increase in wage growth). Keynesian theory finally became the theory of compromise, established in the middle of the twentieth century.[3]

This extended Keynesian theory should not make one lose sight of the pertinence of its central element: explicitly taking a position concerning capitalism and fundamentally evaluating the system's functioning. The content of this theory is still of interest today. It may be summed up as follows.[4] The mechanisms of the capitalist economy were felt to be fairly efficient in allocating resources between different branches, determining the quantities to be produced and fixing prices. Although the question of technological change was never a major concern of Keynesian economics, it may also be added that Keynes found no fault with capitalism's ability to stimulate technological progress. There was, however, something faulty in this system, as it had functioned up until then: nothing guaranteed that production capacities and the workforce would be utilized at adequate levels. To use language closer to that of Keynes, nothing guaranteed that the level of global demand would be appropriate. Above all, the problem was one of insufficient demand, although it could also be excessive. This was how the necessity of state intervention burst into Keynes's reasoning. The creation of money and credit should not be abandoned to private initiative; or, at least, these activities should be supervised. If the credit system could no longer assume its function of lender, the state should step in—this was its function as lender of last resort. If the offer of credit by financial institutions did not find borrowers, there should be no hesitation about resorting to the spending capacities of the state, which would shore up global demand through budget deficits. Thus we can propose a formula symmetrical to the preceding one, that of the state as the borrower of last resort: lender of last resort through its central bank, and borrower of last resort through its budget. The state finances and spends.

Keynes attacked not finance, but conservative policies and coupon clippers. He differentiated between the financier, in his mind an active figure, who senses investment opportunities, and coupon clippers, whom he described as investors without a function, a class of parasites, living off interest payments and dividends. He advocated euthanasia for them. Moreover, he denounced the financial markets, above all the stock market, for provoking a tremendous degree of instability.[5]

The original Keynesian compromise, largely limited to the ruling classes, had much to do with the depression conditions of the 1930s. The relations between Keynes and President Franklin Delano Roosevelt, who was wrestling with the crisis, well illustrate Keynes's point of view. In Keynes's opinion, the New Deal was tangled up in carrying out reforms which he did not reject but which, according to him, were not the priority for dealing with the crisis. The system aimed at mitigating the hardships of competition was unnecessary, according to Keynes. As for the increase in purchasing power for wageworkers, he was not against it, and doubtless it fit into his social philosophy, but the policy he defended was different—a combination of monetary policy and budgetary policy which aimed to set investment at the level necessary for full employment. These policies were justified by the crisis, but Keynes viewed them as having a general importance as well. The state was supposed to control the course of the economy under all circumstances, not by substituting itself for companies or investors in their individual choices, but by regulating global demand.

In the United States this lesson was not learned until 1937, when the ongoing recovery from the Depression was interrupted by a new plunge of the economy, and World War II, when the necessities of the war economy involved the state in managing the economy to an extent far beyond what Keynes had proposed. At the end of the hostilities, the business and finance milieus stood up massively against a possible extension of this state intervention. The Keynesian policies of macroeconomic control then became the compromise solution, but not without leaving frustrations behind, both on the side of the advocates of the market and on the side of those (called "planners" at that time) who wished to pursue and develop the experiences of the New Deal and the war economy.

The Keynesian framework extended to setting up international institutions. Keynes, struck by the monetary disorder and the collapse of international commerce during the depression, realized the need for major international financial institutions. Bodies were needed that could survey the world monetary mechanisms, thus controlling the central state banks. The fundamental idea was the same as at the national level. Capitalism cannot regulate itself in an autonomous manner through the interplay of the market, at least not so far as the great masses of demand are concerned; in the same way that demand can collapse in a national economy if it is not regulated, international commerce can suddenly contract, as during the depression of the 1930s. A world credit institution should supervise the international monetary mechanisms. The capacity of each country to regulate the general activity of its economy and its level of employment should be preserved within these institutions, which implies possible restrictions on capital movements. Such regulation could not be left for private finance to take care of.

The negotiations with the Americans were difficult, particularly because of the opposition of the major New York banks, and the plan adopted at Bretton Woods did not go as far as Keynes's initial project, especially concerning the limits placed on the movement of capital (Box 18.3).

Keynes's ideas were remarkably well adapted to the problems of his time. The analysis we have made of the crises of the end of the twentieth century—both the structural crisis and the financial crises—furnishes an additional demonstration of the correctness and significance of the Keynesian diagnosis: the control over the macroeconomic situation and financial institutions must not be left in private hands, that is, those of finance.

Another major theme of this book is that the structural crisis of the end of the twentieth century did not have the same causes as the Great Depression. The crisis begun in the 1970s did not resemble the virtual collapse of the 1930s. But the opinion of Keynes as to the necessity of centralized, national, or international intervention remains valid today, all the more so because the end of the crisis of the 1970s is similar to the period preceding the Great Depression, and should therefore be seen as bearing significant dangers (Chapter 19).

This Keynesian view of the history of capitalism, including its current problems, is very sensible. One can only regret that the political conditions of recent decades have not made it possible to stop the neoliberal offensive, and put to work alternative policies—a different way of managing the crisis—in the context of other social alliances. Nevertheless, the lessons of Keynes and several decades of macroeconomic policies have not been forgotten or completely put aside. Finance did not utterly destroy the frameworks of macroeconomic policy. Monetary policy is the tool capable of guaranteeing price stability par excellence—one of the arms in the fight against inflation. Finance has taken over control of it. It has separated the central banks from the governments in order to leave them free of the sociopolitical constraints of the former compromise, and it has known how to make its goals prevail. They are registered in the statutes of the relevant institutions. The definition of the functions of the European Central Bank is an example: first and above all it is to guarantee price stability—a discipline that is, at the same time, both reinforced and complicated by the interplay of the monetary and financial markets.

The reign of finance has therefore incorporated some of the lessons of Keynesian theory, although they have been diverted from their original goals and made to serve private interests. The rise in interest rates in the 1980s makes this evident. Of course, monetary policy can be effective in the fight against inflation and Keynes would not have denied that. But Keynes wanted to eliminate creditors by slow death through the decline of interest rates and not reinforce their privileges. His view was poles apart from the views in vogue in the 1980s, when we saw so-called supply-side theories and policies resurfacing, the exact opposite of Keynesian theory. The high interest rates were supposed to favor savings, and, therefore, within the logic of supply-side economics, favor investment, helping to

Box 22.1
The words of a Keynesian: Joseph Stiglitz

Joseph Stiglitz of Columbia University is a leader of the *new Keynesians.* He served as chairman of the president's Council of Economic Advisors during part of the first Clinton administration, and was the main economist and vice president of the World Bank from 1997 to 2000. He won a Nobel Prize in 2001.

In a vigorous article published in April 2000,[a] Stiglitz counterposes two schools of thought, the neoclassical school and the Keynesian school, identifying with the latter. They are responsible for, or are used to justify, two radically different types of policies, whether they involve the management of the monetary and financial crises of the 1990s, or the transition to capitalism in the former socialist countries. But these different theories are not, in his view, disembodied—one can easily see behind the first theory the actions of the IMF, as well as the hand of the U.S. Department of Treasury, and ultimately "American financial interests" and those of the "advanced industrial world"; up against the interests of the affluent, whose center is American, can be found the "populations of the affected countries." He denounces the undemocratic procedures of the IMF and expresses understanding for those who wind up taking to the streets.

The analysis that Stiglitz gives of the East Asian crisis sometimes resembles criticisms by the far left. On the liberalization of capital and its flows, he notes: "In the early '90s, East Asian countries had liberalized their financial and capital markets—not because they needed to attract more funds (savings rates were already 30 percent or more) but because of international pressure, including some from the U.S. Treasury Department."

And on the policies imposed after the crisis: "Most importantly, did America—and the IMF—encourage policies because we, or they, believed the policies would help East Asia or because we believed they would benefit financial interests in the United States and the advanced industrial world? And, if we believed our policies were helping East Asia, where was the evidence? As a participant in these debates, I got to see the evidence. There was none."

---

a. Quotations taken from an article published April 17, 2000 (J. E. Stiglitz, "What I Learned at the World Economic Crisis," The Insider, The New Republic Online, 17-04-2000, http://thenewrepublic.com/041700/stiglitz041700.html). See also Joseph Stiglitz, *Globalization and Its Discontents* (New York: W. W. Norton & Co., 2002).

Box 22.2
Conducting world affairs:
The United Nations Development Program report

The 1999 report of the United Nations Development Program contained a chapter entitled "A New World Governance to Serve Humanity and Equity," which set forth a striking proposal: "Let us recall the remarkable vision and human concerns of the 1940s, when the United Nations and Bretton Woods institutions were created. At that time full employment was a key objective."[a]

This statement is followed by praise of Keynes's draft for the Bretton Woods negotiations and of the way these institutions functioned after the war. What is at stake now is to "build the world architecture of the twenty-first century" and to substitute UN control for American hegemony (exclusive power, derisively called the "G-1"). The idea is to democratize world institutions and to have them serve development and equity.

a. United Nations Development Program, *Human Development Report 1999* (New York: Oxford University Press, 1999), p. 111.

eliminate the stragglers—those were the refrains of the Reagan years—an anti-Keynesian creed.

The risks inherent in the instability of financial institutions are also perceived by contemporary finance, just as they always have been. This concern was at the heart of the monetary system of the nineteenth century, from crisis to crisis; it is still a preoccupation of the private financial sector and the international institutions, such as the IMF, the World Bank, or the Bank for International Settlements. But it is not clear that much progress has been made in this field. The risks have been identified, but crises occur, as the series of monetary and financial crises proves.

The international monetary and financial crises of the 1980s and 1990s—those concerning the debt of the peripheral countries, those concerning Mexico, Japan, Korea, and Latin America, or those concerning the main developed countries (Chapter 11)—reinforced once again the credibility of current Keynesian theory. Although the international monetary institutions inherited from Bretton Woods have been diverted to serving the neoliberal order, they still shelter political Keynesian theory. This Keynesian current is very critical of neoliberalism and aims to reaffirm the preeminence of these institutions, reoriented toward the goals of Keynesian policy (Box 22.1). The same is true of certain UN bodies. Putting aside the strident tone of their criticism, what they say directly echoes the initial draft for Bretton Woods and the general spirit of Keynesian theory: the monetary and financial markets are potentially dangerous and powerful world institutions should guarantee the proper functioning of the world economy. This program defines, in an idealistic but far-sighted manner, the main lines of post-neoliberalism (Box 22.2).

Should Keynes be denounced for his reformism by those who still dream of a revolutionary future? There was undoubtedly something remarkable in the Keynesian point of view, which remains of current interest. A fraction of the ruling classes felt deprived by Keynes's efforts, and limited in its prerogatives. But everything that could be saved from capitalism was saved, even though what changed was far from being insignificant. The concessions required were sizable, but perhaps more limited than anything else that could have been conceived of, given the contradictions in which capitalism had gotten itself entangled under the leadership of finance, and given the rise of popular struggles. Keynes's work is indeed that of a reformist. His brilliantly open, but still socially limited perspectives were nevertheless the only alternative to a more radical road—that of real socialism and social-democratic alternatives—that we have known for decades to have gone wrong, everywhere.

CHAPTER

23

The Dynamics of Capital

It is difficult to reform capitalism, and this difficulty does not simply follow from the complexity of fine tuning basic economic mechanisms and policies, in particular the control of the macroeconomy. There is no perfect and sustainable policy framework. One of the major lessons that can be drawn from Marx's analysis is that capitalism is not a system that was devised to gradually evolve toward perfection. Each of its achievements, each step forward, supersedes the existing relations of production and creates the conditions for new challenges. The essence of history is this patient process of endless transformation.

The power and income of privileged minorities are at stake. History is the expression of the constant struggle to perpetuate this domination by the few, on the one hand, and to attain a new, more favorable social order by the other segments of the population, on the other. Thus class struggle is the engine of history.

The history of capitalism, over the hundred years analyzed in the previous chapters, provides a demonstration of the relevance of this analysis. The twentieth century must be understood as a succession of what we call "power configurations." The existence of these configurations reflects the fact that, because of the power of class struggle itself, class domination is never absolute or straightforward. To various extents, compromises must be made. Relatively stable or precarious social constructions are repeatedly established and destroyed.

This chapter must be understood as a synthesis. It restates and generalizes at a broader level several components of the book's analysis. Various additions are made concerning power configurations, which relate to the main purpose of this summary: focusing not only on the crucial role played by social relations above and beyond basic economic mechanisms but also on the complementary character of these two elements.

The Violence of the Economy

The Keynesian dream of civilized capitalism seemed to become almost tangible in certain countries during the 1960s. Economists hastened to celebrate the end of crises, unemployment, and poverty. But the euphoria was short-lived when the economy entered into crisis in the 1970s. The optimism was unjustified, but the opposing view, which predicted the impending end of capitalism, appears, in hindsight, to have been just as erroneous. Capitalism does not founder in ever-deeper and longer-lasting crises—rather, it goes into structural crisis, transforms itself, and recovers. In a certain manner—which can be strongly criticized—it emerges from its crises and deals with its problems before others arise. The necessary changes depend not on individual behavior, but on collective practices whose political stakes are enormous. This type of functioning is deeply rooted in the very nature of the mode of production.

This book has given several examples of such periods of tension. At stake: the rate and forms of technological change, their repercussions on the rate of profit and wage increases (Part II), the struggles through the maze of financial institutions and the mechanisms for sharing the fruits of exploitation, and the implications for the stability of the system (Part III). For capitalism to function well would require harmonious and regular development of technological progress (which must concern capital and labor), of wages, of increased output and a growing workforce, as well as adjusting the institutional framework in charge of controlling the swings in the general level of activity. In reality, these developments are largely independent, and involve differing interests. The imbalances that result reveal themselves suddenly, although they have already existed for some time. They are finally resolved, but only after violent crises have created the conditions necessary for adjustments—objectively and subjectively—and have exposed reality and overcome reservations. The pattern is always the same:

Tensions → Crisis → Transformations → End of crisis → . . .

At the most general level, these after-the-fact reactions, which do not avoid crises but result from them, explain the structural crises and unemployment, as well as the ability of capitalism to change. Above all, the phases where profit rates decline lead to accumulating tensions.

Paradoxically, the rate of profit is one of the variables that is least measured by the dominant schools of economics, although evaluating profitability and maximizing it are at the heart of private management. Even if the declines in profit rates were identified, the system would have to be transformed in order to turn these unfavorable trends around. Without such declines, companies are not compelled to stimulate the rate and forms of technological change necessary to maintain the balances. The institutions capable of promoting the needed policies concerning industry, research, and training either do not exist or have little power. In an even more fundamental way, the conditions for making progress are not purely technical or institutional, but touch on property forms and the very nature of capitalism.

The way in which the availability of the workforce is collectively regulated is revealing with regard to this after-the-fact dynamic. Periodically, capital accumulation tends to come up against the limits of the available population. Under these circumstances, labor struggles have a much better chance of leading to increases in purchasing power. At other times, the crisis once again swells up the reserve industrial army, reinforcing the conditions for wage discipline. Immigration or work by women may be encouraged at times; under other circumstances, immigration is said to be excessive, and women are encouraged to go back to being housewives. This is how capitalism regulates its march forward and manages its problems.

The Politics of Violence: Finance in the Class Struggle

The historical path along which capitalism evolves is not, however, the mechanical outcome of crises and broad social tensions. This book has repeatedly pointed to the action of a social agent, referred to as "finance." Finance has played a central role in the perpetuation of capitalist relations of production since at least the beginning of the twentieth century. The rise of neoliberalism may be imputed to its action.

Finance

By finance, we mean not a specific industry, the financial sector of the economy such as manufacturing or trade, but the major financial institutions and the superior and active segments of the dominant classes. These segments are the major owners (creditors and shareholders), free from direct management but often still active in the institutions that come to embody ownership (boards of directors, banks, funds, and so on). Finance has asserted itself since the early twentieth century as the main force in the dynamics of capitalism and the class struggle.

The coexistence of social groups and institutions within the definition of finance is not any more disconcerting than mentioning workers' parties and unions in analyzing popular struggles. This is an essential point, just as is the reference to the superior and active segments of the ruling classes acting on behalf of the social group.

Since the splitting up of the capitalist relationship into ownership and management endangered the exercise of power by the owners, it was vital, for the perpetuation of the dominant classes, that this power be concentrated in institutions. In them, the agglomeration of gigantic masses of funds, the ability to buy expertise, and the potential that flows from the organization of these bodies increase the power of the ownership of the means of production, despite the distance between the owners and what they possess. The institutions of property are therefore the essential forces in the practices and struggles of advanced capitalism. Of course, all this does not keep the dominant classes from having their employers' federations and their parties (or more exactly their hold on governmental parties, whose function is to have a wide electoral appeal in the population).

But the agents of capitalist ownership are also individuals, and families. The richest and most powerful play a preponderant role. Around this nucleus a vanguard is formed. Its ownership (quite separated from management, especially in the case of nonfinancial companies) is embodied within securities, stock shares, and credits, and thus takes on a financial character. But these agents are concerned with both the financial and the nonfinancial sectors through combinations that are difficult to decipher.

One can attempt to identify the capitalists who own financial companies and who are thus in some way dual financiers: as owners of the institutions, one of their functions is to concentrate the ownership of capital. American sociologists have identified such a segment among capitalists (stockholders and members of various corporate boards) in postwar American society, whose property and power affect both financial and nonfinancial corporations.[1] It appears that the capitalists of this subgroup belong to the most important ruling-class families, the top of the pyramid.

At the same time these studies show that a significant number of other capitalists do not belong to finance in this sense. For these capitalists, the dichotomy between financial activity, on the one hand, and industry, trade, and services, on the other, remains pertinent. Such an analysis meticulously establishes the link between sectors (financial and nonfinancial), functions (owners and creditors), and individuals or families.

Given this framework, we can now look again at the three main stages that American capitalism has gone through in a little more than a century.

The First Period of Financial Hegemony

At the end of the nineteenth century, the capitalist class was permeated with divisions—big capitalists and small, farmers and industrial capitalists, and so on. The transformation of the relationships of production at the turn of the century came to shape this social matter in a very particular way, stimulating the rise of finance and of the industrial capitalists (the latter were still owners to a great extent but were losing their autonomy), and, progressively, the rise of managerial and clerical personnel. Finally, modern finance, seconded by the high-level executives who managed the big companies, asserted its power. This was the first era of financial hegemony.

The arrival of this social configuration was a time of intense class struggle (Box 16.1). Finance and the big corporations linked to it were confronted with the traditional sector—its bosses, on the one hand, and the labor movement, on the other. Each of the segments of the dominant classes attempted to use the popular struggles to its advantage at the same time that it confronted them. As for the managerial and clerical personnel, they did the work of organizers in their companies. Their political role was not affirmed autonomously, but they played a key role in forming the compromise that was established at the time, and that favored their historical development. This compromise guaranteed the traditional sector a certain degree of protection and the working class certain advantages, opening the way to the new large corporations characteristic of modern capitalism.

Finance kept control over policies in a traditional manner, despite the explosion of monetary mechanisms and the progress made by corporate management. This failure to promote a political framework corresponding to the new economic performances and transformations represented an important weakness of this first era of financial hegemony, as dramatically revealed by the Great Depression.

The Keynesian Compromise

It was the 1929 crisis that placed certain limits on the power of finance, limiting its room for maneuver. Behind the New Deal and World War II should be seen the considerable progress made by managerial personnel, both in corporations and within state institutions. Flowing from this was the Keynesian compromise, often called the New Deal coalition, defining a new era. These experiences resulted in the application of advanced processes of centralized social organization, led by a layer of managers from the public sector. But the most ambitious reforms of the New Deal were fleeting.

For the ruling classes, faced with the Soviet threat, World War II was, as World War I had been in different circumstances, a tremendous tool, extending into the 1950s in order to eradicate revolutionary ferment. The affirmation of the reform-oriented aspect of this strategy of the ruling classes was greatly facilitated by the favorable developments in technology, making possible gains in purchasing power. This movement was also reinforced by the growth of the new middle classes, facilitating the broadening of the social base of the compromise. Thus the violence of the 1930s depression and the establishment of the socialist countries did not lead to a revolutionary surge.

We have already written a great deal on the Keynesian postwar compromise. Clarifying its relationship to classes and struggles only emphasizes its deep significance.

The Second Period of Financial Hegemony with Neoliberalism

The third era saw finance, that is, the capitalists and the institutions of capitalist ownership, recover hegemony in this world where ownership and management are separated. In this period the labor movement was weak, its resistance overcome by the blows of Margaret Thatcher and Ronald Reagan. Finance, which had prepared its return to power through patient and thorough efforts, particularly on the international level (Box 18.4), took advantage both of the crisis of the international monetary system (the crisis of the dollar) and of the structural crisis that began in the 1970s, in order to reassert its hegemony. Hegemony was recaptured under American domination; financial hegemony and American power combined into one dynamic. The compromise alliance between the managerial personnel of the public and private sectors and the wage-earning classes could not be maintained in the face of this offensive, while the top managers of the multinationals were made partners and joined in the prosperity of the rich. The countries in which the most advanced alternatives had been developed for the most part gave in to the new current under outside pressure combined with the intervention of their own national dominant classes or certain portions of these classes. Neoliberalism is the fruit of a victorious comeback of a segment of the ruling classes. The policies applied, their consequences concerning employment, crises, and the end of crises, express the interests of these classes, either simply and directly or within more elaborate social configurations, but always linked to the class structure.

The Politics of Neoliberalism

In the same manner that we speak of a Keynesian compromise, neoliberalism is also based on compromises. From its very first steps, in the 1970s, dealing with the crisis of the dollar and the reform of the international monetary system, the neoliberal order could not have taken over without making partners out of the top rungs of corporate managers (initially in the multinationals). Freeing the movement of capital facilitated world strategies and opened the door to the financialization of these companies.[2] It remained to have the corporate leaders benefit from the new revenues flowing toward the dominant classes, which was accomplished through enormous remunerations. Not all the managerial personnel was integrated into this alliance; on the contrary, tensions also arose because of the pressures placed on the large mass of managers.

The alliance of the owners and the top leaders led certain analysts to see in neoliberalism the strategy of multinational corporations acting as independent entities. This is an indisputable fact, but this analysis should be taken further, and the classes behind these institutions identified. In these companies, the interests of the owners and the top managers are intertwined. The ownership-management interface is the mainspring of this top-level compromise.

Moreover, the power of finance also makes partners, though in a thoroughly different manner, of large layers of pensioners or future pensioners and small investors, who benefit from certain financial revenues or from the rise of stock prices (when there are rises). This is a compromise with the middle classes—the "everyone's a capitalist!" scheme. Such a compromise does not deny the class reality of neoliberalism, but is itself a requirement for class domination and for exercising this domination on a state level within modern democracies.[3] A fall in the stock market, like the one that began in 2000, obviously jeopardizes such a compromise.

Viewing neoliberalism as reinforcing the power of finance does not mean that this social order is the result of a conspiracy on the part of a few big banks or capitalist families, or derives from blatant political conflicts between finance capital and nonfinance capital, or between big and small capitalists. The question of determining the segments of classes whose powers and revenues were reinforced in neoliberalism is linked, but not identical to, the question of how the processes that led to this restoration were guided and how they unfolded. For the first question, what is involved is the result (what the neoliberal order is); in the second case, it is the mechanism (how did we get there).

Neoliberalism has developed as the product of a whole range of processes, ranging from the underlying objective conditions (the crisis and the trends of technological change and of profitability) to deliberate stands of certain groups, individuals, and institutions (such as the decision to support certain parties or policies) within vast historical configurations. For example, in the United States in the 1970s, the convergences created between various economic interest groups by the desire to reinforce America's endangered supremacy were combined with the effects of the structural crisis and its treatment.[4] The interests of the owners were combined with the strategies of the multinationals and their top leaders.

We would be wrong to underestimate the levels of consciousness reached by certain social groups, business milieus, and intellectual centers tied to them (Chapter 18). The political nature of the turnaround leading to the new power of finance was completely obvious, particularly in the United Kingdom and the United States. It was organized and financed in a massive way and more deliberately than can be imagined.[5] Although it is generally difficult to establish a direct link between specific economic interests and the votes of Democrats or Republicans in the United States, the electoral program of Reagan, an emblematic figure of neoliberalism, mobilized the highest-income sections of the population, that is, those who hold financial wealth.[6]

This vision, centered on the United States, should be completed here by a picture of the ways in which neoliberalism has asserted itself on a global level. This process, which is still going on, defines the globalization of neoliberalism, a fundamental feature of the current period. From the early years of the assertion of neoliberalism, Europe played a central role. The interpenetration of the European economies and their insertion in the system of the multinationals and world finance were key elements. Each European country long remained, and still remains, marked by its historical trajectory and its specific features—the United Kingdom with its desire to perpetuate the privileged status of its financial center, Germany with its monetary orthodoxy, France with its retreat from its tradition of state intervention and its subsequent march toward orthodoxy (briefly interrupted by the Mitterrand experience), and so on. The opening of Japan to world capital in the second half of the 1980s represents another decisive stage. What social forces have been at work? What are the national and international dimensions? Can the hand of world finance be seen? To what extent have the special features of these countries survived?

Beyond Neoliberalism

Neoliberalism should be seen as a stage of capitalism that is attempting to revive certain of capitalism's fundamental features, but one that will not stop the course of history. Neoliberalism will not be the last stage of development of human society. The current dynamism of the dominant class is stimulated, in the short term, by the rapid increase in its revenues, but also, more subtly, by the historical feat it has just accomplished. This feat consists in keeping at bay the progress of socialization toward the road to state control (the control of the state of the Keynesian compromise), in favor of a private socialization, along with a state that has to a large extent been put back under this class's boot. Neither expropriated nor exterminated, this dominant class hopes to preserve its privileges for a long time to come. Such is, at least, the option it has taken on the market of the future.

The method by which neoliberalism can be bypassed is not yet determined—will it be one of gradual reform, if capitalism is capable of slowing down the excesses of finance, or violent shift, in the case of a major financial crisis? Needless to say, the method will not be without consequences. If finance wants to keep on course, it must at all costs avoid this descent into the unknown, for history could repeat itself: structural crisis, upheaval, end to crisis, crisis of the end of the crisis, upheaval.

APPENDIX A

Other Studies by the Authors

Virtually no reference has been made in this book to the other studies of its authors. In this appendix information relative to various subjects can be found. Studies that have not been published may be consulted on our website: *http://www.cepremap.ens.fr/levy/*

The following book is referred to below as *La dynamique du capital:* G. Duménil and D. Lévy, *La dynamique du capital: Un siècle d'économie américaine* (Paris: Presses Universitaires de France, 1996).

Macroeconomics

Economic Cycles (Overheating and Recessions)

La dynamique du capital, part III.

G. Duménil and D. Lévy, "Being Keynesian in the Short Term and Classical in the Long Term: The Traverse to Classical Long-Term Equilibrium," *The Manchester School* 67, no. 6 (1999): 684–716.

Unemployment

G. Duménil and D. Lévy, "Structural Unemployment in the Crisis of the Late Twentieth Century: A Comparison between the European and U.S. Experiences," in *Global Money: Capital Restructuring and the Changing Patterns of Labor,* ed. R. Bellofiore (Aldershot: Edward Elgar, 1999).

Consequences of a Decline in Profitability

La dynamique du capital, chaps. 13 and 16.

G. Duménil and D. Lévy, "Why Does Profitability Matter? Profitability and Stability in the U.S. Economy since the 1950s," *Review of Radical Political Economy* 25, no. 1 (1993): 27–61.

Structural Crises

La dynamique du capital, chaps. 20 and 23.

G. Duménil and D. Lévy, "The Great Depression: A Paradoxical Event?" CEPREMAP, Paris, no. 9510 (1995).

G. Duménil and D. Lévy, "La crise de 1929 et la dépression des années trente aux États-Unis: Des événements paradoxaux?" *Économie et Sociétés (A.F. series)* 22, nos. 4–5 (1996): 193–218.

Policies, Keynesian Policies, and Neoliberalism

G. Duménil and D. Lévy, "Dynamique du capitalisme et politiques de classe: Un siècle de capitalisme américain," communication at the symposium "*Karl Marx et la dynamique actuelle du capitalisme,*" Université du Littoral, Dunkerque, October 18–19, 1996, CEPREMAP, MODEM, Paris.

G. Duménil, M. Glick, and D. Lévy, "The History of Competition Policy as Economic History," *Antitrust Bulletin* 42, no. 2 (1997): 373–416.

G. Duménil and D. Lévy, "Keynésianisme américain et social-démocratie suédoise: Quels compromis?" *Actuel Marx* 23 (1998): 117–136.

G. Duménil and D. Lévy, "Pre-Keynesian Themes at Brookings," in *The Impact of Keynes on Economics in the 20th Century,* ed. L. Pasinetti and B. Schefold (Aldershot: Edward Elgar, 1999).

G. Duménil and D. Lévy, "Coûts et avantages du néolibéralisme: Une analyse de classe," in *Le triangle infernal: Crise, mondialisation, financiarisation,* ed. G. Duménil and D. Lévy (Paris: Presses Universitaires de France, 1999).

G. Duménil and D. Lévy, "Costs and Benefits of Neoliberalism: A Class Analysis," *Review of International Political Economy* 8, no. 4 (2001): 578–607.

G. Duménil and D. Lévy, "The Nature and Contradictions of Neoliberalism," in *A World of Contradictions (Socialist Register 2002),* ed. L. Panitch and C. Leys (New York: Monthly Review Press, 2002).

Trends of Technology and Distribution

Empirical Studies

G. Duménil and D. Lévy, *Profit Rates: Gravitation and Trends* (Paris: CEPREMAP, MODEM, 1999).

G. Duménil and D. Lévy, "The Profit Rate: Where and How Much Did It Fall? Did It Recover? (USA 1948–2000)," *Review of Radical Political Economy* 34 (2002): 437–461.

Theories of Technological Change, Models:

G. Duménil and D. Lévy, "A Stochastic Model of Technical Change: Application to the U.S. Economy (1869–1989)," *Metroeconomica* 46, no. 3 (1995):213–245.

G. Duménil and D. Lévy, "Technology and Distribution: Historical Trajectories à la Marx," *Journal of Economic Behavior and Organization* 52 (2003): 201–233.

Periodization and Transformation of Capitalism

Periodization

G. Duménil and D. Lévy, "Periodizing Capitalism: Technology, Institutions, and Relations of Production," in *Phases of Capitalist Development: Booms, Crises, and Globalization,* ed. R. Albritton, M. Itoh, R. Westra, and A. Zuege (Palgrave, London: Basingstoke, 2001).

G. Duménil and D. Lévy, "Sortie de crise, menaces de crise et nouveau capitalisme," in *Séminaire Marxiste, Une nouvelle phase du capitalisme?* (Paris: Syllepse, 2001).

Transformations of Capitalism, the Managerial Revolution

La dynamique du capital, part V

G. Duménil and D. Lévy, *Au-delà du capitalisme?* (Paris: Presses Universitaires de France, 1998).

G. Duménil and D. Lévy, "Rapports de production et structure de classe du capitalisme: 150 ans après," *Cahiers Marxistes* 210, (1998): 131–161.

Managerial and Clerical Personnel

G. Duménil, *La position de classe des cadres et employés: La fonction capitaliste parcellaire* (Grenoble: Presses Universitaires de Grenoble, 1975).

G. Duménil and D. Lévy, "The Emergence and Functions of Managerial and Clerical Personnel in Marx's Capital," in *Bureaucracy: Three Paradigms,* ed. N. Garston (Boston: Kluwer Academic, 1994).

Interpretations of Marx

G. Duménil and D. Lévy, "The Dynamics of Historical Tendencies in the Third Volume of Marx's *Capital:* An Application to the U.S. Economy since the Civil War," in *Marxian Economics, A Reappraisal: Essays on Volume III of Capital,*

Profit, Prices, and Dynamics, ed. R. Bellofiore (London: Macmillan, 1998), vol. 2.

G. Duménil and D. Lévy, "Technology and Distribution: Historical Trajectories à la Marx," *Journal of Economic Behavior and Organization* 52 (2003): 201–233.

APPENDIX B

Sources and Calculations

The data used in this book essentially come from the national accounting systems of the United States and France. These systems constitute integrated frameworks based on common principles, with a few exceptions. To that should be added various accounts drawn up by the Organization for Economic Cooperation and Development (OECD). These statistics provide global information, broken down by agents and operations over long periods. They do not, however, take into account the heterogeneous character of certain agents (for example, large and small companies, or rich and poor households), which significantly handicaps research. In these areas, use must be made of specific studies, where they exist. The problem is then that these studies are limited in time, and their nomenclature does not correspond to that of other frameworks used.

Main Sources by Country

France

1. Institut National de la Statistique et des Études Économiques (INSEE). We use the 1980 classification.
   a. Accounts of institutional sectors
   b. Accounts of holdings
   c. Accounts of the variations of holdings
   d. National quarterly accounts
2. Ministère de l'Emploi et de la Solidarité (SESI): Social protection accounts
3. Pierre Villa: Capital stocks *(http://www.cepii.fr/francgraph/bdd/villa/mode.htm)*
4. Banque de France: Balance of payments and foreign commerce for France (appendixes to the annual report)

United States

1. Bureau of Economic Analysis (BEA)
   a. National Income and Product Accounts (NIPA) tables
   b. Gross Product Originating (GPO) data
   c. Fixed Assets Tables

2. Board of Governors of the Federal Reserve System: Flow of Funds Accounts of the United States

3. Federal Deposit Insurance Corporation (FDIC)
   a. Bank Closings Report
   b. Changes in Number of Insured Commercial Banks
   c. Changes in Number of Insured Savings Institutions

4. Bureau of Labor Statistics (BLS)
   a. Employment, Hours, and Earnings
   b. Consumer Price Index

5. United States Long Term: G. Duménil and D. Lévy, The U.S. Economy since the Civil War: Sources and Construction of the Series, available on our website *(http://www.cepremap.ens.fr/levy/index.htm)*, Cepremap, Modem, Paris, 1994

Europe and the United States

Germany has been limited to the former West Germany in order to avoid discontinuities linked to reunification.

1. OECD
   a. International Sectoral Database (ISDB)
   b. Flows and Stocks of Fixed Capital
   c. Economic Outlook
   d. Annual Labor Force Statistics
   e. Jobs Perspectives

2. Angus Maddison
   a. Monitoring the World Economy
   b. Standardized Estimates of Fixed Capital Stock

France and Japan

1. Board of Governors of the Federal Reserve System: Foreign Exchange Rates

2. OECD, Economic Outlook (for purchasing power parities)

Developing Countries

World Bank: World Development Indicators (WDI)

Korea

International Monetary Fund (IMF): International Financial Statistics

Calculation of Certain Variables

Corrections for the devaluation of debt by inflation and the revaluation of stock shares. The real interest rate is equal to the nominal rate less inflation: $i_R = i - j$. By multiplying this ratio by the stock of net debt (debt minus financial assets), we verify that the real transfer is equal to the amount of interest paid out, iD, less the devaluation of this debt, $jD : i_R D = iD - jD$.

In this calculation, only financial assets estimated at their nominal historical value should be considered, and not those that have been valued at their market value (such as stock shares).

The calculations of profitability do not take into account the appreciations and depreciations linked to changes in stock prices. The distinction between real or potential gains or losses cannot be made in the available statistics.

Net Worth

The calculation of this variable for nonfinancial companies is a bit different for the United States and France.

France. All stock held by the *nonfinancial corporations* sector is counted in the assets of this sector, including the stock issued by the companies within the sector. In order to avoid counting this stock twice when estimating the sector's net worth, the value of this stock should be subtracted. Unfortunately, it is not possible to distinguish between the two types of stock (those of companies from the sector and others). The alternative is therefore either to subtract the value of all stock or to include all of it. Since stock held is mainly from the sector, we have opted for the first solution—subtracting the value of all stock. We subtract all the dividends received from revenue. This gives us:

Net worth = (All assets − Stock held) − Liabilities (debt)

United States. In the American national accounting system, the "flows of funds" database does not take into account shares issued by nonfinancial corporations and held by the same sector. Shares held as assets have therefore not been issued by that sector. In the liabilities column, next to actual debt are listed shares corresponding to direct investments by foreigners in the United States. The net worth of companies is considered independently of the nationality of the owners. This gives us:

Net worth = All assets − (Liabilities − Direct foreign investments in the United States)

France and the United States (finance). We register stock shares as part of assets (and dividends as part of revenues).

Definition of Sectors

1. "All firms" in the figures of Part II refers to all industries as considered by the *International Sectoral Database* of the OECD.
2. *Nonfinancial companies* in France are sector S10 of INSEE statistics and, in the United States, *Nonfinancial Corporate Business* in the BEA's and the Fed's statistics.
3. The definition of the financial sector is more difficult. For France, we call the *financial sector* all the *financial institutions* (sector S40 of INSEE statistics), and the *insurance companies* (sector S50). However, when calculating the profit rate, we consider only the *financial institutions.* For the United States, we eliminate all funds (pension funds and mutual funds) that are not corporations, as well as public institutions, such as the Federal Reserve. This restricted financial sector includes mainly the following agents: *Commercial Banking, Savings Institutions, Insurance Companies,* and *Brokers.* (For more details, see G. Duménil and D. Lévy, "The Real and Financial Components of Profitability (USA 1948–2000)," *Review of Radical Political Economy* (forthcoming).)

Technical Points

1. Statistics have been smoothed out with the help of the Hodrick-Prescott filter.

2. By *nominal,* we mean: in current monetary units (in euros or in dollars). By *real* or in *volume* we mean the result of dividing the nominal variable by the price index of the gross domestic product. The statistics may be expressed either as a monetary unit for a particular year or as an index (with the value of the base year being set at 1 or 100). Average growth rates are calculated by the regression of the logarithm of the variable in relation to time.

Notes

1. The Strange Dynamics of Change

1. United Nations Development Program, *Human Development Report 1997* (New York: Oxford University Press, 1997), p. 3.
2. United Nations Development Program, *Human Development Report 1999* (New York: Oxford University Press, 1999), p. 3.
3. At the same time, in the United States, talk of the new economy was triumphant before the recession of the end of the century; see Council of Economic Advisers, *Economic Report of the President* (Washington, D.C.: Government Printing Office, 1999). The media couldn't stop showering praise regarding the country's growth, wealth, and so on.
4. In turning to the notion of social exclusion, we are referring not to a process that is foreign to the dynamics of capital accumulation, but to the layers of the industrial reserve army, living in what Marx called the "hell of pauperism." Karl Marx, *Capital* (1867; New York: Vintage, 1977), vol. 1, chap. 25.

2. Economic Crises and Social Orders

1. The most radical attempts, as in Latin America, were destabilized by direct actions of extreme violence.
2. See, for example, the introduction to J. Weinstein, *The Corporate Ideal in the Liberal State, 1900–1918* (Boston: Beacon Press, 1968).

3. The Structural Crisis of the 1970s and 1980s

1. A lack of data limits us to a restricted view of Europe. In 1995 the production of these three countries represented 70.2 percent of that of the United States, of which 33.5 percent was for Germany, 21.2 percent for France, and 15.5 percent for the United Kingdom.

2. As noted earlier, the sources and calculations are introduced in Appendix B. We have devoted numerous studies to the analysis of the declining profit rate (Appendix A). See also F. Moseley, *The Falling Rate of Profit in the Postwar United States Economy* (New York: St. Martin's Press, 1992), and "The Rate of Profit and the Future of Capitalism," *Review of Radical Political Economics* 29 (1997): 23–41; A. Shaikh, "The Falling Rate of Profit as the Cause of Long Waves: Theory and Empirical Evidence," in *New Findings in Long Wave Research,* ed. A. Kleinknecht, E. Mandel, and I. Wallerstein (London: Macmillan Press, 1992), pp. 174–195; E. Wolff, "Structural Change and the Movement of the Rate of Profit in the USA," in *International Perspectives on Profitability and Accumulation,* ed. F. Moseley and E. Wolff (Aldershot: Edward Elgar, 1992), pp. 93–121; R. Brenner, "The Economics of Global Turbulence," *New Left Review,* 229 (1998): 1–264; M. Husson, "Après l'âge d'or: *Sur le troisième âge du capitalisme,*" in *Le marxisme d'Ernest Mandel,* ed. G. Achcar (Paris: Presses Universitaires de France, 1999), pp. 49–78.
3. All the growth rates are calculated from variables in volume (that is, corrected for price increases).

4. Technical Progress

1. It goes without saying that we are not discussing here the consequences of this "progress" on lifestyles or the environment.
2. This increase came after five particularly unfavorable years, with the rate dropping to as little as 1.1 percent between 1990 and 1995, which explains the way in which the upturn was greeted. In this analysis, a distinction should be made between a possible underlying improvement in the conditions of technological change and the effect of swings in activity (overheating and recessions) whose effects are recorded by labor productivity.
3. This reasoning is undergirded by the formulas introduced at the end of Box 3.1.
4. Séminaire Marxiste, *Une nouvelle phase du capitalisme?* (Paris: Syllepse, 2001).

5. America and Europe

1. In such an international comparison, it is more difficult to measure the relative levels of the different countries than the specific trends for each country. One may question whether the rates attained in Europe now exceed those of the United States. For the most recent years, the levels and trends doubtless reflect the characteristics of each area more than mere catching up.
2. Examining the number of hours worked confirms this structural difference

between Europe and the United States. The number of hours worked has increased less, due to the reduced workweek. In the three European countries, the number of hours worked in the private sector has decreased significantly, from 105 billion hours in 1974 to 92 billion in 2000.

3. In the 1990s the number of public employees represented roughly 20 percent of the number of private employees in Europe and 15 percent in the United States.
4. This growth in jobs should be linked to the much greater natural increase in the population, compared with Europe. In 1999 the birth rate in the United States was 15 per 1,000 and the death rate 9 per 1,000. For the three European countries, these rates were: Germany, 10 and 10; France 12 and 9; United Kingdom 12 and 10.
5. Had the rates of capital accumulation been exactly the same for the United States and Europe, the growth in the capital-labor ratio would explain the totality of the difference in job creation (employment is equal to capital over the capital-labor ratio). The rates of accumulation were not the same (Figure 3.2), but it is indeed the rates of technological change that explain the profiles observed in terms of job creation.

6. Controlling Labor Costs and Reining in the Welfare State

1. In a country such as France, employing a worker necessarily leads to paying social taxes that give access to a series of benefits (retirement pensions, health care, family and unemployment allocations) within a system, which is globally called "social security."
2. In Figure 6.1 it is possible to note the increase in labor costs in the United States during the very last years of the 1990s. With regard to its causes, this observation should be linked to the decline in unemployment and the increase in jobs, and with regard to its effects, to the slight upturn in the growth rate of labor productivity and the decline in the profit rate.
3. An employee who earned 100 cost 142. Social taxes therefore represented 42 percent of what the employee received and 29 percent of the total (of 142) paid out by the employer.
4. Notably at the beginning of the 1980s and the 1990s.
5. A fraction of social benefits is not financed by social taxes: in 1999 it was 14 percent.
6. That the relative affluence resulting from the prosperity of the first postwar decades may have led to a certain degree of waste is a fact that we shall not attempt to discuss here. However, these supposed excesses should be measured against those made possible by other types of consumption (for example, cars and clothing).

7. Unemployment

1. Everything else being equal, an increase in the jobs growth rate of 0.5 percent per year would have created, over twenty years, about 10 percent more jobs than there were at the end of this period (the growth rate over twenty years is calculated as approximately: 0.5% × 20 = 10%).

8. The End of the Crisis?

1. This slow growth of the stock of capital, in spite of a recent limited increase, seems to contradict the observation, which is sometimes put forward, of a resumption of investment in the United States. Investment referred to here is gross investment, that is, it does not take into account capital depreciation. As far as the share of net private investment outside of housing is concerned, we see that this resumption represents merely a catching up after the decline that was observed all during the 1980s and until 1993. The levels reached at the end of the 1990s were mixed. The distinction between "gross" and "net" investment is important. Gross investment is one of the components of demand (next to consumption). It is adequate when studying an economic cycle for which the creation of demand is an explanatory factor. In order to deal with the changes in productive potential, as is the case in the present discussion, it is necessary to consider net investment, which is obtained by subtracting capital depreciation from gross investment.

9. The Interest Rate Shock and the Weight of Dividends

1. Why does an agent not prefer to pay a share of his debts by using his monetary and financial assets? There are several explanations for this. In certain cases, financial assets correspond to a commercial necessity (such as credit to clients); in other cases, the investment may bring in more than the debt costs and the company makes a profit from it (in this case it functions as a financial intermediary); holding liquid assets also corresponds to the requirements of current transactions.
2. The profit rates used in Chapter 3 (Figure 3.1) were adapted to the study of the effects of technology and wages. These evaluations related profits in a very *broad* sense (output less the total cost of labor) to fixed capital (buildings, equipment, and so on). We are now taking up profitability on a level closer to what companies receive. Two changes have been made. First, capital is no longer measured as fixed capital, but as net worth, that is, assets of companies (fixed capital, inventories, and monetary and financial assets) less their debts: their capital that has not been borrowed. Second, we deduct taxes and net in-

terest from profits and add the devaluation of net debts (the difference between debts and monetary and financial holdings; how stocks held and dividends received are treated is presented in Appendix B).

3. This relationship indeed corresponds to the results of certain econometric studies. For France, Germany, and Japan, see L. Bloch and B. Cœuré, "Profitabilité, investissement des entreprises et chocs financiers: France, Allemagne, États-Unis, et Japon, 1970–1993," *Économie et Statistiques,* nos. 268–269 (1993): 11–30.
4. Studies based on direct questionnaires or on econometric methods confirm that the desire to reduce indebtedness represented a specific factor in the slowdown of investment and therefore of growth: P. Artus, "Les entreprises françaises vont-elles recommencer à s'endetter?" *Revue d'économie financière* 46 (1998): 143–162; H. Michaudon and N. Vannieuwehnhyze, "Peut-on expliquer les évolutions récentes de l'investissement?" *Notes de conjoncture de l'INSEE,* March 1998. This reduction in indebtedness was more difficult for small companies: B. Paranque, "Compétivité et rentabilité des entreprises industrielles," *Banque de France,* Paris, 1995.
5. Michel Husson, discussing this same divorce between the rate of profit and the rate of accumulation in France, explains it as the result of capitalism's inability to extend its markets: "Après l'âge d'or: sur *Le Troisième âge du capitalisme,* in *Le marxisme d'Ernest Mandel,* ed. G. Achcar (Paris: Presses Universitaires de France, 1999), p. 74. See also M. Husson, *Les ajustements de l'emploi: Pour une critique de l'économétrie bourgeoise* (Lausanne: Page deux, 1999).

10. Keynesian State Indebtedness and Household Indebtedness

1. The high value of this rate in France does not mean that retirement pensions or health care insurance costs more in that country than elsewhere, but flows from the obligation on the part of every employer to finance, in the form of social tax payments, these social security systems.
2. See the dossier on overindebtedness from the *Revue d'économie financière* 46 (1998), and J. J. Hyest and P. Loridant, "Surendettement, prévenir, et guérir," *Rapport d'information* 60, Sénat (1997).

11. An Epidemic of Financial Crises

1. In this chapter we make broad use of Federal Deposit Insurance Corporation, *History of the Eighties: Lessons for the Future* (Washington, D.C.: Federal Deposit Insurance Corporation, 1997).
2. We leave aside here the political aspects of these events, which go beyond the ambitions of this book. See especially Eric Toussaint, *La Bourse ou la vie, la*

finance contre les peuples (Brussels: CATDM, 1998), chap. 9, which places the rise in debts in the framework of the actions by Robert McNamara within the context of the fight against communism.

3. On all these subjects, see J. Lambert, J. Le Cacheux, and A. Mahuet, "L'épidémie de crises bancaires dans les pays de l'OCDE," *Observations et diagnostics économiques* 61 (1997): 93–138.
4. The most spectacular bankruptcy filing by a bank was that of the Continental Illinois National Bank and Trust Corporation in 1984.
5. The discussion of American hegemony in Chapter 12, which underlies this analysis, will provide us with the opportunity to examine these variations of exchange rates (Figure 12.1).
6. United Nations Conference on Trade and Development (UNCTAD), *Trade and Development Report* (New York: United Nations, 1999), p. 101. Although James Tobin's idea was older, new interest arose in the idea to tax international capital movements; see F. Chesnais, *Tobin or not Tobin?* (Paris: L'esprit frappeur, 1998).

12. Globalization under Hegemony

1. This situation has given rise to a renaissance of analyses relating to imperialism; see G. Duménil and D. Lévy, eds., *Le triangle infernal: Crise, mondialisation, financiarisation* (Paris: Presses Universitaires de France, 1999), part 2. See also numerous works devoted to neoliberal globalization, including S. Amin, *Les défis de la mondialisation* (Paris: L'Harmattan, 1996); M. Husson, *Misère du capital: Une critique du néolibéralisme* (Paris: Syros, 1996), part 2; F. Chesnais, ed., *La mondialisation financière: Genèse, coût, et enjeux* (Paris: Syros, 1996), and *La mondialisation du capital* (Paris: Syros, 1997); M. C. Esposito and M. Azuelos, eds., *Mondialisation et domination économique: La dynamique anglo-saxonne* (Paris: Économica, 1997); J. C. Delaunay, ed., *La mondialisation en question* (Paris: L'Harmattan, 1999).
2. This is the central thesis of Eric Helleiner in his remarkable book: *States and the Reemergence of Global Finance: From Bretton Woods to the 1990s* (Ithaca, N.Y.: Cornell University Press, 1994).
3. Actuel Marx, *L'hégémonie américaine*, vol. 27: dossier prepared by Gilbert Achcar, 2000.
4. See the picture painted in B. Hoekman and M. Kostecki, *The Political Economy of the World Trading System: From GATT to WTO* (Oxford: Oxford University Press, 1996).
5. The price of exported goods and the price of the GDP differ substantially. The value of the yen in relation to the dollar as expressed in Figure 12.1 does not reflect with sufficient precision the conditions of the competition between the

economies of the United States and Japan. The relative price of Japanese exports, expressed in dollars, was maintained until the 1990s, before exchange conditions deteriorated. In assessing these evolutions, one must evaluate what technological progress and the limitation of margins made possible respectively.

6. Refer to the point of view of Joseph Stiglitz (Box 22.1).
7. See the detailed and particularly bleak account laid out by Peter Gowan in *The Global Gamble: Washington's Faustian Bid for World Dominance* (London: Verso, 1999).
8. R. Altbach, "The Asian Monetary Fund Proposal: A Case Study of Japanese Regional Leadership," *Japan Economic Institute Report,* 47A (1997).
9. Going back a bit, we can add to the list the rise in the price of crude oil in 1974, in which some observers saw a deliberate attempt by the United States to weaken its rivals, notably Japan. Gowan, *The Global Gamble,* is among these.
10. Savings is generally defined by the difference between income and consumption in the strict sense, that is, a broader definition of savings than the one used here. For households, for example, savings in the usual definition in France finances their housing purchases, which are not part of their consumption. Our definition, applied to households, corresponds to financial savings.
11. The multiplication of *fiscal paradises* has blurred these configurations; see R. Palan, "Trying to Have Your Cake and Eating it: How and Why the State System Has Created Offshore," *International Studies Quarterly* 42 (1998): 625–644.
12. R. Hilferding, *Finance Capital: A Study of the Latest Phase of Capitalist Development* (1910; London: Routledge and Kegan Paul, 1981); V. Lenin, *Imperialism: The Highest Stage of Capitalism* (1917; Peking: Foreign Language Press, 1973).

13. Financialization

1. For France it is necessary to isolate institutional investors, such as the *sociétés d'investissement à capital variable* (SICAV) and other *fonds communs de placement* (FCP), from other financial companies.
2. The proportion of shares in the securities held by the funds, around 37 percent, has remained fairly stable since the 1950s despite large fluctuations, which reflect those of stock market prices.
3. A central theme in recent studies by Robert Boyer is the *diversity* of contemporary capitalism. In a study devoted to financialization, "Deux enjeux pour le XXIe siècle: Discipliner la finance et organiser l'internationalisation," *Techniques financières et développement* 53 (1998): 8–19, he emphasizes the gaps between countries: "The degree of financialization of the American economy is exceptional." The picture that he paints, for 1997, establishes a much more siz-

able gap than what we have measured. The ratio of the wealth of stocks and bonds to available income would be, according to his sources, 1.45 in the United States and 0.20 in France.

4. The curves here stop in 1997. Longer-term statistics concerning the themes treated in this chapter are in preparation. See A. Friez and P. Branthomme, "Les tableaux d'opérations financières, 1995–1998," *Banque de France,* Paris, 2000.
5. The stock prices are presented in Figure 15.4. It is striking that the increase in prices for the second half of the 1990s is not apparent for France in Figure 13.3. The reason for this is that French households possess fewer and fewer shares (shares are above all acquired by French nonfinancial companies and by foreign funds)—contrary to what might be supposed from the way in which the themes of "popular" or "salaried shareholding" are insisted upon.
6. N. Chabanas and E. Vergeau, "Explosion du nombre de groupes d'entreprises," *Les notes bleues de Bercy* 130 (1997): 1–8.
7. This practice of national accounting, which is the counterpart of consolidation in corporate accounts, reflects the desire to avoid counting something twice. The idea is that the sector is not richer because one firm possesses part of another.
8. It is deceptive to estimate the debt of firms by considering only their total debts, and not their net debts. Complete confusion may result if firms are calculated to have a dangerously high level of debt because the mass debt level has increased.
9. Some large nonfinancial firms now manage credit cards, as banks do.

14. Does Finance Feed the Economy?

1. These analyses only take into account the effect on companies as a whole, which may hide quite a bit of heterogeneity, with capital leaving certain companies and contributing to the development of others. In such a case, finance would be taking on a function in capital reallocation, which may be contrasted to its negative influence on global accumulation (the development of risk capital is an indication of this mobility).
2. We have already illustrated these various evolutions: (1) the growth of securities, other than stock shares, held by households, although it is not possible to distinguish the credits extended to nonfinancial corporations from other investments (Figures 13.3 and 13.4): (2) the growth of borrowing by American households (Figure 10.4); (3) budget deficits (Figures 10.1 and 10.2); (4) exporting of capital by the United States (Figure 12.3); (5) extraordinary growth of the net worth of financial institutions (Figure 13.1).
3. Banking or parabanking institutions create credit and money at the same time.

15. Who Benefits from the Crime?

1. The strong rise in stock prices during the second half of the 1990s does not appear. This observation is in conformity with that concerning the stagnation of the value of stock held by households in France, despite the rise in stock prices (Chapter 13).
2. The financial holdings of households in both countries are presented in Figures 13.3 and 13.4.
3. United Nations Development Program, *World Report on Human Development* (Brussells: De Boeck, 1999), p. 39.
4. F. Arrondel, F. Guillaumat-Taillet, and D. Verger, "Montants du patrimoine et des actifs: Qualité et représentativité des déclarations des ménages," *Économie et Statistiques,* nos. 296–297 (1996): 145–164.
5. E. Wolff, *Top Heavy* (New York: New Press, 1996); and Wolff, "Who Are the Rich? A Demographic Profile of High-Income and High Wealth Americans," University of Michigan Business School, Working Papers series, no. 98-6 (1997). See also D. Henwood, *Wall Street* (London: Verso, 1998), chap. 2.
6. Wolff, "Who Are the Rich?" p. 11.
7. Institut National des Statistiques et Études Économiques, "Revenus et patrimoines des ménages," *Synthèse,* no. 28 (1999): 81–94; S. Lollivier and D. Verger, "Patrimoine des ménages: Déterminants et disparités," *Économie et Statistiques,* nos. 296–297 (1996): 13–31.
8. F. Berthuit, A. Dufour, and G. Hatchuel, *Les inégalités en France: Évolution 1980–1996* (Paris: CREDOC, 1996).
9. Alain Bihr and Roland Pfefferkorn, *Déchiffrer les inégalités* (Paris: La Découverte et Syros, 1999), provides a fairly complete picture of social inequalities in France and the gap between the 1960s and the 1970s on the one hand, and the neoliberal decades on the other: a reduction of the wage hierarchy in the wake of May 1968, then an increase during the neoliberal years; social inequalities when faced with unemployment; and so on. See also J. P. Fitoussi and P. Rosanvallon, *Le nouvel âge des inégalités* (Paris: Seuil, 1996). Few studies by sociologists have been devoted to the bourgeoisie and its holdings, except for those by Michel Pinçon and Monique Pinçon-Charlot, *Grandes fortunes* (Paris: Payot, 1998), especially chapter 1.

16. Historical Precedent

1. This evolution was not specific to the United States. Historians note a major depression in Europe, and especially in France, between 1873 and 1895. A lack of data prevents us from saying whether it came about following a drop in the profit rate, as in the United States.

2. A relationship that gave birth to the notion of finance capital à la Hilferding, *Finance Capital: A Study of the Latest Phase of Capitalist Development* (1910; London: Routledge and Kegan Paul, 1981).
3. H. B. Thorelli, *The Federal Antitrust Policy: Organization of an American Tradition* (Baltimore: Johns Hopkins University Press, 1955).
4. A. D. Chandler, *The Visible Hand: The Managerial Revolution in American Business* (Cambridge, Mass.: Harvard University Press, 1977).

17. The End of the Structural Crises

1. Ernest Mandel underlined the importance of this aspect in the historical dynamic of capitalism; see his *Long Waves of Capitalist Development: The Marxist Interpretation* (Cambridge: Cambridge University Press and Éditions de la Maison des Sciences de l'Homme, 1980).
2. Concerning this question, in chapter 20 of G. Duménil and D. Lévy, *La dynamique du capital: Un siècle d'économie américaine* (Paris: Presses Universitaires de France, 1996), we left the question open but drew on this historical comparison: "It seems premature to draw too optimistic conclusions. But we must also remain very prudent, because the experience of this end of the nineteenth century and of the beginning of the twentieth century shows that it is very difficult to detect such turnarounds in their initial stages" (275).
3. For a striking portrait of labor conditions and their transformation, consult S. Beaud and M. Pialoux, *Retour sur la condition ouvrière: Enquête aux usines Peugeot de Sochaux-Montbéliard* (Paris: Fayard, 1999).
4. "You can see the computer age everywhere but in the productivity statistics." R. Solow, "We'd Better Watch Out," *New York Times*, July 12, 1987, Book Review, 36.
5. But discipline was already fierce on the shop floor, and the old management procedures already required the services of employees who were subject to strict rules, repetitive jobs, and an exhausting pace.
6. F. M. Scherer and D. Ross, *Industrial Market Structure and Economic Performance* (Boston: Houghton Mifflin, 1990).
7. Which is not limitless, as the case of Microsoft has shown.

18. Two Periods of Financial Hegemony

1. The statistics reproduced in Figure 15.6, which show the portion of national holdings in the hands of the richest 1 percent of households, represent the only quantitative sign we possess of a possible modification of the hierarchy of holdings between the 1920s and the postwar period. That is a weak basis, but it gives a quantitative dimension to the notion of financial repression. The rela-

tive wealth of this 1 percent declined significantly after the Great Depression and World War II. According to this simple criterion, after its erosion during the 1970s, neoliberalism reconstituted a hierarchy of the type that prevailed in the first post–World War II decades, but less concentrated than before the Great Depression.

2. "The main opposition to the plan came from the banking community, especially from big banks in New York [who proposed an alternative plan]. [This opposition] was based first of all on a desire to maintain the large influence of monetary policy that traditionally had been enjoyed by large banks, and secondly on a fear that overly liberal currency policies might lead to postwar inflation." G. W. Domhoff, *The Power Elite and the State: How Policy Is Made in America* (New York: Aldine de Gruyter, 1990), p. 178.
3. The Bank for International Settlements is the bank of the central banks. It contributes to the cooperation of these banks in the stabilization of exchange rates and to the development of international commerce. It is also a place of discussion and information.
4. This is a theory recently repeated by Robert Brenner, who explains the decline of the profit rate in the United States and then in the world, by very strong competition in the manufacturing industry. "The Economics of Global Turbulence," *New Left Review*, no. 229 (1998): 1–264.
5. The last major attempt to stimulate the economy in the United States was made by Jimmy Carter after the 1974–75 recession.
6. They advocated regular monetary issuances in accordance with goals that could seldom be revised, and the end to rapid reaction policies for imbalances.
7. Obviously in an imperfect way—for example, the rise in prices reached an average of 1.5 percent per year between 1897 and 1914. This is different from zero, but not by much.

19. Inherent Risks

1. The deep difference in nature between the crisis of the end of the nineteenth century and the Great Depression leads us to remain fairly prudent vis-à-vis interpretations in terms of long waves. Concerning such interpretations, one may consult P. Dockès and B. Rosier, *Rythmes économiques, Crises et changement social: Une perspective historique* (Paris: La Découverte/Maspero, 1983).
2. T. F. Bresnahan and M. Raff, "Intra-Industry Heterogeneity and the Great Depression: The American Motor Vehicles Industry, 1929–1935," *Journal of Economic History* 51 (1991): 317–331.
3. Explanations of the Great Depression often cite the conditions in which demand was created. There are several variants. Just as old as the depression, and still the most widespread in France, is the theory of the lack of consumption,

linked to a relatively excessive level of profits in relation to salaries. See M. Leven, H. G. Moulton, and C. Warburton, *America's Capacity to Consume* (Washington, D.C.: Brookings Institution, 1934); M. Aglietta, *A Theory of Capitalist Regulation* (London: New Left Books, 1979). In a recent study, Isaac Joshua joins us in refuting this theory—profits were not particularly high in the 1920s; see Joshua, *La crise de 1929 et l'émergence américaine* (Paris: Presses Universitaires de France, 1999). To this explanation Joshua opposes the instability of demand, linked to the development of a structural feature of capitalism, which makes demand depend more and more on the market and on employment. We do not deny this transformation and the instability that it lets ferment. The explosion of monetary and financial mechanisms played, in our opinion, an even greater role. We have argued in other studies (under the rubric of the theory of the "trend to instability") that there is a historical trend toward increased instability within capitalism, which must be countered by improving institutions and policies capable of remedying it. Our interpretation is that this adjustment was not adequately made during the 1920s.

4. J. A. Miron and C. D. Romer, "A New Monthly Index of Industrial Production, 1884–1940," *Journal of Economic History* 50 (1990): 321–337.
5. H. Stein, *The Fiscal Revolution in America* (Chicago: University of Chicago Press, 1969).
6. C. P. Kindleberger, *The World in Depression, 1929–1939* (Berkeley: University of California Press, 1973).
7. America's incontestable domination in the current period could just as well be interpreted as fermenting instability (Chapter 12).
8. M. Friedman and A. Schwartz, *A Monetary History of the United States, 1867–1960* (Princeton: Princeton University Press, 1963).

20. Capital Mobility and Stock Market Fever

1. Capitalization appears as the denominator. Since it varies more than profits or dividends, both ratios are high during the crisis and weak in 2000.
2. W. A. Brown, *The International Gold Standard Reinterpreted* (New York: NBER, AMS Press, 1940).
3. Keynes saw in monetary policy the primary determinant of macroeconomic stability, as long as private agents agree to borrow (and, one may add, as long as the banking system agrees to make loans). A public deficit can be used in all circumstances, but is essential when the situation has deteriorated to such an extent that credit is not sufficiently requested by private agents or granted by the banking system because of the risks or the weak level of interest rates. On these issues, see J. M. Keynes, *The Means to Prosperity*, in *The Collected Writings*

of John Maynard Keynes (London: Macmillan, St. Martin's Press for the Royal Economic Society, 1933), 11:335–366.

21. Between Two Periods of Financial Hegemony

1. Here we should distinguish between what the "thirty glorious years" made possible and what enabled them to be. We don't think that wage growth represented one of the factors of prosperity, rather, conversely, we believe that prosperity created the conditions for winning wage demands without endangering growth. This is a difference with the Regulation school, which explains the prosperity of the first postwar decades by the simultaneous growth of labor productivity and wages, contrasting that period with the 1920s. See R. Boyer, *The Regulation School: A Critical Introduction* (New York: Columbia University Press).
2. See, for example, A. D. Chandler, *The Visible Hand: The Managerial Revolution in American Business* (Cambridge, Mass.: Harvard University Press, 1977); J. K. Galbraith, *The New Industrial State* (London: Penguin Books, 1969).
3. The inevitable reference is A. Berle and G. Means, *The Modern Corporation and Private Property* (London: Macmillan, 1932).
4. Galbraith, *The New Industrial State.*
5. F. Bloch-Lainé, *Pour une réforme de l'entreprise* (Paris: Éditions du Seuil, 1963).
6. In France the term "mixed economy" or "third road" was used.
7. See C. Johnson, *MITI and the Japanese Miracle: The Growth of Industrial Policy, 1925–1975* (Stanford: Stanford University Press, 1982); C. Sautter, *Les dents du géant: Le Japon à la conquête du monde* (Paris: Oliver Orban, 1987).
8. Alice Amsden insists on the preponderant role of technical personnel, the engineers; see *Asia's Next Giant* (Oxford: Oxford University Press, 1989). Her analysis therefore continues along the preceding lines concerning managerial autonomy.
9. A. Begounioux and B. Manin, *Le régime social-démocrate* (Paris: Presses Universitaires de France, 1989); G. M. Olsen, *The Struggle for Economic Democracy in Sweden* (Aldershot: Avebury, 1992).

22. A Keynesian Interpretation

1. J. Crotty, "On Keynes and Capital Flight," *Journal of Economic Literature* 21 (1983): 59–65; J. M. Keynes, *National Self-Sufficiency,* in *The Collected Writings of John Maynard Keynes* (1933; London: Macmillan, St. Martin's Press for the Royal Economic Society, 1972), 21:233–246.
2. "The world is *not* so governed from above that private and social interests al-

ways coincide. It is *not* so managed here below that in practice they coincide. It is *not* a correct deduction from the principles of economics that enlightened self-interest always operates in the public interest." Keynes, "The End of Laissez-Faire" (1926), *Essays in Persuasion,* in *Collected Writings of Keynes,* 9:287–288.

3. In many respects, this broader compromise extended the one made at the beginning of the century (Box 16.1).
4. Keynes, *The Means to Prosperity,* in *Collected Writings of Keynes,* 11:335–366; J. M. Keynes, *The General Theory of Employment, Interest, and Money* (London: Macmillan, 1936).
5. Keynes had suggested taxing market operations, thus anticipating the Tobin tax, even though he wasn't specifically thinking of international transactions (Keynes, *General Theory*). This instability of financial markets extends to the instability labeled as structural with regard to the financial institutions. See H. Minsky, *Stabilizing an Unstable Economy* (New Haven, Conn.: Yale University Press, 1986).

23. The Dynamics of Capital

1. M. Soref and M. Zeitlin, "Finance Capital and the Internal Structure of the Capitalist Class in the United States," in *Intercorporate Relations: The Structural Analysis of Business,* ed. M. Mizruchi and M. Schwartz (Cambridge: Cambridge University Press, 1987), pp. 56–84. To our knowledge, this study has not been brought up to date.
2. See E. Helleiner, *States and the Reemergence of Global Finance: From Bretton Woods to the 1990s* (Ithaca, N.Y.: Cornell University Press, 1994), pp. 115ff.
3. Here we find an essential aspect of the Marxist analysis of the state, which perceives two facets of democracy: the internal democracy of the ruling classes—the relatively free expression of their internal contradictions—and a form, also called "democratic," of how power is exercised over the other classes, which is an expression of an economic and political compromise. These two uses of democracy maintain certain links (institutional and juridical). Dictatorship is the negation of these two elements, which it can alter in specific ways.
4. In this sense the analysis of Thomas Ferguson draws a very broad picture of the foundations of the neoliberal turn, with all the necessary historical perspectives and documentation. See Ferguson, *Golden Rule: The Investment Theory of Party Competition and the Logic of Money-Driven Political Systems* (Chicago: University of Chicago Press, 1995).
5. See, for example, M. Useem, *The Inner Circle: Large Corporations and the Rise of Business Political Activity in the U.S. and U.K.* (Oxford: Oxford University Press, 1984), especially chap. 5.

6. T. B. Edsal, "The Changing Shape of Power: A Realignment in Public Policy," in *The Rise and Fall of the New Deal Order, 1930–1980,* ed. S. Fraser and G. Gerstle (Princeton: Princeton University Press, 1989), pp. 269–293. It would be naive to see in these changes of attitude by the electorate the expression of spontaneous movements of opinion. They were largely the product of the investments by business milieus in the electoral campaigns. See T. Ferguson and J. Rogers, *Right Turn: The Democrats and the Decline of American Politics* (New York: Hill and Wang, 1986), and Ferguson, *Golden Rule.*

Index